The Illustrious Dead

Empire of Blue Water
*Captain Morgan's Great Pirate Army,
the Epic Battle for the Americas,
and the Catastrophe That Ended
the Outlaws' Bloody Reign*

Mulatto America
*At the Crossroads of Black and White Culture:
A Social History*

The
Illustrious
Dead

The Terrifying Story of How Typhus Killed

Napoleon's Greatest Army

Stephan Talty

THREE RIVERS PRESS   NEW YORK

Published in the United States by Three Rivers Press, an imprint of the
Crown Publishing Group, a division of Random House, Inc., New York.
www.crownpublishing.com

THREE RIVERS PRESS and the Tugboat design are registered trademarks of
Random House, Inc.

Originally published in hardcover in the United States by Crown Publishers,
a division of Random House, Inc., in 2009.

Library of Congress Cataloging-in-Publication Data
Talty, Stephan.
The illustrious dead / Stephan Talty.—1st ed.
1. Napoleonic Wars, 1800–1811—Campaigns—Russia.
2. Napoleonic Wars, 1800–1815—Campaigns—Russia—Medical and
sanitary affairs. 3. France Armée—History—Napoleonic Wars, 1800–1815.
4. Napoleon I, Emperor of the French, 1769–1821—Military leadership.
5. Russia—History, Military—1801–1917. I. Title.
DC235.T27 2009
940.2'742—dc22   2008050646

978-0-307-39405-7

DESIGN BY LEONARD HENDERSON
MAPS BY JEFFREY L. WARD

First Paperback Edition

146119709

For Asher and Delphine

Note to the Reader

In these pages you'll find a handful of place-names and military terms specific to the Napoleonic era. If you're unclear about any of these, please consult the short glossaries found at the back of this book.

Contents

French Empire

French Client
Countries

French Allies

NORWAY
(Danish)

Christiana

SCOTLAND

Edinburgh

*North
Sea*

DENMARK

IRELAND UNITED

Copenhagen

Dublin KINGDOM

OLDENBURG

Hamburg

WALES

Bremen Berlin

ENGLAND

Amsterdam

Hanover

London

Cologne

Cassel

English Channel

CONFEDERATION

Frankfurt

Prague

Paris

OF THE

Strasbourg

A T L A N T I C   O C E A N

F R E N C H

RHINE

E M P I R E

Zurich

Innsbruck

Geneva

KINGDOM

Bordeaux

Milan

OF ITALY

Turin

Venice

Genoa

Illyria

PORTUGAL

Salamanca

Marseille Nice

Florence

Corsica

Madrid

Lisbon

Barcelona

Rome

S P A I N

KINGDOM OF

Naples

SARDINIA

Balearies

Cadiz

M e d i t e r r a n e a n   S e a

Palermo

Gibraltar

KINGDOM

A F R I C A

OF SICILY

Europe, 1811

St. Petersburg

Stockholm

*Baltic
Sea*

Moscow

Riga

Konigsberg • Tilsit
Vilna
Smolensk

Danzig
Friedland
Minsk

Poznan
Warsaw
**GRAND DUCHY
OF WARSAW**

**R U S S I A N
E M P I R E**

Kiev •

Cracow

A U S T R I A N   E M P I R E

Vienna
Buda • • Pest
HUNGARY

M
O
L
D
A
V
I
A

Odessa

TRANSYLVANIA
Brasso

**FRENCH
EMPIRE**
Spalato

WALLACHIA
Bucharest
Belgrade
Ruschuk

Black Sea

Provinces

• Sofia

Constantinople

O T T O M A N   E M P I R E

**KINGDOM
OF NAPLES**

0 Miles   200   400
0 Kilometers   400

Corfu

Athens

Ionian Islands (Br.)

© 2009 Jeffrey L. Ward

The Grande Armée
Command Structure

NAPOLEON

BERTHIER
Chief of staff

Imperial Guard	I Corps	II Corps	III Corps
LEFEBVRE, MORTIER	DAVOUT	OUDINOT	NEY

IV Corps	V Corps	VI Corps	VII Corps
PRINCE EUGÈNE	PONIATOWSKI	SAINT-CYR	REYNIER

VIII Corps	IX Corps	X Corps
JUNOT	VICTOR	MACDONALD

Austrian Corps	Cavalry
SCHWARZENBERG	MURAT

The Russian Army
Command Structure

TSAR ALEXANDER I
(Political head of Russia)

GENERAL MIKHAIL BARCLAY DE TOLLY
(Minister of War, acting head of army until August 20)

FIELD MARSHAL PRINCE MIKHAIL ILARIONOVICH KUTUZOV
(Commander in chief, appointed August 20)

First Army	**Second Army**	**Third Army**
BARCLAY DE TOLLY	BAGRATION	TORMASOV

I Corps	**VII Corps**	
WITTGENSTEIN	RAEVSKY	
II Corps	**VIII Corps**	
BAGAVOUT	BOROZDIN	
III Corps		
TUTCHKOV		
IV Corps		
TOLSTOI		
V Corps		
CONSTANTINE		
VI Corps		
DOKHTUROV		

Coalitions Against France During the Napoleonic Era

First Coalition (1792–97)
Austria, Prussia, Great Britain, Spain, and the Piedmont

Napoleon emerges from obscurity to conquer Italy. France gains Belgium, the Rhineland, a partitioned Venice, and most of Italy.

Second Coalition (1798–1801)
Russia, Great Britain, Austria, the Ottoman Empire, Portugal, Naples, and the Vatican

Napoleon returns from Egypt to defeat the Austrians at the Battle of Marengo, France gains control of the Netherlands, and Austria accepts French domain over Italy and territories as far north as the Rhine.

Third Coalition (1805)
Austria, Great Britain, Russia, and Sweden

England smashes the French and Spanish fleets at Trafalgar and rules unchallenged over the waters. Napoleon triumphs at Austerlitz against Austria and Russia. The German states are organized into the Confederation of the Rhine as a redoubt around France.

Fourth Coalition (1806–7)
Prussia, Great Britain, Sweden, Saxony, and Russia

Napoleon crushes Prussia at the Battles of Jena and Auerstedt. The French fight the Russians to a draw at Eylau. France occupies Prussia, including Berlin. The Treaty of Tilsit gives France half of Prussia's land as well as the Kingdom of Westphalia. The Grand Duchy of Warsaw, which includes most of modern-day Poland, is created.

Fifth Coalition (1809)
GREAT BRITAIN AND AUSTRIA

Napoleon triumphs at the Battle of Wagram. Austria loses Carniola, Carinthia, and the Adriatic ports to France; Galicia to Poland; and Tyrol to Bavaria.

Sixth Coalition (1813–14)
GREAT BRITAIN AND RUSSIA, JOINED BY PRUSSIA, SWEDEN, AUSTRIA, AND THE GERMAN STATES

France is driven out of Germany and the nation is occupied. Napoleon is exiled to Elba.

Seventh Coalition (1815)
GREAT BRITAIN, RUSSIA, PRUSSIA, SWEDEN, AUSTRIA, AND THE GERMAN STATES

Napoleon returns from exile but is defeated at Waterloo and is exiled to St. Helena, where he dies in 1821.

The Illustrious Dead

Introduction: Old Bones

IN LITHUANIA, LATE IN THE WINTER OF 2001, CONSTRUCTION crews began clearing a piece of land in that part of the capital, Vilnius, known as Northern Town, digging trenches for phone lines and demolishing the old Soviet barracks that had stood on the land for decades. Vilnius was booming, with new money flooding in and decades of oppression under Moscow and Berlin seeming at last ready to vanish along with the last physical traces of imperialism. Real estate developers had snapped up the old troops' quarters to be made into luxe new homes for the computer programmers and regional managers who would soon turn this forbidding collection of buildings into a sparkling hub of the new Europe.

The work had gone smoothly until one bulldozer scraped up a layer of soil and uncovered something white underneath its blade. The operator looked down and saw bones, bones that were quite clearly human: femurs, ribs, skulls. One worker later told a reporter that the white things "wouldn't stop coming out of the ground." There were thousands of them.

Word spread to nearby neighborhoods, and men and women came hurrying across the fields, their boots crunching in the hoarfrost and their breath blowing white. There had been whispers for years about this place, rumors that the KGB had used the barracks as torture chambers for political dissidents. Many believed that those who hadn't survived the questioning had been buried in mass graves somewhere on the grounds. Eight years earlier, a grave filled with seven hundred KGB victims had been found a few hundred yards away. The local people looked down into the freshly dug hole, looking for missing lovers, sisters, or sons.

Or perhaps these were the corpses of Jews murdered by the Nazis. Hitler's bureaucrats had set up two ghettos in the city after occupying it in June 1941 and then slowly drained them of men, women, and children, eventually killing 95 percent of the country's Jewish population.

When archaeologists from the University of Vilnius arrived, they saw that the bodies had been stacked three-deep in a V-shaped trench and quickly realized that the men had been buried in the same pits they had dug to defend themselves. Clearly, the men were soldiers, not dissidents or civilians. And they were robust specimens, many of them tall and broad-shouldered, most between fifteen and twenty years old, with a few women mixed in—prostitutes was the early guess.

As they excavated the 2,000 skeletons, the archaeologists found a plaque that had once adorned a helmet, decorated by an eagle and a cockade in faded red, blue, and white. There were curious belt buckles inscribed in several languages, buttons with regiment numbers such as "29" and "61." And there were, crucially, 20-franc coins that dated from the early 1800s. The remains were too old to be the victims of either Stalin or Hitler.

After quickly calling to mind the history of Vilnius, called "the city built on bones" because of its past as a minor bauble for conquerors and tyrants, the scientists realized they could only be looking at the remnants of one force: the Grande Armée. One hundred and eighty-nine years before, Napoleon had led 600,000 men into Russia in an attempt to conquer his last major opponent on the Continent. These corpses were the remnants of that invasion force.

The dead were from every corner of Europe—Holland, Italy, Spain, Germany, Westphalia, and other duchies, kingdoms, and states. Napoleon had ruled all of them and had in 1812 been at the coruscating height of his power, leading an army unlike anything that had been seen since the days of the Persian conqueror Xerxes in the fifth century BC. The soldiers were the paragons of their time, and on their march to Moscow they had been considered unstoppable. But they had clearly encountered something beyond their power to overcome or outrun.

What had killed these men? None of the remains had the crushed skulls or telltale bullet holes of men who had been executed and dumped in mass graves. The bodies were curled into the fetal position, the normal human response to extreme cold, which had certainly played a part in their demise. Hunger, too, had ravaged the city in the winter of 1812. The archaeologists remembered the stories of Napoleon's troops breaking into the local university and eating the human and animal specimens suspended in formaldehyde. Some of these men had starved to death.

But something else had clearly been at play in that awful year. The soldiers had been physical specimens, the toughest of a gargantuan, battle-hardened army who had managed to escape the fate of their less determined or less robust comrades lying in roadside graves all the way to Moscow and back. These men were the *survivors* of something even more cataclysmic that had occurred many weeks earlier. In a sense, they were the lucky ones.

The archaeologists drilled into the teeth of the corpses and extracted samples of dental pulp, placed it on slides, and slid them under microscopes. In the DNA of a number of the soldiers, they discovered the signs of the hidden killer that had done so much to bury not only the Grande Armée but also Napoleon's hopes of world domination.

Older than France or Europe or *homo sapiens* themselves, its causative agent had arisen millions of years ago. It had mystified—and slain—its scientific pursuers for centuries, complicating the race to understand and defeat it. And it had a past as fearsome as any of the mass killers of the twentieth century, only more illustrious and strange.

CHAPTER I

Incarnate

IT WOULD BE A REMARKABLE THING TO LOOK AT A MAP OF THE world in 1811 and not be struck by how much of it was controlled by France and its forty-two-year-old leader, Napoleon Bonaparte. His writ ran from the Atlantic Ocean to the borders of Russia and from southern Spain to northern Germany. Some 45 million subjects lived under his rule. One exhausts superlatives in talking of his kingdom: He held sole command of a nation that was the richest and most powerful on earth. His empire was larger than the Roman emperors' or Charlemagne's, and it had every promise of expanding in the near future. And Napoleon commanded it with such rigor that no detail, down to the opening time of the opera in Paris, escaped him.

The emperor had not only conquered territory, he had remade societies. Coming of age during the reign of Louis XVI, Napoleon and his generation grew disgusted with a nation where the accumulated layers of tradition and artifice clogged one's path in life, and money and prestige flowed to the amoral and the cunning. They felt suffocated by the weight of the past, its irrationalities, its injustices. After taking power in France, Napoleon had streamlined the nation's administration, rationalized its civic laws and its economy to free up long-suppressed energies, and exported these innovations to the satellite nations under his control. He'd famously declared that careers should be open to the most talented, and in many ways he'd succeeded in moving European societies toward a future where merit, brains, and hard work counted.

When the young general took power, he was seen across much of Europe as a kind of mythological creature: half warrior, half idealist. For those with any progressive ideas whatsoever, he was the strong man who would give order and structure to the best instincts of the French Revolution. Emerging from the whirling blood feuds of the Terror, during which thousands were executed on the slightest pretext, when men ran through the streets hoisting the body parts of princesses stuck on pikes, Napoleon had saved the nation.

Our politics today are divided between left and right, liberal and conservative. But those notions gain their heat and shape from Napoleon's times. He came of age during the birth of those concepts: between the French Revolution's insistence on individual dignity, rights, and freedoms, and the Anglo-American conservative response, inaugurated by Edmund Burke in his landmark *Reflections on the Revolution in France* (1790), which stressed the value of tradition, caution, and social norms built up over time. The temperature of the early 1800s burned much hotter than that of the early 2000s: the eruption of the Revolution threatened to sweep away all accumulated notions of social place and long-held values and to leave in their place pure chaos. Rulers eyed their subjects nervously, and subjects eyed their kings with the new idea that they were hateful and unnecessary. Europe in Napoleon's time seemed ready to fly apart.

This goes a long way toward explaining why Napoleon aroused such intense admiration early on. Like George Washington, with whom he was often compared, he had taken a hot revolution and cooled it into a rational system without reverting to the abuses of the tyrant-kings. "Peoples of Italy!" the young general had cried after beating the Austrians there in 1796. "The French army comes to break your chains. . . . We shall wage war like generous enemies, for our only quarrel is with the tyrants who have enslaved you." Words like that hadn't been heard in Europe before the Revolution. Even some monarchists swooned, at first.

Napoleon took power in a 1799 coup d'état, midstride in a series of wars that the French Republic claimed were fought to protect its borders and export freedom. For sixteen years he ran roughshod over opposing generals and kings. In 1797 the general had seized control of northern Italy from the Austrians. In 1800 he returned to Italy and defeated the Austrians; in 1802 he was named first consul for life; in 1804 he became emperor; in 1806 Napoleon faced the Fourth Coalition—Russia, Sweden, Great Britain, Saxony, and Prussia—and defeated them soundly; in 1807 he signed the Treaty of Tilsit with Tsar Alexander of Russia; in 1808 he invaded Spain; in 1809 he stumbled against the Austrians but stormed back with a punishing victory at Wagram.

Napoleon's conquest had pitted him in a battle to the death with the monarchies of Europe. But even the opponents who considered him an Antichrist saw him as an almost miraculous figure. "He wanted to put his gigantic self in the place of humankind," wrote Madame de Staël, and even the young tsar of Russia, Alexander I, at first regarded Bonaparte with admiration bordering on a kind of worship.

It wouldn't last.

THE EMPEROR'S GIFTS were numerous and mutually reinforcing: an exacting self-discipline; a memory that was close to photographic; an ability to read people and fit their unspoken desires to his aims; a gut-level genius for inspiring men and leading them in battle; an openness to new ideas so long as he could benefit from them; a farseeing, flexible, and often breathtakingly daring mind. His less appealing qualities were clear but not yet fatal: he was as superstitious as an old Corsican widow, petulant, headstrong, and, most of all, increasingly blind to the flaws in his thinking. His self-intoxication grew by the year.

Napoleon had come to power through the military, and his career there was divided by a bright sharp line. There was before Italy and after Italy. His unexpected victories there in 1796 against the Austrian army as an obscure general had changed his idea of himself and launched him into a career where he could seemingly do anything he set his mind to.

It hadn't always been that way. Napoleon had emerged from his Corsican boyhood as a solitary, workaholic dreamer with immense, far-reaching gifts but a slim chance at greatness. He was also superstitious, tetchy, and prone to childish rages, a man who rated his natural abilities very highly and grew suicidal at the thought that, as an obscure gunner, he would never get the chance to realize them. But Italy changed that, confirming to him that he not only had genius but would be given a chance to display it. "From that moment, I foresaw what I might be," he wrote later. "Already I felt the earth flee from beneath me, as if I were being carried into the sky."

Napoleon's military capabilities began with a near-total knowledge of tactics used in past wars; he was a walking database on every major battle in history, and knew what had worked or failed and why. But the young Corsican also reimagined the standard tenets of military science. He constantly gathered intelligence and used it to formulate his plans. He honed his communications systems to give his divisions an edge in speed, and he specialized in flanking and enveloping maneuvers that concentrated overwhelming firepower on the enemy's weakest point. Napoleon also organized his armies into independent corps that were designed to march against and defeat enemy forces three times their size, which they regularly did.

The Grande Armée also had a technological edge, especially in the areas of infantry guns and lighter muskets. The French had long poured money into developing better big cannons that could be maneuvered into position more quickly and brought to bear on crucial zones on the battlefield. And the carbines carried by the Grande Armée's sharpshooters, snipers, and forward skirmishers were state of the art (a relative term in relation to notoriously inaccurate muskets of the period), giving his units an advantage in marksmanship, especially in the early stages of the battle where, under the pall and roar of an artillery bombardment, Napoleon would send sharpshooters forward to take down officers and members of the first line poised for the attack.

Napoleon's classic approach to battle was kinetic and precise. He designed a battle as a watchmaker would a fine chronometer. One corps, usually heavily outnumbered so as to allow other units to execute the rest of Napoleon's plan, would engage the main body of enemy troops, freezing them into position and often suffering horrible casualties. Then other divisions, in sequences timed down to the minute, would pin down the opponent from unexpected angles, isolating and cutting apart individual divisions while at the same time cloaking from view a hidden force that was marching rapidly to a weak flank or an exposed rear guard. Then, at a crucial moment, Napoleon would drop these unseen divisions into the battle, backed by cavalry and artillery, overwhelming the enemy and scattering its forces to the wind.

To the outmatched generals who faced him, Napoleon's armies always appeared larger than they actually were, because the emperor maneuvered them for maximum striking power on the battlefield. And they were ghostly, appearing from behind a hill or over a ridge at a time when they were supposed to be miles away.

Napoleon's debut was a perfect illustration of his tactical brilliance as a force multiplier. In the first Italian campaign, he took a demoralized, ill-equipped collection of 100,000 soldiers and led them on a breathtaking series of victories, cutting the Piedmontese-Austrian enemy into its component parts and then chasing, catching, and defeating each segment in turn. He captured 160,000 men, 500 cannon, 39 ships, and wagon-trains worth of booty, including Michelangelos and Titians. Like many geniuses, he seemed to have no apprenticeship. General Napoleon emerged onto the world stage fully formed.

AS HE REVOLUTIONIZED THE big-picture aspect of war, Napoleon became a master at motivating the individual soldier. "You must speak to his soul in order to electrify him," he famously said. But his attention went deeper than oratory. He remembered hundreds and hundreds of his troops' names, tweaked their ears and joked with them during reviews, led them brilliantly, and promoted and rewarded them on the spot for acts of bravery that would have gone unnoticed under another general.

Stoked by a feeling of personal devotion to their leader, his soldiers did things that no other men in modern European warfare had done, things that modern Navy SEALs would struggle to equal. "The belief that they were invincible made them invincible," remarked Karl von Funck, a German officer on Napoleon's staff. "Just as the belief that they were sure to be beaten in the end paralyzed the enemy's sprits and efforts." During a stretch of four days during the first Italian campaign, one division under the former cabin boy André Messéna, the son of a tanner risen to general, fought three brutal pitched battles on successive days, marched nearly sixty miles through darkness and snow, and killed or captured thousands of the enemy. Messéna's division helped Napoleon turn a competent Austrian force of 48,000 men into a terrified mob of 13,000 in a matter of 120 hours. This was not an isolated incident: Napoleon raised the standard of individual performance in the Grande Armée to levels thought unachievable before he arrived.

. . .

BY 1811 THE EMPEROR was the undisputed master of the Continent, with only the Portuguese, the Spanish rebels, and the old bugbear of England still providing outright resistance to his dominion. By that time, too, the patina of his early rhetoric had been rubbed through and now what Europe saw, by and large, was bright steel: Napoleon's promise to free those he conquered had gone unfulfilled. He was more and more a traditional conqueror.

By seeking further territories, Napoleon was reverting to a native form. From the days of the illustrious "Sun King," Louis XIV, in the late seventeenth century, the French army was considered to be the vanguard of a progressive society conquering backward nations in order to bring them freedom, art, and science. For over a hundred years before the ascent of Napoleon, France had seen itself as the citadel of civilization. As expansionists and Christian visionaries would claim throughout American history, empire building was more than an economic good. It was a duty.

The makers of the French Revolution called a pause in the acquisition of colonies and satellites, asking for an end to all "wars of conquest." But Napoleon, driven by a new utopian ardor, rampaging personal ambition, and the need to safeguard his borders, reignited the drive to empire. "The genie of liberty," Napoleon wrote, "which has rendered the Republic since its birth, the arbiter of all Europe, wishes to see it mistress of faraway seas and foreign lands." The 1798 invasion of Egypt had been disguised as a scientific mission to rediscover the secrets of the ancient world. But by 1812 the hostile response of many of the recipients of their "liberation" had hardened French attitudes into something far older and more recognizable: what one historian called "egotistical nationalism." Success had proved to the French that they were better and stronger than their rivals, and that they deserved whatever they could take. By the time they headed for Russia, the banner of intellectual and cultural progress was faded and torn.

. . .

THE NORMATIVE NINETEENTH-century leader of a European empire would have been more than satisfied with Napoleon's
achievements. His enemies were chastened and his empire at least
reasonably secure. Napoleon saw things differently. Five-eighths
of the world's surface—the oceans—was controlled by his enemy,
England, whose navy outmatched France's in every way. His ally,
Russia, "the barbarian North," was slipping outside of his sphere,
having recently broken its agreement to stop English ships from
entering its harbors and trading with its merchants, a key defec-
tion in Napoleon's intent to strangle England commercially before
defeating it militarily.

Bonaparte didn't compare himself to his contemporaries, none
of whom (except perhaps for the French diplomat Talleyrand) could
match his intellect or energy. Instead, he saw himself in a world-
historical continuum, with Alexander the Great and the Caesars of
Rome as his peers. "I am the successor," Napoleon said, "not of
Louis XVI, but of Charlemagne." He believed that he had been chosen to remake human society. To do that, first he must grasp and
then control the levers of power. Ruthlessly, if necessary.

To accept peace and turn to the work of civic administration
(which he always claimed that he yearned to take up full-time)
would be to spurn his own gifts. Napoleon was enough a child of
the Revolution to see warfare not only as a practical means to
power but as a test of himself as a whole man. He believed that
every person should exhaust his possibilities, and his were near-
infinite. To turn away before a perfect empire was created, an empire stronger and more enlightened than any that had gone before,
was unacceptable.

England for the moment was out of reach. But Russia, too ob-
stinate and too powerful for its own good, was not.

ALEXANDER I OF RUSSIA was much closer to a recognizable
nineteenth-century monarch than his counterpart in Paris: bright

but intellectually lazy; an aesthete who played at military affairs and never really mastered the basics; a vain man not cut out for leadership who could nevertheless on very rare occasions take a position and hold it against everything. Raised in the hothouse climate of the royal palace at Tsarskoye Selo, Alexander had led a cosseted life unsettled only by the murderous strains between his father and grandmother. He was more fluent in English and French than he was in his native language and was completely unfamiliar with the Russia of the steppes or the brutal degradation of the serfs on the estates. Napoleon would say later that he found Alexander to be deeply intelligent but that there was a piece of his character missing. The tsar rarely had the will to carry out intentions to the end, no matter how bitter. Deeply curious, he read prodigiously, but rarely finished a book.

Alexander led from fear: fear of the military, of his father's fate, of his mother, and of his people, who were so often a mystery to him.

Soon after Alexander's accession in 1801, Napoleon attempted to pry him from his alliance with the Kingdom of Prussia and neutralize Russia as a player in the game for Europe. But Alexander, with his own ambitions for empire, eventually came to regard Napoleon as all the European monarchs did, as a usurper who had enslaved half of Europe and unsettled the rest. He turned down Napoleon's proposals and joined forces with Austria for a climactic battle on December 2, 1805: Austerlitz.

Austerlitz was Napoleon's apogee. There he faced highly rated generals and outthought them at every turn in a battle that unfolded so seamlessly it was as if he had written out the events in longhand the night before. His army proved to be deft and maneuverable, even swelled to the then-unprecedented size of 75,000 men (a figure that would be dwarfed by the Grande Armée in 1812). The emperor fought a new kind of warfare, emphasizing speed, concentrated power, surprise, and improvisation.

After another crushing victory over Russian forces at Friedland in June 1807, Napoleon and Alexander finally met at Tilsit the following month for a peace conference and the emperor laid siege to him as if he were a romantic conquest. The satanic elf that Alexander had been warned about turned out to be a fascinating charmer, a seducer of great intellectual skill and apparent honesty. Napoleon for his part allowed himself to believe that Alexander was a kindred soul, at least for his present purposes. "He is a truly handsome, good and youthful emperor," he wrote, and the two spent nearly two weeks firming up their alliance.

The main result was the humiliation of Prussia, which was cut down to almost half its size, and an uneasy stalemate over Poland, which Alexander and the political class in Moscow had always considered to belong to the homeland. Napoleon wanted to keep Poland outside of Russian control, as a buffer against any ambitions Alexander might have on his empire. Not only that, he had proposed enlarging the grand duchy with the 1.3 million citizens of western Galicia. This would turn Poland into a significant nation-state and a staging ground for Napoleon's armies.

Despite himself, Alexander was swayed by Napoleon and left Tilsit hopeful of a long-lasting alliance. But the return to Moscow dashed cold water in his face. Almost every segment of his power base was against the treaty—from his mother the empress, who hated Bonaparte to her marrow; to the business class, worried about French merchants expanding into their traditional markets in the Baltic; to the military elite, largely French-speaking but traumatized by two wars in which Napoleon had shredded their ranks. "Love for the Tsar has changed to something worse than hatred, to a kind of disgust," wrote a Russian observer in his diary. There were warnings that Alexander would be assassinated like his despised father. A wave of Russification swept through the upper classes, with traditional arts and language finding a new popularity in the face of what was considered a French humiliation.

Napoleon's true target in courting Alexander was, of course,

England. He had contemplated an invasion of the British Isles almost as soon as he came to power, but the inherent difficulty of the enterprise, and the looming power of the Royal Navy, had foiled his plans at every turn. What he'd failed to do militarily he tried to do commercially with the Continental System, an economic blockade instituted in 1806 and adopted by Alexander's Russia after the Tilsit conference. But the blockade was a failure. Smugglers carrying English goods regularly skirted the French authorities and their lackeys and did a booming business in Portugal, Spain, and Italy, often with the corrupt approval of Napoleon's handpicked rulers. Even his brothers Joseph in Naples, Louis in Holland, and Jérôme in Westphalia, who had been placed on the throne by the emperor, allowed British merchant ships into their harbors to trade freely.

French manufacturers simply couldn't supply the finished goods that England did. Russia was hit especially hard: its thriving export market in raw materials such as tallow, pitch, wood, corn, iron, and leather collapsed under Napoleon's regime. England responded with its own blockade, a much more effective one, as it was enforced by the Royal Navy. Rich barons in Paris had to smuggle in tobacco and coffee, and even aristocratic families hung a single lump of sugar from their ceilings on a string and allowed their members only a single dunk of the sweetener into their coffee. In Hamburg, all but three of the city's four hundred sugar factories closed as a result of the embargo, and one of Napoleon's administrators there had to turn to England to get warm uniforms for the emperor's troops, without which they would have "perished with the cold." England had woven itself into the fabric of international life, and even Bonaparte couldn't unravel its ties.

In December 1810, the young Tsar Alexander, under pressure from his merchants and after watching the value of the paper ruble fall 50 percent, opened Russian ports to ships from neutral countries (which were sure to be filled with British goods) and slapped steep tariffs on French luxury products. The Continental System

was effectively dead in Moscow. The blockade was almost universally hated, but it was Napoleon's only real weapon against England. If he let Russia openly flout the embargo, it would become
an "absurdity," in the emperor's opinion. That couldn't be allowed
to happen. "Sooner or later we must encounter and defeat the
Russians," Napoleon had written as early as 1806, and now the
case for him became even more pressing.

For his part, the tsar eventually saw Napoleon clearly, not as a
monster or a soul mate (a notion he had briefly entertained) but as a
conqueror who demanded obedience, pure and simple. Concessions
on Poland and the embargo were Napoleon's main demands now,
and Alexander knew he couldn't relent on the first issue. "The
world is clearly not big enough for us," he wrote in the buildup to
the war, "to come to an understanding over that country."

The emperor was intensely frustrated by Alexander's stubborn-
ness. From speaking of the young man as an underrated ruler,
Napoleon began to revert to the old chestnuts of anti-Russian invec-
tive: Alexander was inscrutable, a Tatar, a barbarian. He repeated to
his advisers ridiculous stories and accounts of conspiracies hatched
by the Russian imperial court to overthrow or undermine him. Perhaps as in every war, the enemy used many of the same tropes in de-
scribing Napoleon, especially that of a barbarian.

But disillusionment with Alexander didn't necessitate war with
Russia. The tsar was flouting the embargo on English goods, but
so were Napoleon's own brothers. Poland was still securely in the
French sphere, and Alexander had been sufficiently cowed by two
defeats not to attempt anything in the near future. Still, Napoleon
(like Alexander) had domestic concerns that would be alleviated
by a new war: the nobles were pressing the emperor for reform,
and a crop failure in 1811 had exacerbated tensions and depressed
the economy. Fresh victories would turn the public's mind away
from the increasing authoritarianism of his rule.

There are a hundred theories as to why Napoleon began to contemplate war with Russia, from Freud's speculation that he was driven by guilt over his recent divorce from the empress Josephine to mental complications from his declining health. Napoleon said that the speculation that swirled around him even during the lead-up was frivolous. "I care nothing for St-Cloud or the Tuileries," he said of two of his magnificent residences. "It would matter little to me if they were burned down. I count my houses as nothing, women as nothing, my son as not very much. I leave one place, I go to another. I leave St-Cloud and I go to Moscow, not out of inclination or to gratify myself, but out of dry calculation." Dry calculation, of course, in the service of a fantastic ambition.

LETTERS FLEW BETWEEN Paris and Moscow in 1810 and 1811, the tone getting progressively colder and more threatening. War drew closer and Alexander knew it was going to be costly. "It is going to cause torrents of blood to flow," he wrote. In addition to the disagreement over the blockade, Alexander fumed at Napoleon's refusal to divvy up the Ottoman Empire as promised; his installation in 1810 of Jean-Baptiste Bernadotte as king of Sweden, which Alexander viewed as an aggressive French threat on his border; and France's swallowing up of the Duchy of Oldenburg in northwest Germany, which was supposed to fall to Alexander's brother-in-law. These actions inflamed age-old stereotypes of French arrogance and gave an increasingly hostile Alexander little room to maneuver with his nobles or military advisers. He felt that war was coming and that it would decide the fate of his empire.

France was already at war with Spain and England on the Iberian Peninsula, a vicious, seesaw campaign that gave birth to the concept of the guerrilla war. Spain had included some brilliant successes, but over the course of three years it had shown Napoleon's weakness as a political strategist: he repeatedly concluded that the revolt had been quashed when it hadn't, never comprehended the nationalistic fervor of the rebels, and failed, crucially, to set up an adequate supply system for his 350,000 troops. His "live off the land" philosophy had worked in the emperor's blitzkrieg victories, but when extended over time, it led to an embittered populace, fueling the resistance.

The quagmire of Spain only made a fast victory in Russia seem more attractive. But this war would be different from all the other Continental campaigns Napoleon had fought: the musket cartridges that, as 1811 ended, were being packed into knapsacks from Brittany to Rome would be superseded by a force being carried to the battlefield by the soldiers themselves, secreted in the folds of their clothes. The killing agent that the scientists would discover two hundred years later in Vilnius was already present in the Grande Armée's ranks.

CHAPTER 2

A Portable Metropolis

THE ARMY THAT THE EMPEROR MOBILIZED TO THREATEN Russia was enormous: all told, 690,000 men were under arms, including reserves, of whom between 550,000 and 600,000 would actually cross the Niemen River into Russian territory. Over the corps of veterans had been layered green recruits, who would hopefully learn enough from their peers to make it to and then over the battlefields. It was a staggering collection of men from a dozen different nations and duchies and kingdoms, speaking a babel of languages, overseen by a legendary administration that could move semaphore signals at 120 miles per hour and staffed by veterans who had fed, clothed, and nursed Napoleon's armies from Italy to Spain to Egypt.

As it assembled, the army and its trail of approximately 50,000 wives, whores, sutlers, and attendants represented more people than lived in the entire city of Paris. (To accomplish that today would take over 2.1 million men.) It formed the fifth-largest city in the world, after Tokyo and before Istanbul. The Grande Armée had become a portable metropolis, with its own courts of justice, its own criminals, its own hospitals and patois. The small mercenary armies that had fought in Europe at the service of kings for centuries were gone, replaced by a behemoth.

Most of the men were, unlike their mercenary predecessors, motivated to serve under Napoleon by more than compulsion or gold. It wasn't a volunteer army by any means—Napoleon had sent teams to force French conscripts from their town halls and homes—but many of the men wanted to have an adventure, to squeeze some loot out of their enemies, to honor France or their own brief lives, or to write their name in glory on the battlefield. Napoleon guaranteed that one could burst from the ranks and become an officer for a single act of bravery, and that spoke to many of his soldiers.

The Grande Armée was divided into three components. The 250,000-strong First Army Group was made up of three battalions, along with the Imperial Guard and the cavalry. The Second and Third Army groups, totaling 315,000 men, would play a mainly supporting role, guarding supply lines, patrolling the rear, and being called on to reinforce depleted battalions.

Napoleon led the Imperial Guard of 50,000 handpicked troops known as the "immortals." These were the reserves, to be utilized to tilt a battle at the crucial moment. The Imperial Guard, essential to the outcome of so many battles past and to come, were Napoleon's elite: Each had to be able to read and write and stand above five foot six (in a time when most Frenchmen were closer to five feet). Each had served in at least three campaigns and bore the scars of at least two wounds. They looked the part of the military beau ideal in their two-foot shakos: mustached, young, and strapping.

If you wanted to find living, breathing examples of what changes Napoleon had wrought, you could do worse than look to the ranks of this army, especially the men who led them, his marshals. They were the new aristocracy. The title of "marshal" had existed before the Revolution as part of the vast system of favor currying and court intrigue that had so depressed the young Napoleon and his peers, but the emperor refashioned it into an order of real accomplishment, open to anyone. He named twenty-six marshals between 1804 and 1815. In Louis XVI's time, many of them would have toiled away in obscurity. Under Napoleon, they made his army even more formidable. Among them, Davout, Murat, and Ney, along with General Junot, stand out.

Louis-Nicolas Davout was the exception among the four: he would most likely have played a leading role in the French army if Napoleon had never been born. A strict taskmaster and disciplinarian, he was descended from a blue-blooded line of patrician warriors that extended back to the Crusades. Known as the "Iron Marshal," the balding general was the archetype of the committed professional soldier that forms the backbone of any great army. Many commanders envied him, as Davout had been the first among them to achieve fame in France. He was as hated for his perfectionism and his temper as he was admired, but his troops knew at least that he would see to their every need and would suffer every hardship they suffered. He commanded I Corps.

Joachim Murat was a different kind of personality entirely. He had grown up around horses, working in the stables of his father, a country innkeeper, until he was sent away to join the priesthood, a perfectly respectable career. But it was the wrong one for Murat, who with his almost feminine good looks and thirst for fame wanted a career in the cavalry. Murat ran away to join the King's Chasseurs at the age of twenty and became Napoleon's aide-de-camp in the Italian campaign. Dressed in his trademark outré costumes—scarlet thigh-high leather boots, a tunic made of cloth of gold, a sky blue jacket, and a sword belt crusted with diamonds was a typical combination—he consistently matched his daring on the field with an instinctive flair for tactics, especially in a brilliant flanking maneuver in Egypt that won him his own division. Napoleon once snapped at the young general, "You look like a clown," but he favored boldness in his generals and Murat exemplified it.

Murat did lack Davout's almost genetic loyalty to his leader. He had flirted with Josephine, and he was thrown into a fit of depression and jealousy when Napoleon failed to name him king of Spain, instead awarding him Naples. The former seminarian was a brilliant field leader but nakedly ambitious and often reckless to a dangerous degree. He commanded the Grande Armée's cavalry units.

At the head of III Corps, Michel Ney was known even before Russia as "the Bravest of the Brave." His father was a poor cooper who couldn't afford to set him up in a profession, so Ney took up arms. Imperturbable, vulgar, badly educated, he rose by a native talent for battlefield strategy and sheer fearlessness. One of his typical exploits dated from 1799, when Ney entered a town occupied by enemy Austrian units disguised as a Prussian civilian. Wandering the streets, he took note of every guard post and every tent, then strolled back across the picket lines to plan his offensive. Had he been caught, he would have been executed as a spy, but Ney seemed indifferent to the danger. The outnumbered French regiment attacked the next day and took the town easily.

A peasant in the best sense, Ney was also difficult to command and sometimes rash in his hurry to engage the enemy, but the emperor couldn't resist his toughness. "That man is a lion," he remarked to his staff at the Battle of Friedland as Ney marched by with his troops. From the emperor, it was high praise.

One key player without a marshal's baton was Jean-Andoche Junot, who had been with Napoleon from 1793, and had been seriously wounded in the head at Lonato in 1796. Erratic, fearless, and loyal, Junot hated the fact that he had never become a marshal. Some said that the head wound had altered his personality. But Napoleon stood by him. It would prove to be a risky decision.

The men Napoleon had assembled to lead the Grande Armée in Russia had all proved themselves in battle and believed in daring over caution. Napoleon had no pure theorists or rear-echelon generals in his key commands. His leaders had risen largely through their own instincts, and they, like their leader, loved risk.

They were an apt expression of his reign, and no one had been able to match them.

THE MAKEUP OF DIFFERENT units varied based on availability of men, casualties, illness, and the role of the particular force, but certain parameters were common throughout the Grande Armée. The smallest infantry unit was the company of 100–140 men. Six companies on average formed a battalion, which averaged around 600 men (but which could fluctuate down to 300 and up to 1,200). Four battalions made up a regiment of approximately 2,500 men. Two regiments on average made a division of 5,000 men or so, including an attached artillery unit. The largest force in the Russian campaign was the corps, made up of several divisions, allied with cavalry units and artillery.

The size of the corps varied from the 10,000-strong force under Prince Eugène, Napoleon's stepson (from his marriage to Josephine) and ruler of Venice, to Murat's 40,000 cavalrymen to Davout's mammoth I Corps, which fielded 70,000 men at the start of the campaign, more troops than many armies had put into the field a generation before, and a force that underlined Napoleon's confidence in the Iron Marshal. Attacks were most often carried out at the corps and division level, depending on how broad the field of battle was.

Napoleon was the undisputed head of the Grande Armée. Beneath him on the command chart was his chief of staff, Louis-Alexandre Berthier, who was closer to an exalted secretary, dispensing his orders and running the organization. Under Berthier were the marshals and a few high-ranking generals, each commanding one of the eleven corps put into the field. Each marshal or corps commander had a complete hierarchy under him: generals, majors, down to the commanders of the individual infantry battalions, artillery units, and cavalry regiments.

In all, Napoleon commanded 522,300 infantry, 94,000 cavalry, 47,000 artillery, and 21,000 miscellaneous troops. Some 449,000 of these were first-line troops intended for battle.

The deeper statistics were telling: Two-thirds of the troops were non-French. Napoleon had insisted that his allies bear a large share of the burden of his ambitions. That 80,000 were mounted on horseback indicated that Napoleon intended to strike fast and end the war quickly. (But with a sure hand—all the corps were commanded by French generals or marshals, apart from the Polish and Austrian forces.) The unprecedented size of the army meant not only that it would be a monumental task to keep it fed and organized, but that Napoleon, who had throughout his career maneuvered his regiments like an admiral commanding a fleet of highly maneuverable light cruisers, darting and speeding to arrive at an unexpected position at a crucial moment in time, was now at the helm of a massive and unwieldy ship.

These figures make Napoleon's uncanny relationship with his soldiers even more impressive. Most of his troops, it has to be emphasized, were from nations *he had conquered by force*. The emperor had humiliated Austria in war after war, and yet its men fought for him; he had forced Holland to accept his brother Louis as its king (later to remove him), but the Dutch would have enthralling moments in Russia. Certainly he had coerced their leaders, but most of his troops ought to have been sabotaging him at every turn, or performing only well enough to avoid being shot for desertion. But they would fight, for the most part, like lions. It was as if, in 1945, General Patton had convinced the conquered Germans to fight the Japanese in the South Pacific. Very few leaders throughout history could have done it.

Some have suggested that the emperor's army was, in fact, *too* large. Napoleon biographer Frank McLynn argues that Napoleon had become an expert in winning with armies of 100,000 troops, "which permitted the speed and flexibility that produced an Austerlitz." McLynn suggests that Napoleon failed to do the correct math: increasing his army's striking ability sixfold increased his command and supply problems not by a similar number but exponentially. "It was an impossible dream," McLynn writes, "something impracticable before the advent of railways and telegraph."

But had Napoleon begun with one-quarter of the force he assembled and not won a quick and devastating battle, the killing agent that would turn up in those bones in Vilnius, and which was already filtering through his ranks, would have quickly whittled those numbers down to a pittance. Each strategy, in retrospect, had its risk.

ALEXANDER'S FRONTLINE FORCES in the beginning numbered only about 162,000, giving the French a three-to-one advantage at the beginning of the war. His army was strong at the bottom, dissolute in the middle, and often chaotic at the top. The ordinary Russian soldier was typically poorly fed, poorly equipped, but decently trained and ferocious in battle, especially in a defensive posture. Nowhere else would Napoleonic troops encounter soldiers who fought as fanatically or bravely when defending a position; a famous epigram said that you not only had to kill the Russian soldier, you had to then push him over.

The officer corps was a glaring weakness. Officers gambled, whored, and drank when they should have been drilling their men. Commanders weren't held to account for the performance of their troops or junior officers. They treated the common soldiers more like automatons or serfs they had inherited than men to be inspired and led.

And the Russian high command, although it contained some brilliant officers, was riven with dissension. "The headquarters of the Emperor were already overrun with distinguished idlers," wrote Carl von Clausewitz, the brilliant German strategist attached to the Russian headquarters staff. Petty intrigues, nationalist posturing

between the Russians and Germans and Austrian commanders, co-
teries and cliques all contributed to an atmosphere where decisions
were made and unmade in hours. Alexander lacked the backbone to
stop the intriguing that every general, sensing the chance to mold
the tsar to his wishes, engaged in.

The Russian army was divided into two forces. General Mikhail
Barclay de Tolly led 160,000 men of the First Army in a line opposed to Napoleon's northern positions. Barclay was an unspec-
tacular but highly competent general, a straight-backed, balding,
reserved man who suffered from several disadvantages in the position and historical moment he found himself in: He was descended
from a Scottish clan and spoke German as his first language,
deeply suspect credentials for a man defending a country that was
whipping itself into a nationalist fervor. And although he had
made his name in a thrilling battle during the 1809 Finnish war by
marching his army over the frozen Gulf of Bothnia, an exploit
worthy of the young Napoleon, he was conservative by nature.

The man who would quickly emerge to be his closest rival was
General Pyotr Bagration, a hot-tempered nationalist eager for a
confrontation with Napoleon. Bagration commanded the 60,000
troops of the Second Army, which would face the French positions
in the south. Four years younger than Barclay, he was a firebrand,
tetchy, capable of plunging into ecstasies of despair or joy depending on the progress of the battle (and of his career). He was as ambitious for himself as he was for his nation, and in his deeply
emotional responses to the progress of the war, he would prove to
have an innate understanding of the Russian mind that the phlegmatic Barclay often lacked.

Napoleon planned to drive between them east along the Orsha-
Smolensk-Vitebsk land bridge, which would lead him almost directly
due east toward Moscow, should he need to go that far. His plans
were straightforward: keep the two armies separated; drive forward
and encircle them separately; cut off their supply, communication,

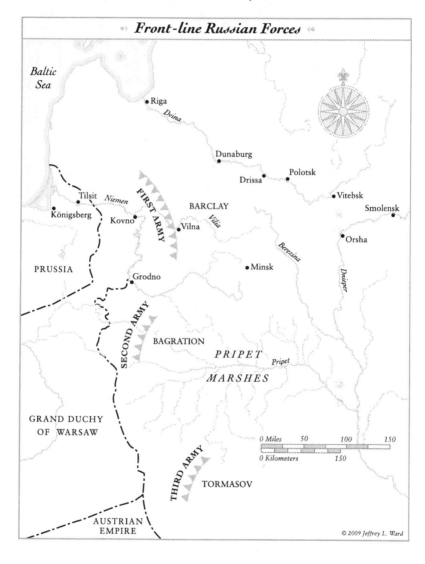

Front-line Russian Forces

Baltic
Sea

● Riga

Dvina

Dunaburg ●

● Polotsk

Drissa ●

Vitebsk ●

Smolensk ●

Tilsit   *Niemen*   FIRST ARMY   BARCLAY

Königsberg   Kovno ●   *Vilia*

● Vilna

Orsha ●

Berezina

PRUSSIA

Grodno ●

● Minsk

Dnieper

SECOND ARMY

BAGRATION   *PRIPET*   *Pripet*

MARSHES

GRAND DUCHY
OF WARSAW

THIRD ARMY

TORMASOV

0 Miles   50   100   150

0 Kilometers   150

AUSTRIAN
EMPIRE

© 2009 Jeffrey L. Ward

and reinforcement lines to the east; force them into a defensive posture near Grodno; and then annihilate them. Napoleon continued to believe that Alexander would sue for peace after a convincing French victory.

But in one respect Napoleon had radically misjudged Alexander. He was thinking in terms of empire. Alexander was mobilizing his people for another kind of conflict entirely. The tsar was convinced he was facing an Antichrist, a millennial figure who would destroy Russia itself. For him, the coming war was a religious crusade.

Two ANCIENT WARS set the stage for the kind of conflicts the two men planned for and mark the vicious debut of the lethal pathogen that was already deeply embedded in the Grande Armée.

In 1489 the Catholic monarchs Ferdinand and Isabella fought a decisive battle with the Islamic forces of the Moors. The Moors had ruled Spain ever since crossing the Strait of Gibraltar in A.D. 711, leaving only a few lonely outposts of Christians in the north of Spain along the Bay of Biscay. The Christian warriors bided their time, taking advantage of dissension among the Muslim rulers, looking to the Crusades for inspiration in their slow war of toppling one Islamic stronghold after another. By the late 1400s, only the citadel of Granada was left.

During the siege of the city in 1489, a third combatant entered the field: a "malignant spotted fever" began carrying off Spanish soldiers at a fast clip. When the Catholic forces mustered their soldiers in the early days of 1490 to regroup, their commanders were shocked to learn that 20,000 of their men had gone missing. Only 3,000 had fallen in battle with the Moors, meaning that a full 17,000 had died of the mysterious disease. In an age when small armies of 30,000 to 40,000 were the rule, that figure represented a devastating loss of fighting power.

But this was the illness's first foray into war, and it didn't have the decision-changing impact it would later carry. The Spanish recruited more soldiers to replenish their ranks and returned to the campaign. On January 2, 1492, the last Muslim ruler of Granada, Abu 'abd Allah Muhammad XI, departed the ancient province and left Spain to the Christians. January 2 remains a black day in the minds of Islamicists today.

Ferdinand and Isabella had fought a religious war in the context of empire (or, equally true, a war of empire in the context of religion). It was a template that fit Alexander's view of the battle to come. The Spaniards had overcome the fatal disease that struck their armies primarily by luck and persistence: The battles were being fought on their territory, meaning their commanders could quickly replace troops lost in the epidemic. Alexander, whose religious mania exceeded that of the Spanish king and queen, would have the same advantage against the despoiler from France.

FORTY YEARS LATER, THE MALADY that would meet the emperor on the road to Moscow emerged from the shadows to fulfill its role as an arbiter of empires.

The conflict drew together the depressive King Charles of Spain, the greatest power on the Continent; King Francis I of France, a young ruler who wished to retrieve ancestral lands claimed by Charles (and his two sons, held for ransom in a previous war); and King Henry VIII of England, who had territorial ambitions in the war but also sought, by taking control of Italy and Rome, to gain control over Pope Clement VII and to obtain a divorce from Catherine of Aragon so that he could marry Anne Boleyn. Drawing in the continent's three most powerful monarchs, this was a war for control of Europe's future.

King Charles expressed the ethos of the war they would fight. It was a contest between honorable knights, and Charles longed to live up to the code they shared:

> Therefore I cannot but see and feel that time is passing, and I with it, and yet I would not like to go without performing some great action to serve as a monument

to my name. What is lost today will not be found to-morrow and I have done nothing so far to cover myself with glory.

It was a passage that Napoleon could have written nearly three centuries later.

In 1527 the forces of King Francis (bolstered by a contingent from Henry VIII) met Charles's mercenary army at the Italian port city of Naples, the French army with 30,000 men, the Imperial army of Charles with 12,000. If Francis could destroy the army inside the walls, Spain's power, so dominant for so long, would be broken at least for the near future and perhaps for centuries.

But then a pathogen appeared in the ranks and began to kill wantonly. "There originates a slight internal fever in the person's body," wrote one ambassador, who later died of the illness, "which at first does not seem to be very serious. But soon it reappears with a great fervor that immediately kills." It was the same inscrutable microbe that had emerged at the Spanish siege of Granada.

Bodies began to pile up. The Italian sun beat down on men who had fallen into stupors or raving fevers. Each day brought more cases, and soon the sick began to die in terrible numbers. "The dangers of war are the least we have to think about," wrote one commander. The French lieutenants, convinced the air in the plain had turned bad, urged their commander to retreat to the hills, where the atmosphere was cooler and fresher. But he refused and the epidemic "literally exploded." Desertions increased; men faked illness to get out of the death zone. Out of a force of 30,000, only 7,000 were fit for duty. Soon two out of every three of the soldiers had died, most of them from the nameless pathogen.

At the end of August, the French forces broke from their camps and fled in panic, leaving their artillery and their sick comrades behind. The siege was broken. Charles's forces ran them down on the road from Naples to Rome, stripping, robbing, and killing the remnants. "Without a doubt," one observer wrote, "one would not find in all of ancient and modern history so devastating a ruin of such a flourishing army." Francis's men were skeletal, sick, some of them clothed only in tree leaves. The disease claimed more on the way and bodies could be seen heaped on the side of the road. Of the 5,000 who started the retreat, perhaps 200 arrived safely in the holy city; from there, some French troops were forced to walk all the way back to their native land.

The effects unspooled for years. Spain dominated the Continent, King Francis was humiliated and France radically weakened. Pope Clement VII rejected Henry VIII's petition for divorce as a direct result of the defeat. Infuriated, the king broke with Rome and led his country into the Church of England.

Even today, a believer kneeling to pray in a High Anglican Church worships, at least partly, in a structure built by an invisible microbe.

The conflict revealed crucial aspects of the epidemic disease: It seemed to need large groups of people to thrive. It left dark spots on the torsos of many of its victims, sparing the hands and face (making it harder to detect in men who wore full uniforms). It had a terrifying mortality rate, up to 95 percent, among the highest of any epidemic disease known to humankind. And it had a decided predilection for war. It was almost as if nature had invented a biological sleeping agent to combat the wishes of ambitious men.

NEARLY THREE HUNDRED YEARS after the siege of Naples, Napoleon reclaimed Francis's sword after conquering Spain and brought it back to Paris in glory. He'd revenged the monarch's humiliation. And now Napoleon imagined he was about to embark on a war that would share in the same codes of war.

The historian David Bell has argued persuasively that in the years 1792–1815, the modern concept of "total war" came into being, ushered in by Enlightenment ideas about the perfectibility of society and the political upheavals that followed the French Revolution. The "culture of war" was transformed so that the struggle between France and the successive coalitions against it became, in the words of one French supporter, "a war to the death, which we will fight so as to destroy and annihilate all who attack us, or be destroyed ourselves."

The description fits Alexander's view of the coming battle. The transformation of national conflicts into all-out, apocalyptic duels, a notion that has come cleanly down to us as a clash of civilizations in which one side must win or die, would be realized on the road to Moscow. And there, as in the modern version, faith would play a huge role.

Certainly Napoleon endorsed such an all-encompassing view of war, especially early in his career. Still, he genuinely imagined the coming invasion would have certain limitations, especially in the endgame. He believed Alexander was a nobleman who would fight, be measured on the battlefield, and then settle according to the results of arms, as had Francis I and Charles of Spain. The emperor had badly misjudged the situation in Russia.

But his war machine made the error seem irrelevant. If ever there had been an armed force built for total, annihilating war, it was the Grande Armée. No divisions on earth, arrayed against it in a straight-ahead confrontation, had a remote chance of winning.

Except if they had a hidden, undetectable ally in the fever that had burned at Naples.

CHAPTER 3

Drumbeat

A S WAR APPROACHED, ADVISERS BEGAN TO WARN NAPO-
leon. His statistical expert, a Captain Leclerc, looked at the
demographics and resources of Russian society and told the
emperor that, if he invaded, his army would be "annihilated." Others recounted in detail the deprivations suffered by the last army to
invade the Russian hinterland: that of the strapping and enigmatic
Charles XII of Sweden, whose forces were almost completely
wiped out by cold, Cossacks, and disease in 1709. Charles would
come to haunt Napoleon, as he paged through Voltaire's history of
the campaign on his way to Moscow. But more and more a smashing victory seemed an answer to Napoleon's problems. By the first
months of 1811, the emperor had ordered his Topographical Department to supply him with accurate maps of western Russia.

Early in 1811, Napoleon assured both his advisers and Alexander's representatives that his intentions were peaceful. "It would be
a crime on my part," he told Prince Shuvalov in May, "for I would
be making war without a purpose, and I have not yet, thank God,
lost my head. I am not mad." But he contradicted himself by returning to the language of threat and provocation again and again.
Indecision, which would plague every phase of his conduct of the
war, also muddied his thinking when it came to starting it.

The first unit to move on his command was a Polish cavalry regiment, which left Spain on January 8, 1812. On January 13, Napoleon ordered his War Administration department to be ready to provision an army of 400,000 frontline troops for fifty days. That broke down to 20 million rations of bread and 20 million rations of rice, along with 2 million bushels of oats for the horses and oxen. Some 6,000 wagons, either horse- or ox-drawn, were requisitioned to carry enough flour for 200,000 men for two months. The customary card index, which Napoleon kept on all opposing armies, detailing strengths and weaknesses down to the battalion level, was quickly pulled together.

The emperor wrote Alexander on February 28, 1812, warning him to abide by the Continental System or face dire consequences, a threat that Alexander brushed off by saying he was only protecting Russian business interests. Alexander included a list of demands required for his return to the Continental System, including a French evacuation of Prussia, which Napoleon regarded as impertinent. The emperor railed at his advisers and predicted that a prospective war would last only twelve days. "I have come to finish once and for all with the colossus of Northern barbarism," he shouted. Napoleon's advisers were horrified. He had never approached a campaign with so few backing opinions from those around him.

"Whether he triumphs or succumbs," observed the German-Austrian diplomat Count von Metternich, "in either case the situation in Europe will never be the same again." The emperor ratcheted up the rhetoric against Alexander, and he began to embroider his vision of a quick war with grand designs: if the tsar fell or was assassinated, the Grande Armée could pivot south and march to the Ganges, taking India and its rich markets and dealing a crushing blow to English maritime commerce, crippling the trade that funded the British Empire. Napoleon was wandering even deeper into self-delusion.

The emperor wasn't the same man he had been ten years before. He had grown stout, his skin had turned sallow, the lean, hawklike face had developed the hint of jowls, and his almost forbiddingly intense expressions had mellowed and grown more querulous. "He spoke more slowly and took longer to make decisions," writes historian Adam Zamoyski. "Something was eating away at the vital force of this Promethean creature." Whether this decline was caused by the effects of middle age or physiological problems, but Napoleon was a less commanding figure, physically and intellectually, just as he began his most exhausting mission.

IN RUSSIA, THE CALLS for war escalated almost monthly. The country was, in its own way, deeply imperialistic, a rising power probing west (in Sweden) and south (toward the increasingly feeble Ottoman Empire) for new sources of wealth and territory. Its upper classes and its army officer corps were fluent in French, the only language many of them spoke, and their bookshelves were lined with volumes of Voltaire and Montesquieu. Still, they deeply resented Napoleon's encroachment upon Russian power and national pride.

As rumors of war spread, waves of revolt rippled through the society. French tutors lost their jobs and it became fashionable for boyars and aristocrats to spice their conversations with Russian phrases. When Alexander appeared on the Kremlin's Red Steps, he was greeted by thousands of ordinary Russians shouting, "We will die or conquer!"

In the early months of 1812, Napoleon's armies began streaming toward the Polish border from France, Italy, Hungary, and other garrisons. Even the Austrians and Prussians were forced to contribute 30,000 and 20,000 men, respectively, to face their former ally. Napoleon had clearly made up his mind on war, though he kept his target a secret from the general public and even his own marshals.

But Alexander stole a march on the emperor. In quick succession, he formed an alliance with his old adversaries the Swedes in the north and signed a peace treaty with the Ottoman Turks in the south, securing his most troublesome borders and eliminating the possible division of his armies for war on two fronts. Napoleon meanwhile dithered and made a halfhearted attempt to sign a treaty with the British in Spain, without, however, offering much of anything to end a disastrous war. The British sensibly refused. In the months before the Moscow campaign, it was Alexander who looked like the master political player and Napoleon who looked like a distracted novice.

ON MAY 9, 1812, the emperor left Paris and began a processional through his client kingdoms, a display of his wealth and power that he'd remember as the happiest time of his life. He traveled with an army of 300 carriages filled with crystal, plate, tapestries, and his own personal furniture, sweeping into the king of Saxony's castle and putting hundreds of chefs to work creating a Pan-European menu that was testament to his reach. Nobles, kings, and queens came to pay homage.

The German poet Heinrich Heine remarked on how the army's veterans, passing in review before the emperor, "glanced up at him with so awesome a devotion, so sympathetic an earnestness, with the pride of death." The army itself was a pageant, gaily outfitted in all the colors of the peacock. Cuirassiers, the cavalrymen who were the successors of medieval knights, pranced on their chargers, their mirrorlike steel helmets capped by black horsehair manes. The carabiniers were dressed in crisp white jackets, while the lancers wore crimson shapkas with white plumes a foot and a half high. The rapid-response chasseurs wore kolbachs with green and blood-red feathers, while the hussars strutted in their tall peaked shakos topped with red feathers. Dragoons sported turbans cut out of tiger skin and brilliant red coats, and the grenadiers of Napoleon's elite unit, the Imperial Guard, wore the traditional French blue uniform covered by great bearskins, the sun glinting off their gold earrings.

AS MORE AND MORE units from the empire marched toward the Niemen River to assemble for the invasion, in Germany one of the millions who would be deeply affected by Napoleon's decisions prepared to leave. Franz Roeder was a captain in the First Battalion of the Lifeguards of the Grand Duke of Hesse, a German principality. Roeder was typical of the soldiers who would form the core of any assault on Russia: he was non-French; experienced in battle, having nearly died in the Russo-Prussian War; and fiercely loyal to his men and his reputation, if not to the emperor. Roeder was handsome, with a long aquiline nose, an intense gaze, wavy hair that fell over his collar, and a mouth that seemed to be holding back some outrageous remark. He had entered the barracks after punching a schoolmaster as a boy and running from a flogging, never to return. And as war approached, he was trying to get on with his life despite the rumbles from Paris. The captain expressed as well as any soldier readying for battle what it would mean in the terms of a single life.

For Roeder, the most pressing dilemmas were romantic: His beloved wife Mina, a direct descendant of Martin Luther, had died of consumption that year and he was left with two young children to care for. Still steeped in grief, he was nevertheless thinking of asking a young woman named Sophie, who lived in a city miles from his hometown, to marry him. His children needed a mother, and he, in his loneliness, needed someone to love. Letters and short visits added up to a courtship against the gathering clouds.

As Napoleon rattled his saber, Roeder read the signs. "Nobody believes that it will really come to war," he wrote in his diary. "This

hope helps the good souls to overcome the pain of parting and ob-
scures for them the danger which looms so close, which may well
lead, not to long absence, but to parting forever." One night, feeling a departure approaching, he rushed to the neighboring town
where Sophie lived, pulled her out of the opera between the second
and third acts, and asked her to marry him. He didn't even have a
ring to offer her, but she said yes. The veteran campaigner was relieved. At least the children, if he died, wouldn't be orphans.

BY APRIL, CAPTAIN ROEDER was marching his 181 men through
the roads of eastern Germany. In the bigger towns, his men were
feted at balls, and Roeder, although just married to a new wife and
haunted by a dead one, flirted with the local beauties. His men were
mostly healthy but suffering from diarrhea, "which may be partly
caused by the water," he wrote from the German town of Doberan,
"through which they frequently have to march up to the knees." A
more worrying case was that of his quartermaster, who, on May 21,
died of "creeping nervous fever," most likely an early sign of the approaching epidemic.

But the general mood was good. "I share the thoughts of the
whole army. It has never shown itself more impatient to run
after fresh triumphs," wrote Captain Louis-Florimond Fantin des
Odoards, a veteran grenadier who had fought at Austerlitz and
Friedland. "Its august leader has so accustomed it to fatigue, danger, and glory that a state of repose has become hateful. With such
men we can conquer the world." Roeder, too, despite his love for
Sophie, relished being out with his men, throwing his cape under a
tree and falling asleep under the stars. Many of the young recruits
saw the 1812 campaign as the finale in a long link of adventures,
the last chance for rapid advancement and glory. Some 10,000
wills were drawn up by Parisian notaries before the commence-
ment of hostilities, and the famous coachbuilder Gros Jean churned
out carriage after carriage for the marshals and generals.

. . .

NAPOLEON PLANNED FOR a spring/summer offensive that would allow the fields to ripen with oats for his horses and wheat for his men. As he attended to the thousands of details necessary for a campaign involving half a million troops and more, he made a shocking discovery. His much-vaunted medical service was in disarray, with even the basic necessities for a campaign—dressings, linens, splints—in short supply. His surgeon in chief, the legendary Dr. Dominique-Jean Larrey, rushed from Paris to Mentz, Germany. But the forty-six-year-old surgeon was being sent "doctors" so inexperienced that he was forced to give them crash courses in battlefield medicine.

Despite Larrey's sterling reputation ("the worthiest man I know," the emperor once said), Napoleon didn't trust doctors. He could be progressive when it came to new techniques, such as Edward Jenner's smallpox vaccine, discovered in 1796, which the emperor embraced, even having his two-month-old son inoculated and spearheading a vaccination campaign for the young and new army recruits. But for the most part he despised physicians, shouting at his guests "Medicine is the science of assassins!" during one memorable party. He was a fatalist when it came to epidemics. He believed that if one wasn't strong enough to resist disease, it would claim you. Mental fortitude was the only remedy.

These attitudes were rooted in Napoleon's youth. At the age of twenty, while walking across the Ajaccio salt flats near his birthplace, he'd come down with a serious fever, but he had survived with no aftereffects. While stationed in Auxonne as a poverty-stricken junior officer, Napoleon had survived a bout of malaria while still managing to put in eighteen hours of study every day. A second wave hit after the first had subsided, and Napoleon blamed it on the *miasme* (or "bad air") from a river close to his lodgings. Still, he worked furiously through the headaches and pain. "I have no other resource but work," he wrote. "I dress but once in eight days; I sleep but little since my illness; it is incredible." For the young Corsican—penniless, friendless, obscure but driven—those days were his refining fire. Disease had been just another test. Why couldn't other men overcome it?

Instead of physicians he believed in portents, lucky omens, as any true Corsican of the time would have. March 20 and June 14 were particularly good days for him; he hated Fridays and the number 13. He had a "familiar" called Red Man, a conduit to his lucky star, which visited him only on important occasions. In Egypt, the Red Man had told him that success was guaranteed despite his reversals, and in Italy, at Marengo, the spirit assured him that he was soon to be emperor of France. As he contemplated the invasion of Russia, the ghost had appeared to him and told him the war was a mistake, but after considering the warning, he disobeyed. To rebel even against the spirit world would prove he was equal to the gods themselves. "I'm trying to rise above myself," he confided to his officers on the campaign. "That's what greatness means."

Later in his career, he learned to use disease. When the English took the island of Walcheren off the coast of the Netherlands in 1809, he refused to send his troops in. "Walcheren has for its defense fever and poor air," he told his marshals. "In this season the island is one of the unhealthiest places on earth." The British fell in droves to Walcheren fever, a mixture of dysentery and assorted fevers. "Health is indispensable in war" became one of the emperor's maxims.

Napoleon had actually overseen a host of advances in war medicine, including Larrey's invention of the "flying ambulance," which, combined with his insistence that doctors bring their field hospitals close to the lines of battle, reduced the time that doctors could reach and treat wounded men from many hours to fifteen minutes. (For these innovations, and his policy of treating enemy wounded in the same way he treated French ones, Larrey is often considered the spiritual father of the modern Red Cross.) The doctor was genuinely loved by the soldiers; when in 1808 a rumor shot through the Army of Spain that Larrey had been killed by enemy fire, the troops of the elite Imperial Guard broke down and swore to avenge him. The rumors turned out to be untrue.

But when it came to funding his army, Napoleon's prejudices came through. On the Russian campaign, the surgical corps was a shell of its former self. Young men unfit for army service, the dregs of the French population, could get an appointment as a junior regimental surgeon after only three months at a medical school. One medical student remarked on how many of his classmates were "hunchbacks and cripples." Napoleon had systematically cut at the control that doctors had over their own work, handing supervision over to bureaucrats and even stripping physicians of the epaulettes they had worn on their uniforms. A significant portion of his doctors were regarded as cowards, malingerers, or hacks.

THE FRENCH HAD FACED the killer that was gathering power in its ranks before. It had struck the French army during the wars in Spain (where 300,000 of Napoleon's men died of disease, and only 100,000 in battle). The pathogen had aided them immensely at the siege of Saragossa in the summer of 1808, when 54,000 of the city's 100,000 citizens died of the disease, along with 18,000 of the 20,000 Spanish soldiers within its walls, forcing the city to surrender. After Austerlitz, a bout of the illness struck that Dr. Larrey described in the complex nosological formulation of the day as "a malignant, nervous and putrid hospital fever (adynamico-ataxic)." During the epidemic, a Polish officer, Heinrich von Brandt, caught the disease and was taken to a military hospital. "[The dead] were thrown from the windows stark naked," he wrote, "and they fell, one on top of the other, with a muffled thud just as though they were sacks of corn."

In 1796, during the siege of Mantua, Italy, the malady, along with malaria, killed or incapacitated 14,000 of Napoleon's force of 24,000. The French still managed to prevail during the Italian campaign, but afterward one army surgeon reported the cost. "Like an enormous fire [the illness] is sweeping our hospitals," he wrote. "That mortal plague afflicting all campaigning armies is caused by the filth of these quarters, the lack of fresh air, the negligence of the troops, and the total lack of concern by our own general staffs."

Public health officials in France knew the disease. Spanish prisoners sent back from the ongoing war there brought the pathogen with them; they were forbidden to fraternize with the local French inhabitants, and after they left the straw they had slept on was burned and their barracks fumigated. The precautions weren't thorough enough, however: in one hospital, the nuns who nursed the prisoners, the guards, the porters, the gendarmes who guarded the convoys, the medical students, the chaplain, and even the secretary of the War Commissioner—nearly everyone who came in contact with the Spanish patients even for the briefest time—caught the illness. Many of them died.

During the Wars of the First Coalition, while Napoleon was making his name, an especially lethal strain swept through the Prison du Bouffay in Nantes, killing twenty-one of twenty-two sentinels and most of the committee sent to investigate. Even the grave diggers hired to bury the victims succumbed. Any doctor with long experience in France would have been familiar with the disease. In a popular medical journal, a physician wrote in April 1812: "I warn all military physicians not to congregate all their fever patients in a single room by themselves, for few would come forth from such a room alive."

In its encounters with French society, the pathogen had confirmed further clues about itself: Once entrenched in a population (how it achieved that was still a mystery), it appeared to be highly contagious. And the evidence showed that it was, as the army surgeon suspected, intimately connected with hygiene. Those two simple facts could have given Napoleon's doctors a key insight into the malady's nature and radically altered their approach to it, if they had learned the correct lessons from the outbreaks. Those bits of information would, a century and a half later, help to solve the riddle of the disease's origin, a riddle unraveled by a French doctor at another hospital in another far-flung colony of empire.

CHAPTER 4

Crossing

THE FIRST OF NAPOLEON'S SOLDIERS CROSSED THE NIEMEN River into Russia on a beautiful summer's day. Napoleon's army, the greatest he had ever led, in fact the greatest since the time of the Persian conqueror Xerxes, tramped above the rushing waters that marked the border between Poland and Russian Lithuania on June 24, 1812. Crossing the river was itself the signal, the trigger for war. It would take only hours for the news to reach Tsar Alexander I, reclining in a chair at a party scented by groves of orange trees in bloom, seventy miles to the east.

Anticipation and uncertainty and dreams of riches swirled in the minds of everyone from the emperor to raw privates pulled away from sleepy Normandy farms. The towns in Germany, the natural staging ground for an attack on Russia, had for months been full to bursting with troops waiting to know if it would be war or not. In his diary, Captain Roeder, the veteran Hessian soldier with a new wife back home, wrote how he was drinking in a restaurant when a passing Frenchman cried out on seeing him. They had tried to kill each other five years before at the Napoleonic Battle of Altenkirchen, when they were fighting on different sides. But the emperor's reach was now so all-encompassing that ancient enemies marched shoulder to shoulder. The two men fell into each other's arms.

In the noise and billowing clouds of dust and the percussive tramping of thousands of horses' hooves, the shouts and orders in a half-dozen different languages, the men who staggered out of the ranks and collapsed by the roadside were hardly noticed. A few remarked on the bodies. No one was unduly alarmed. Napoleon was already ensconced in his richly appointed carriage, pulled by six horses and equipped with volumes of history and literature, scores of maps, a writing table, and candles for reading.

The deaths could easily be attributed to exhaustion or bad alcohol. The Grande Armée had swelled enormously beyond its core of veterans for the attack on Russia, and the new recruits weren't as well conditioned as the survivors of Austerlitz and other campaigns. Cossacks, long distances, the Russian winter: these were the things that worried the men, if they worried at all. Supremely confident in its leader, the army bore down on its enemy.

For the sick, falling behind and watching their regiments disappear into a cloud of dust, the disease announced itself in various, even contradictory ways. Some victims felt at first a brush of giddiness; they became dizzy and light-headed with an almost pleasant sensation, as if they had taken a quick drink of schnapps after a long march. But this was often followed by "a very uncommon feeling . . . which is impossible to describe," as if the pit of the stomach had dropped suddenly and the heart had stopped for a few seconds, then began vibrating instead of beating. Afterward, the symptoms could disappear for hours at a time, and the person would feel perfectly healthy and perhaps dismiss the episode as a spell of heatstroke or something equally benign. But the sickness was only gathering strength, and when it returned, as it always did, its wounding and malignant nature was impossible to miss.

A blinding headache shut the men's eyes tight. Nausea and

chills racked the entire body, soon followed by "universal pain," body aches so excruciating, especially in the back muscles, that they could drop a man to the ground. Heat followed cold, as after three or four days a "river of fire" spread from the stomach upward across the chest and then shot along the pectoral muscles to the fingertips. The heat pulsated like a bonfire onto which fresh timber was being thrown every few hours or so; dying down, it was replaced by chills that could cause the teeth to knock together, then the river of fire would flame up again. A fever arrived and the temperature rose quickly to 105 degrees or higher (109 was recorded), where it would stay for days. Some patients grew so weak that they could barely move their head or stick out their tongue when asked by a physician. Others raved or laughed uproariously.

The army's doctors could do little for the men. The disease was feared, but little understood. The best the physicians could offer was bleeding and folk cures such as bark or other herbs. The men were carried to hospitals along the route or put up in houses of local peasants, so filthy that they shocked even the poor French farm boys who had enlisted for adventure or a chance at an army career. In their beds, the symptoms appeared, disappeared, mutated, reversed into new areas of the body, drawing on a seemingly unlimited repertoire of agonies. Sunlight caused knifelike jabs in the eyes; "flying, wandering, or shooting pains" arced across the body, especially the groin and back; the voice coarsened and dropped; the face grew darker and puffy; the eyes lost their affect and appeared corpselike. Some patients reported "sensations of gnawing or tearing" in their bodies, and the headache was constant. "It felt to me as if an immense weight were pressing down the bones of the head," wrote one survivor of the disease, "and as if the brain were reacting against this pressure by violent and rapidly successive throbs."

As early as the second or third day, the mind began to be affected, with men muttering to people who weren't there or singing nursery rhymes in ghastly voices. Complete exhaustion set in; if raising a cup of water to his lips could have saved his life, one sufferer recalled, he couldn't have managed it. Others during the brief respites found it unbearable to stay in their beds and wandered constantly. The appetite disappeared and the men began to lose weight. Around the fifth day, tiny red spots usually appeared and spread from the chest and groin all over the body, except for the face and the palms of the hands.

These are the classic, unmistakable signs of a disease known by many names: famine fever, the Hungarian disease, hospital fever, *hauptkrankheit* ("head disease"), and the most famous alias, "war fever." But it is most commonly known as epidemic typhus.

After ten to twelve days, the illness entered its crucial phase. Some of the severely affected saw their toes and fingers blacken with gangrene. Death came slowly. "Spotted typhus is beyond description, the patient wastes to nothing under your eyes," wrote one woman watching her famous lover die in a Russian epidemic. "Of the illness I can scarcely write—there was so much pain." Guessing who would die was a kind of hobby. One theory held that the number of tiny spots on the body could predict the end: the more there were, the deadlier the strain. Another school held that it was the *color* of the spots that gave the best clue: the closer the pea-size eruptions came to purple, the more certain it was that the patient wouldn't survive. It was a long, often terrible death.

Gathering the ill together and mixing them with men afflicted with other, milder ailments was the worst thing Napoleon's doctors could have done. The mistake was compounded by the fact that the bodies of the dead (left unburied in heaps in the army's haste) were often stripped by local peasants and the clothes sold or worn. Many recipients of the uniforms soon fell ill and died; entire families were found dead in their homes. In the clothes was the answer to the riddle that had eluded doctors and thinkers for centuries, the cause of the deadly illness that was incubating in the Grande Armée as it advanced toward Moscow.

For centuries, typhus had excelled in attacking large armies. Now as Napoleon attempted to force Tsar Alexander to heed his singular rule, the signs of a new epidemic began to appear.

And Napoleon's doctors could do almost nothing to stop it.

To UNDERSTAND WHAT the Grande Armée's doctors were thinking as they tried to save these dying men, one must understand the complex and often contradictory state of medical thought on disease in the early nineteenth century. The theory of the humors developed by Hippocrates in the fifth century B.C. was still the dominant mode of understanding health and sickness. According to it, black bile, yellow bile, phlegm, and blood were perfectly balanced in the healthy person. When diet or routines introduced an excess or a shortage of one of the humors, disease appeared.

But competing theories, superstitions, and straight-out quackery were layered over this belief. Medicine was very much an intuitive art as opposed to a rigorous science, and what treatment one received could vary widely, depending on what school of thought one's physician favored. There was no universal cure for certain diseases. Age, occupation, living situation, physical build, and even temperament were key factors in determining the cause and cure for diseases. In addition, one had to consider the circumstances under which the victim had fallen ill: Was a northwest wind blowing? Was he depressed? Had he been exhausting his vitality by drinking to excess? Each patient was a world unto himself. This was a concept called "specificity."

Specificity was fatal to the idea of common diseases and common treatments. One man's cure was considered useless for the next patient, who had a different set of life factors to consider.

When it came to infectious diseases, there were two working theories: miasmism and contagion. Miasmism remained the dominant disease theory of the seventeenth through the nineteenth centuries. The influential English doctor Thomas Sydenham championed the idea beginning in the mid-1600s and developed the notion that noxious vapors emerged from the earth's rotting center and infected the air of towns and villages, which were then struck by epidemics. It was a dark view of Mother Earth, much different from our own. Odor was a telltale sign of danger to one's health. "All smell is disease," wrote the English sanitary activist Edwin Chadwick.

The theory dissipated through European and American life. In *Jane Eyre,* the orphan asylum where Jane and her sisters live sits in a forest dell that is a "cradle of fog and fog-bred pestilence" and that eventually causes a typhus epidemic that kills a number of the girls. Edgar Allan Poe's 1839 short story "The Fall of the House of Usher" contains perhaps the most palpable description of miasmism in modern literature. The twenty-first-century reader might interpret the passage as a gothic premonition of death, but the nineteenth-century one would also see something else—a realistic portrayal of airborne disease:

> But the under-surfaces of the huge masses of agitated vapor, as well as all terrestrial objects immediately around us, were glowing in the unnatural light of a faintly luminous and distinctly visible gaseous exhalation which hung about and enshrouded the mansion. "You must not—you shall not behold this!" said I, shuddering, to Usher, as I led him, with a gentle violence, from the window to a seat. ". . . The air is chilling and dangerous to your frame."

The doctors who advocated miasmism weren't only following tradition, they were obeying common sense. Who could believe disease was spread by invisible organisms that somehow floated from body to body, instead of the odors from rotting corpses that one could smell and even taste on the tongue? Which made more sense? The idea of contagion was more radical in its view of a hidden world of germs. The miasma theory fell in easily with centuries of folklore about the dangerousness of swamps and bogs, and it chimed with the evidence of one's own senses. It's no wonder that it proved remarkably resilient.

Contagion—the idea that disease spreads by direct or indirect contact—was the father of modern germ theory. Its roots went back to the Muslim statesman and medical thinker Avicenna in the eleventh century. By the nineteenth century, it had many supporters but just as many detractors.

MOST OF NAPOLEON'S doctors followed the categories of illness invented by Philippe Panel, a groundbreaking French specialist in mental illness, in *Nosographie philosophique ou méthode de l'analyse appliquée à la médecine* (1798). Panel divided illness into five categories: fevers, phlegmasias (inflammations), hemorrhages, neuroses, and organic lesions. Fever was divided into antiotenic, meningogastric, adenomeningeal, adynamic, ataxic, and adeno-nervous, each with subdivisions and each requiring its own course of treatment. But as to cause, the miasmatic model ruled.

During the Egyptian campaign of 1798–1801, Napoleon's future surgeon general, Dr. Larrey, spoke of winds "loaded with the putrid effluvia of animal and vegetable substances decomposed by the heat in the lakes." A hot southwest wind was believed to bring the plague, while a brisk wind from the north brought health. In a study of the 1806–7 Prussia-Poland campaign, an army doctor reported that "one cannot give a good history of the diseases which are epidemic in the army without having first described the medical topography of the theater of war and the state of the atmosphere whilst the army was in the field." The doctor had to be an amateur surveyor and meteorologist to diagnose an epidemic.

But Larrey also conceded that *once plague had rooted itself in the ranks,* it could become contagious. The rapid spread of the plague in Egypt, in differing meteorological circumstances and across different terrains, made it clear that disease wasn't just arising from bad air. He and other doctors borrowed from both theories to fit the patterns they observed.

CRUCIALLY, THERE WAS no accepted way to test which theory was true. Nor was there a way to find out which treatments worked best: the rest cure, the bark cure (using the outer layer of trees, the original source of aspirin), the cold-water cure, cupping, bleeding, and the split carcasses of small animals applied to the body—all of these were common treatments for typhus in the early 1800s, each with its own followers and detractors. There were fad causes and fad cures. In 1811 the American doctor Elisha North was compelled to study typhus by the dread it was causing in his patients. "Upon [its] first appearance," he wrote, "in any place, so many fall sudden victims to the jaws of death, that a universal terror seizes the minds of all, and of physicians among the rest." He began to study the illness.

After months of research, he published his results. The disease wasn't the result of outside causes, North found, of bad air or invisible creatures passed from victim to victim. Instead, he blamed "the typhus temperament." Certain qualities made a person susceptible to the disease: a vigorous constitution, a rich and highly seasoned "animal diet," living in a dry environment, and frequent alcohol intake, along with an "ardent spirit."

The idea took its place in the medical literature. But no one could definitely say what was true and what was bunk.

One physician had attempted to change that. On May 25, 1747, twenty-two years before Napoleon's birth, an experiment took place on board the Royal Navy warship *Salisbury* that would change the course of medicine.

The doctor's name was James Lind, and he was a Royal Navy

surgeon and a specialist in diseases that affected mariners. Just thirty-one, the Scottish-born doctor had sailed all over the world as a surgeon's mate, watching men die from typhus and scurvy from the west coast of Africa to the ports of Jamaica. He knew that the two maladies killed far more sailors than the king's enemies ever managed to. Lind would do remarkable work in the understanding of both.

Lind's 1747 experiment looked at scurvy. Twelve sailors who had the illness were divided into six groups. The accommodations and diet of all the sailors were identical, but each received a different remedy: one group received cider; one got seawater; another, "elixir of vitriol"; the fifth group, two oranges and a lemon; and the sixth, a mix of spices with barley water. It was the first documented clinical trial in medical history.

"I shall propose nothing dictated merely from theory," wrote Lind. "But shall confirm all by experience and facts, the surest and most unerring guides." This in itself was revolutionary, in an age when so much superstition and ancient theory overlay the world of medicine. When the sailors who received the citrus recovered completely, and the others did not, Lind had proved that orange and lemon juice was the true and universal corrective for the disease. He had created a blind test whose results were irrefutable.

It wasn't the oranges and the lemons that constituted the breakthrough, as using citrus had been one of the folk remedies against scurvy for well over a century. And, in fact, Lind didn't propose that scurvy was a deficiency disease caused by lack of a mineral (vitamin C, as it turned out) contained in the fruit. He thought that moist air blocked the pores in scurvy patients, and that lemon juice helped toxins escape the body through the skin. But he didn't need to know *why* the cure worked so long as he knew that it *did*. This is what the blind test proved. He had invented a way of evaluating medical knowledge.

When it came to the other great killer of mariners, typhus,

Lind made a signal contribution in a 1763 paper. The Royal Navy at the time took anybody for its ranks, often by force: slums, criminal courts, and taverns were swept for new recruits, who often came to the ships infested with lice and bacteria. The surgeon recommended that the newcomers be sent to a receiving ship and quarantined there for a few weeks to see if any diseases revealed themselves. They were given hot baths, and their old clothes were thrown away and a fresh set provided. By the time the men went on board their new ships, the sick had been culled from their ranks.

The British Admiralty didn't implement the typhus-defeating quarantine until 1781 and didn't fully provide an allotment of citrus until the 1790s, but when these measures were implemented piecemeal, the results were astonishing. In the months before the 1795 Battle of Quiberon, Lind instructed that provision ships carrying fresh vegetables and citrus fruits be ferried to the twenty-three ships of the line blockading French ports. On the day of battle, out of 14,000 men, only about 20 were listed as sick and unfit for duty, an unheard-of number for an eighteenth-century fleet. One of Lind's biographers estimated that his recommendations added the equivalent of six warships to the British fleet that day, in which the British decimated the French. The Royal Navy's policy of blockading ports, so devastating to Napoleon's plans for defeating the English commercially, would have been unthinkable had scurvy or typhus been allowed to ravage its crews.

Taking Lind's warning about noxious air seriously, British captains paid attention to the cleanliness of their ships, regularly airing them out and scouring the bedding and sailors' clothing. The incidence of typhus in the Royal Navy dropped dramatically. Lind remarked that for the first time in history, sailors "enjoy a better state of health upon a watery element, than it can well be imagined so great a number of people would enjoy, on the most healthful spot of ground in the world."

The navy's procedures proved that a large military institution could keep infectious disease at bay indefinitely. In a sense, typhus had been "cured." But there were many times when the mystery of typhus was believed to be solved; in fact, it was "solved" over and over again, but the insight kept slipping away.

Why didn't Lind's insight hold? Why didn't Dr. Larrey and his colleagues adopt Lind's protocols for preventing typhus? And why, at the very least, didn't they use his idea of the blind test to evaluate different treatments and prevention methods?

Simply put, because the breakthrough Lind ushered in—the idea of an empirical test that measured the effects of disease on all men uniformly—went so radically against the reigning ideas of the time: specificity and miasmism. The blind test entered a different mental and theoretical world than exists today. Medicine was not the uniform place we know, where a discovery in Berlin or California is tested, reviewed, published, put through clinical trials, and then adopted worldwide. Lind couldn't with one stroke realign centuries of thought on the humors, on the origins of different kinds of fevers and the effects of the weather. Medicine was a spooky art, and Lind's insights would need many decades, and further breakthroughs in the areas of disease theory, to change history.

In 1812, his theory was one among many. If Lind had found success with strict hygiene and quarantine, Dr. Larrey could point to his colleagues' work that produced results through other methods (although he himself was not averse to keeping patients clean and their clothing disinfected). Standard practices for avoiding and treating diseases did exist, but they were far less ironclad than they are today, and a doctor was free to pick and choose among them. Medicine was still a bespoke pursuit, still decades away from being a true science.

And even if Larrey, convinced that the Englishman was right, had come to Napoleon with a plan for defeating contagious diseases—which would have slowed the Grande Armée down and required a huge infrastructure and an infusion of money—he would have been dismissed out of hand. A century later the Russian army, knowing the cause of typhus, would be unable to stop it during World War I. Lind's protocols were far easier to implement in a fleet of ships than in a massive, multinational army.

So the pathogen that the English surgeon had successfully revealed and defeated was free to strike again.

AND NOW SOMETHING never noted by Dr. Lind was happening within the army. The massing of an unprecedented number of troops meant that typhus suddenly had an almost unlimited selection of potential hosts, and an easy way to infect them. The disease was spreading fast and becoming deadlier by the week.

After millions of years, the fatal mechanism had found its most efficient form, its ideal expression.

CHAPTER 5

Pursuit

WHEN THE ARMY CROSSED THE NIEMEN ON JUNE 24, 1812, a shocked Alexander wrote Napoleon a hurried note as he scrambled to retreat. The tsar had been preparing for the possibility of war but still couldn't quite believe Napoleon had initiated it. His note offered a solution: If the French turned around and retired behind the Niemen, the two sides would settle their problem amicably. "Alexander is laughing at me," Napoleon said, astonished at the apparent mock-naïveté of the letter.

The Grande Armée swept east. X Corps headed northeast to confront General Barclay, the German-speaking commander of all the tsar's forces, while V and VII Corps, at the southernmost tip of Napoleon's lines, moved east toward the Berezina River, chasing the Russian divisions under General Peter Wittgenstein, which were now in full retreat. Napoleon and the main body of troops headed for Vilna (modern-day Vilnius), where Alexander had attended a ball among the fountains and cultivated gardens of a country estate. The emperor arrived there on June 28 and found signs that the Russians had prepared to defend the city but then had left hastily, burning the bridge over the Vilia River as they retreated. The bridge was the first tangible evidence of Alexander's

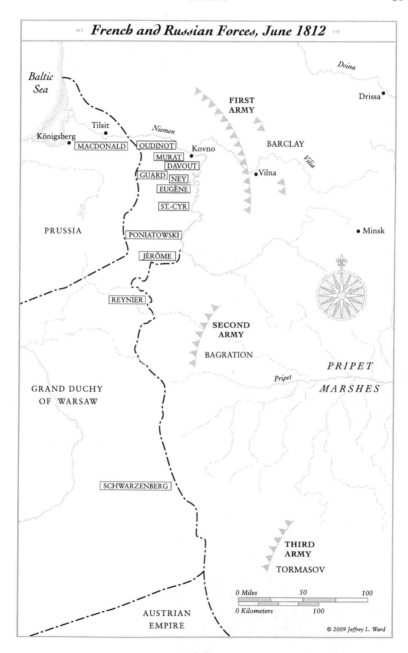

French and Russian Forces, June 1812

Baltic
Sea

Dvina

Drissa

**FIRST
ARMY**

Tilsit

Niemen

Königsberg

MACDONALD

OUDINOT

Kovno

BARCLAY

Vilia

MURAT

DAVOUT

GUARD

NEY

Vilna

EUGÈNE

ST.-CYR

PRUSSIA

Minsk

PONIATOWSKI

JÉRÔME

REYNIER

**SECOND
ARMY**

BAGRATION

PRIPET

Pripet

MARSHES

GRAND DUCHY
OF WARSAW

SCHWARZENBERG

**THIRD
ARMY**

TORMASOV

0 Miles   50   100

0 Kilometers   100

© 2009 Jeffrey L. Ward

AUSTRIAN
EMPIRE

evolving strategy of retreat-and-lay-waste, the first sign of total war. But Napoleon believed the withdrawal could be the prelude to a counterattack that would give him a chance at a quick, decisive victory. He had much to learn about the young campaign.

The timing of the invasion had come as a surprise to Alexander, and his forces were too widely dispersed to mount a serious defense. Nor did he have accurate information on the numbers or positions of Napoleon's forces. The analytical General Barclay, knowing that he would be annihilated if he attempted to stand and fight, ordered the hotheaded General Bagration in the south to fall back and avoid contact with the French, already causing friction with his rival. Napoleon's forward units managed brief encounters with the fleeing troops, but anything resembling a decisive battle evaded Napoleon in the first weeks of the campaign.

Alexander, whose words to his people during the campaign were consistently more effective and rousing than the French emperor's, issued a proclamation telling the Russians what Napoleon had done: "He has come with treachery in his heart and loyalty on his lips to enslave us with the help of this legion of slaves. Let us drive this plague of locusts out! Let us carry the Cross in our hearts, and steel in our hands! Let us pluck the fangs out of the lion's mouth and overthrow the tyrant who would overthrow the earth!" The biblical imagery was clear. The fusing of the campaign into a combination of nationalist struggle and holy war had begun.

The Grande Armée's mood was buoyant, even though a series of bad omens had plagued the beginning of the march. When Napoleon went to review the army, huge thunderheads rolled in, hail pelted down, and the sky darkened so that soldiers could see only by the flashes of lightning. "I have never witnessed so horrific, so frightful a storm," wrote Dr. Larrey. Napoleon, superstitious to a fault, canceled the review. But it would be hard to overestimate the faith that Napoleon's veterans placed in his leadership, and the lengths they were willing to go to win him another victory.

Alexander had placed all his hope in a strategy devised by his German general Karl Ludwig von Phull, who had settled on the idea of creating a fortresslike camp at Drissa, 140 miles northeast of Vilna, which would tempt Napoleon into a disastrous siege. Once the French, eager for a single overwhelming victory, attacked this impregnable position, the emperor's flanks would be crushed from the north by General Barclay and the First Army and from the south by General Bagration and the Second Army. For eight months before the invasion, fortifications were built and entrenchments dug at a spot devoid of a natural defensive feature—a hill or a stream—to give the Russians an advantage against the hordes that would sweep down on it. When the German strategist Carl von Clausewitz was sent to inspect Drissa, he reported to Alexander on July 8 that the work had been a complete waste of time and that the camp offered no tactical advantages to the troops who would defend it. Drissa was a trap not for Napoleon but for the Russians.

The tsar was crushed. Phull had left him defenseless against an invader already on the march. On July 12, he ordered his bewildered troops to abandon Drissa and retreat west to the city of Vitebsk, near the border of modern-day Latvia.

Napoleon could hardly contain his joy. The Italian general Rossetti, who was assigned to the cavalry corps under the dashing Marshal Murat, gave the emperor the news of the Russian withdrawal from their defensive prize, and Napoleon began striding back and forth, galvanized, preening. "You see, the Russians no longer know how to make peace or war!" he cried. "It's a degenerate nation. What! They abandon their 'palladium' without striking a blow! Let's go! Let's go! One more final push and my brother will repent for having followed the advice of my enemies."

As the Russian defense collapsed, typhus and other diseases were beginning their work. The army's health had been excellent when the soldiers began their march to their rendezvous in

Germany. The Belgian doctor J. L. R. de Kerckhove accompanied III Corps led by "the Bravest of the Brave," Marshal Ney, and kept a lively diary that would closely mirror the condition of the troops. At the beginning, he rated the men highly: "The army was not only the most beautiful," he wrote in his medical account of the campaign, "but there was none which included so many brave warriors, so many heroes." During the march to the Niemen River, he had noted "with astonishment" how low the sick rate was in such an immense army. "Nothing announced a disastrous future." The bountiful food of the Dutch lowlands and Germany had delivered an unusually fit force.

But when they were deep into Poland, Dr. Larrey reported disturbing news. He noted in his memoirs, "60,000 [troops] were admitted by their commanding officers to be sick. The true figure was probably double this." Clausewitz, on the Russian side, was also hearing disturbing reports about the French forces. "The French, in the first weeks of their march," he wrote, "had undergone an enormous loss in sick and stragglers, and were in a state of privation which gave early warning of their rapid consumption." The Bavarian soldiers of VI Corps, to choose one element of Napoleon's forces, were hit hard: one colonel reported a "terrible epidemic" had swept through their ranks, infecting almost every last recruit and killing thousands.

When the normally imperturbable Marshal Ney of III Corps reviewed his infantry, which had yet to fire a shot, he was shocked to find that half the effective troops had vanished. Sir Robert Wilson, a British soldier of fortune who had been expelled from Russia for spying, only to return to fight against Napoleon in the 1812 invasion, wrote that in late June, the Grande Armée "was already stricken with a calamity which seemed to be a prelude to its future catastrophe." He estimated that 30,000 men had already fallen out of their ranks after "numbers fell sick." Nor was this a matter of leaving garrisons along the route they had passed, as the French had "scarcely made" any such arrangements.

Soon after crossing the Niemen, the Belgian surgeon de Kerck-hove reported that a crowd of soldiers had separated from their regiments and, unable to keep up with the blistering pace, "dragged themselves behind" the main group. By Vilna, nunneries and churches were converted into makeshift hospitals, without bedding or adequate supplies or basic provisions. Napoleon was losing 4,000 to 6,000 soldiers a day, and 30,000 sick packed every inch of space in the converted sick houses, which were really staging grounds for fresh infection. Another 30,000 men (and possibly many more) had deserted the ranks.

Based on journals of the army doctors, memoirs of the soldiers themselves, and epidemiologists' subsequent analysis of the campaign, the Grande Armée was clearly under attack from a host of pathogens. By July it had become a vast petri dish in which microbes competed for supremacy. Pleurisy, jaundice, diarrhea, hepatitis, enteritis, and other ailments all preyed on the tired, hungry men. But it was dysentery and "nerve fever" *(fièvre nerveuse),* as typhus was often called by the French doctors, that rose to epidemic conditions during the summer. "Under these circumstances," wrote one lieutenant, H. A. Vossler of the Würrtemburg Chasseurs, "it wasn't surprising that within two or three days of crossing the Niemen the army and in particular the infantry was being ravaged by a variety of diseases, chief among them dysentery, ague, and typhus."

Dysentery ruled for the first weeks, with 80,000 sick by the beginning of August. The bloody diarrhea that the men suffered from was causing "the most horrible infection in our hospitals," as the men were packed so closely together, with little available cloth to wash them or keep them clean. Epidemic dysentery is caused by a bacterium, *Shigella dysenteriae* type 1, which enters the system through contaminated food or via contact with an infected person. Its telltale symptom is bloody diarrhea, with rectal pain, fever, and abdominal cramps also frequently present. But even at its deadliest, dysentery most often has a mortality rate of 5 to 15 percent (although recent outbreaks in Africa have found that raised to 30 to 40 percent), which doesn't match up with the huge numbers of sick who were dying on the march. And one of the most common symptoms mentioned in diaries and memoirs of soldiers on the road to Moscow—extreme exhaustion and stupor—is not common to the illness.

Dysentery certainly killed men early on. Johannes von Scherer, a surgeon with the Württemberg regiments, would later write his doctorate on the 1812 campaign and included details of the diseases racking the men. At one hospital, where he served for six weeks, the doctor recorded 902 dysentery patients, of whom 301 died during the first three weeks. When the care and nutrition improved in the next three weeks, only 36 died. The doctors used anything they could find to treat the soldiers, including the huckleberries and root of tormentil, as well as plants such as common sweet flag, which has been used for thousands of years.

Typhus would soon overtake its rival infection. De Kerckhove remembers the beginning of the epidemic, painting it as an example of pure miasma.

> Typhus was present among us. It first appeared spontaneously from the dirtiness of the clothes, which one could not change or even take off at night, and from bad food, from deprivations, from exhaustion, from tiredness and congestion. It became more frequent and more serious as a result of the large assemblies of men. We were breathing putrid smells all the time along roads that were full of dead bodies and rotting animal remains. . . . Typhus began to stand out because it was so infectious.

The French commanders were appalled by the losses but felt powerless to stop them; the bulletins and hurried conferences called to address the epidemic that one would expect from a modern army simply never happened. Illness and hunger were a cost of making war in the nineteenth century. Disease, in the miasmatic worldview, was an inescapable part of conquering backward territory full of gloomy swamps swept by drenching rains and towns pocked by filthy, malodorous hovels. One major, Friedrich Wilhelm von Lossberg, who saw thousands of troops dying by the roadside and fell desperately ill himself, became convinced that it was merely a case of simple callousness on the part of an emperor who believed he had men to spare. "Napoleon doesn't give a damn how many of his soldiers collapse by the roadside," he wrote to his wife.

Most Napoleonic historians have noted the drastic reduction of the French forces on the road east, attributing it to a combination of sickness, hunger, and thirst—and the last two certainly played a significant part. But almost no histories of the war, or of Napoleon's fall, probe deeply into the outsized role of typhus. The disease, as it preferred, remained remarkably hidden, both to the army itself and to its chroniclers.

As the Grande Armée marched east, the sun burned down during the day, with cold and thick fogs moving in at night. Rains drenched the roads, turning them into rivers of mud. Artillery guns had to be dragged through marshes and along rutted lanes. The marching became brutally hard, but nothing worse than Napoleon's troops had seen crossing the Alps. The army's horses were dying in greater numbers than its men: they needed almost twenty pounds of oats a day to survive and weren't getting anything close to that. When their own supplies ran out, the cavalry and supply units substituted the local rye, which was green and unripe, causing the animals to die by the thousands. Their swollen bodies lined the route and threw off a noxious odor as they decomposed. It was a heavy blow for an army that depended on animal power to pull what supplies remained to the next camp and for the lightning cavalry charges that Napoleon expected to turn the tide in upcoming battles.

The French, growing desperate, often turned friendly locals into enemies within a matter of hours. Nobles who offered the troops the ancient welcome of bread and salt found that the troops had soon harvested and eaten their rye, stolen their cows and horses, and pillaged their homes for anything they could use. "The path of Attila in the age of barbarism cannot have been strewn with more horrible testimonies," wrote one Polish officer. The mistake that Napoleon had made by not promising the Poles their freedom was compounded on the ground by men acting as if they were conquering territory instead of liberating it.

Captain Roeder, the diarist-soldier with the Hessian Life-guards, was shocked by what he saw on the march. He passed bodies along the road and kites and vultures feasting on the eyes and entrails. The locals were poor to begin with, but the movable city that was the Grande Armée had taken everything they owned. "What misery prevails already in these wretched houses and hovels," Roeder wrote in his diary. One day he came across a town swept by smallpox. "The parents were ready to tell the Lord God in secret how many children they wished Him to leave them," Roeder recorded. "And looked upon it as a blessing if He took a few to Himself, especially in these hard times." The soft-hearted captain gave out a few loaves of bread to the peasants and kept his men moving.

To his wife Sophie, he wrote about the extreme youth of those around him, so different from other campaigns, and told her that many of the eighteen-year-olds were already in the hospital. Roeder, despite his fearlessness in battle, was "obsessed by the fear of falling sick" (as his niece would later attest) ever since nearly dying during the 1807 Russo-Prussian War. "Beloved, it is so hard to be parted from you," he wrote to Sophie from the road, "harder still not to know if it is only for a little while or if we have lost each other forever."

The enemy took careful note of what was happening inside

Napoleon's ranks. Alexander's spies and scouts reported on the thinning of the Grande Armée's numbers. "This did not remain concealed from the Russians," wrote the German strategist Clausewitz, who was close to the decision makers at headquarters. "General Schuwalow . . . returned to Widzy full of astonishment at the state of the route of the French army, which he found strewn with the carcasses of horses, and swarming with sick and stragglers." French soldiers captured by Cossacks or peasants were questioned, and the reports hardened Alexander's resolve to fight. Napoleon began to feel the mounting pressure. "I am already in Vilna and I don't know what we're fighting over," he told a Russian emissary after arriving in the city on June 28.

In terms of sheer military momentum, Napoleon was succeeding brilliantly, driving his enemy before him. Epidemiologically, he was in mortal danger. A month after Sir Robert Wilson's estimate of 30,000 deaths from sickness and desertion, Clausewitz wrote that already by the time he reached Vilna, less than a week into the campaign, Napoleon had lost 100,000 men, a full quarter of his frontline forces.

BUT DISASTER FOR the French represented an unprecedented success for the pathogen. It was fulfilling its own biological destiny.

Every epidemic disease from plague to cholera has its own patterns. Malaria is ancient and familiar, the tropical cliché, a carryover from the time of humankind's ape relatives, limited by its heat-loving vector, the mosquito. Bubonic plague, with a top mortality rate of 75 percent—one of the few epidemics that can compete with typhus in sheer killing power—seems designed to terrorize, with its victims turned to a gangrenous pulp. Just as ruthless, typhus was now ready to join the ranks of the major pathogens.

It's not inappropriate to talk about the "mind" of a contagious disease. Its habits, preferences, strategies, and alliances with the natural and human world result in a pattern that resembles strategic thought. Typhus favored chaos, deploring the stability of the towns and the nation-states that could enforce quarantines. It hated prosperity, for its ability to raise living and cleanliness standards, although it favored the movement of traders, which carried it to new population centers. The disease was enamored of mariners and seafarers, because they carried the bacillus around the world, truly founding its global empire but it despised learning, as its secrets were so obvious, so exposed, that it seemed that at any moment medical thinkers would discover the root of its power. Curiously, typhus formed an alliance with doctors, who tended to gather patients together with the uninfected, accelerating the pathogen's spread, as was already happening on the road to Moscow.

Typhus was closely allied with the poor and criminals and the corrupt wardens that kept them in filthy hellholes that formed a reservoir where the disease could build its strength for mini-epidemics. It favored cold snaps, when people gathered in their hovels and wore layers of clothing, where its accomplices could burrow. It was fervently pro-religion, as religion was the spur to war after war, while priests and ministers lectured their followers that bathing was an indulgence and nakedness a mortal sin. If pressed, it favored Catholicism, which abhorred washing, over Protestantism. Politically, it was a monarchist to the core (there was really no other choice in the early nineteenth century) and favored corrupt kings who went to battle to replenish their coffers and drove their people to famine and misery. Typhus was, above all, a lover of war, the single greatest propagator of its survival and its rapid spread. The disease hungered for new territory. It had, in this way, the mind of a conqueror.

It's also fair to say that typhus was inherently conservative, or at least pessimistic. It placed large bets on the belief that tradition counted: Men who made war on each other yesterday would continue to make war on each other tomorrow. They would continue to commit crimes punishable by prison terms and those terms would be served in filthy cells. Societies would fall victim to famine and the poor would always be with us. That humanity was basically incorrigible was a gamble written into its genetic code. If nations such as France made a head-spinning moral turn and stopped invading each other's borders, and if men stopped committing felonies, typhus's core constituencies would disappear.

Jails and ships and villages were the basis, in a way, of typhus's domestic policy. There would always be a population there to infect and form a stable reservoir to keep the microbe alive. But those populations were unlikely to spread far enough to appreciably expand the microbe's range. War and conquest, then, formed the center of its foreign policy. Along with shipborne trade, they were the most effective ways it could extend its reach to the corners of the earth.

By this quirk of the mind, the preference for attacking armies, typhus had acted as a check on great power. King Francis I's mercenaries had been stopped by it in the plain that lay before Naples. Napoleon, however, was a different kind of ruler in a different time, driven by more audacious motives. Crucially, too, he led soldiers who would follow him anywhere, even into a raging epidemic.

But this was something typhus, in its very makeup, had wagered on: that war would prove irresistible to certain leaders. That insight was life itself to the microbe.

FROM THE MOMENT the first soldier died of typhus, a clock began ticking. Now that the scourge had arrived, the question of the hour became: Would the pathogen leave Napoleon enough time to catch and destroy Alexander's army?

CHAPTER 6

Smolensk

AT VILNA, NAPOLEON CALLED A HALT TO THE MARCH AND began meeting with Polish emissaries looking for a promise of independence. At the same time, he mulled over Alexander's intentions. "It was truly heartbreaking for him to have to give up all hope of a great battle before Vilna," wrote his former ambassador to Russia, the perceptive Armand de Caulaincourt. "He was anxious for trophies . . . and no one sent him any." The first real doubts about the offensive had snaked into Napoleon's mind by this time, but he wouldn't allow himself to believe that he was engaged in a new kind of war.

Meanwhile, his southern forces under his youngest brother, Jérôme, king of Westphalia, along with three corps of Polish, Westphalian, and Saxon troops, were in pursuit of Russia's Second Army under the hotheaded Bagration. The Russian commander on June 28 began moving north to link up with General Barclay, but a week later his scouts brought the information that the ever dependable Davout, the "Iron Marshal," had dived south from Vilna and was moving southeast to force a battle.

Each was hoping to reach the Russian city of Minsk, approximately 110 miles southwest of Vilna, before the other. The French won the race. Bagration was now caught between Jérôme and

Davout and faced the possibility of a pincer battle he was sure to lose. As the Second Army raced to escape, Jérôme failed to spring the trap, complaining to Napoleon that the roads were impassable and the weather brutal. Napoleon was furious with his brother, but many of the mistakes were his: Jérôme had started from a rear position and even on good roads couldn't have been expected to march the hundred miles to stop Bagration's retreat in the time given him. The emperor had also failed to coordinate the command structure between Jérôme and Davout, which resulted in conflicts between the two, wasting valuable hours. Bagration took advantage of the delay and ducked away south and out of the two-sided snare.

Napoleon blew up. "You know nothing, and not only do you consult nobody, you allow yourself to be guided by selfish motives," he wrote his brother. The outraged Jérôme, who was commanding his first army in battle, turned around with his squad of guards and headed for home, abandoning the campaign on July 16.

The pattern was set for the first part of the war: French advances, minor clashes in which the Russians won as often as the French, and retreat of both Russian armies toward a unified stand deeper in the heartland. Napoleon's decision to drive a wedge between Russia's First and Second armies instead of herding them together against the Drissa River and then fighting a decisive battle had failed. And the Russians by mid-July had sussed out the French strategy, prompting Tsar Alexander to give orders for the two armies to withdraw to Vitebsk and unite there. Almost by accident, a Russian strategy had emerged: withdraw and suck the Grande Armée deeper and deeper into a ravaged landscape.

After Vilna, Napoleon headed northeast to try to outflank General Barclay, hoping to place himself between the two Russian armies and snap the First Army's supply and communication lines to the country's heartland. When the Russians fled from their fortified camp at Drissa, Murat and his cavalry turned south and then east again, hoping to cut them off before they reached Vitebsk. On July 25, the flamboyant, hard-charging marshal confronted the Russian rear guard of 12,000 men at Ostrovno. Dressed for battle in a powder blue coat laced with gold braid, cinched tightly at the waist by a silk cord, and a fetching hat covered with feathers over his lustrous black curls, Murat charged into the Russian lines, driving his horse forward with the enormous gold spurs he wore on his deerskin boots. The first real blooding of the campaign, the encounter left about 3,000 dead on each side. The French broke through the Russian line several times and captured Russian artillery pieces, but the bruising battle allowed Barclay to slip away toward Vitebsk.

As Napoleon approached that city on July 27, he was thrilled

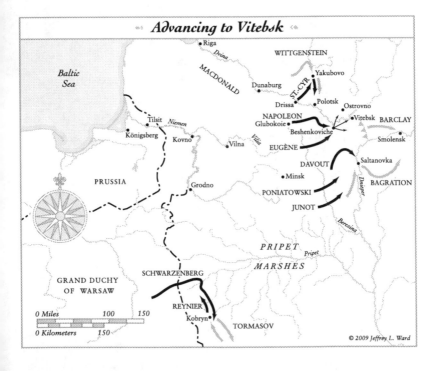

to see the First Army arrayed for battle. French advance elements sent ahead were met with volleys of musket balls in a series of skirmishes that broke out throughout the evening. Still not convinced of his ability to take on Napoleon, the cautious Barclay was anxiously waiting for word from Bagration and the Second Army, who he hoped would arrive just in time to reinforce his ranks. But that night Barclay received dispatches telling him that the Second Army, which had been hurrying north, had finally encountered Davout. The Iron Marshal wouldn't let Bagration pass without a clash.

Davout, as loyal and competent as ever, had complied with Napoleon's orders to engage the enemy wherever and whenever possible. Attempting to stop Bagration's northward flight, he dug in on a high bank near the Dnieper River and waited for the Russians to attack. Already the depletion of the ranks by disease and other factors was telling: Davout's original 70,000 men at the crossing of the Niemen had been reduced by illness—and a contingent of 28,000 men sent to Murat—to 30,000 by July 8. Now, as the fiery Bagration approached with about 45,000 men, the Iron Marshal was down to 17,000 soldiers, partly due to skirmishes and garrisoning towns along the way. But most of his losses had come from illness and desertion. "Each night of rest does extraordinary harm," wrote one of his men, "and costs us many men sick and horses dead. Misery has brought on many suicides, and our column resembles more a transport of sick than of warriors."

The Russians appeared at the Dnieper and Bagration sent one of his divisions smashing into Davout's line, which crumpled in several places and then re-formed, beating the enemy back. Some 3,400 men fell on the French side to the Russians' 2,400. Unwilling to test Davout further, Bagration looped south and then turned northeast toward Smolensk. The Iron Marshal had prevented the two Russian armies from linking up, but he had only delayed

Bagration. He had failed to stop him or even significantly decrease his fighting power. With the men left to him, he could hardly have been expected to.

For the first time, typhus and the other diseases in the French ranks had a clear tactical impact on the battlefield and on the campaign. Without the troop strength to attack Bagration's main body, Davout was unable to stop the Second Army from escaping. The Russians slipped away toward a rendezvous with the First Army.

With Bagration delayed, Barclay and his 80,000 men faced the prospect of a two-front battle against Napoleon in the west and Davout, who was now rushing toward Vitebsk from the south. It was a recipe for annihilation. After convincing Napoleon that July 28 would bring the long-awaited battle, Barclay slipped his forces out of Vitebsk during the night and stole eastward. As clear-minded as always, Barclay knew he faced impossible odds; the numbers were not with him.

Once again the Grande Armée was being drawn deeper into the Russian heartland. But the constant retreat was also fraying nerves on the Russian side, especially between the conservative Barclay and the firebrand Bagration, who wanted desperately to score a blow against the French invader, if only a symbolic one.

A GRAPH OF THE troop strength of both armies would have shown the French line, which had started at a very robust level, steadily diving, with the Russian line, which had commenced at a low point, rising weekly. Russia's army was close to its supply depots and to an almost inexhaustible supply of reinforcements. Napoleon surely knew that the lines would have to cross eventually and his crushing numerical advantage would be gone.

Numbers hadn't been crucial at the beginning of the campaign; with no major battle, it was the Grande Armée's lack of maneuverability and Napoleon's missed chances that let the Russians escape. But going ahead, that would change. "Nothing is more dangerous to us than a prolonged war," Napoleon said. Total war demanded masses of men, and the French were hemorrhaging them at an alarming rate.

Suicides became more frequent, a result of the lack of food and the "terrifying" increase in the sick rolls, according to the Belgian doctor de Kerckhove. Those who couldn't keep up with the main body of troops faced being left behind to the mercy of the Russian serfs. And that was a grim option.

The attitudes of the peasants toward the invaders were complex. Ninety percent of the population were serfs who could be beaten, killed, transported away from their family, or sold for a gambling debt or as collateral for a loan (a healthy male at the time would fetch between 200 and 500 rubles in the Moscow market; a good-looking young female, several times that). Before the invasion, Napoleon had threatened to free the serfs, but it was a ploy. He needed to make peace with the royal families of Europe, and igniting a social revolution in Russia would have deepened their hatred of him.

Any rabble-rousers among the serfs were routinely killed or imprisoned, but the prospect of an invasion by the forces of Revolutionary France inspired freedom-minded peasants to act. The historian Adam Zamoyski found records of sixty-seven minor uprisings across Russia in 1812, more than twice the average amount. Clearly, there was a deep reservoir of anger within the serf population, much of it directed at their masters.

But once the Grande Armée arrived to ransack the peasants' hovels, steal their rye, and rape their women, that rage was increasingly vented on their supposed deliverers. The atrocities committed by the peasants on the French during the advance were trifling compared with what awaited them on the retreat, but no Frenchman wanted to be caught out along the road by a band of Cossacks or the local villagers.

Church officials, aristocrats, and Alexander himself painted the invasion as a desecration of the homeland, an attack by an Antichrist on the Orthodox Church and the religious traditions of Russia. One Bavarian officer recalled the reaction he got when he and some members of a cavalry regiment swept into a small village called Rouza. The peasants, armed with poles and scythes, were quickly scattered by volleys of musket fire, but the mayor of the town stood his ground. "How can I survive the dishonor of my country," he cried. "Our altars are no more! Our empire is disgraced! Take my life, it is odious to me!" Armed only with a small dagger, he bellowed at the invaders to kill him.

The upper classes were firmly behind the tsar's war policy. When Alexander, who remained far back from the front lines throughout the war, traveled to Moscow's Sloboda Palace in late July to address the assemblies of nobles and merchants, the former pledged men— 10 percent of their serfs for the cause, as well as provisions to feed them, totaling 50,000 men—and the latter contributed huge sums of money. Fresh funds poured in: 2.4 million rubles were donated to the tsar's coffers. Count Mamonov, whose father had risen rapidly in the military ranks due to his liaison with Catherine the Great, only to betray her with a sixteen-year-old, pledged 800,000 silver rubles and a cache of diamonds.

ON JULY 29, Napoleon marched into the recently abandoned Vitebsk, an ugly, depressing city partially redeemed by its beautiful churches. He delayed here, unable to make up his mind whether he should keep moving forward or stop for a time, allowing his food trains to catch up, knitting together his lines of communication, and giving his men a much-needed rest and the sick a chance to recover. The diplomat Caulaincourt, along with Murat and his other advisers, urged Napoleon to station the army in the city of Smolensk, sixty miles to the northeast, until the coming spring. His forces were simply too small and run-down after their harrowing in the field, and the prospect of wintering in Moscow, should he conquer it, gave him no strategic advantages against an army that could renew itself over a long winter.

The condition of the army was one of the main topics of debate, as it would be at each stop during the campaign. "War's a game you're good at," the head of Napoleon's commissariat snapped at the emperor. "But here we aren't fighting men, we're fighting nature." "Nature" here refers to the lack of food, the weather, and distance—and disease, which emanated from the bogs and swamps.

With the momentum of the invasion momentarily stilled, Napoleon spent hours reviewing statistics from the various corps, detailing the losses to their ranks and the reinforcements flowing to each division. Many believed his generals were downplaying the deaths to typhus and other causes, hoping to escape charges of neglect or mismanagement (and fearing that, undermanned, they would be left out of coming battles). Dr. Larrey mentioned discrepancies between actual and reported number of sick, and one officer wrote darkly of "the cruel way in which [Napoleon] was being deceived by the reports made to him."

The emperor contemplated stopping at several points during the advance. This was as close as he came to addressing the losses to typhus, as part of an overall plan to give his men a chance to recuperate. The lack of a strong response mystifies the modern mind, but Napoleon was ill-informed and his options were vanishingly small. He also knew that even diagnosing the problem as an epidemic would solve nothing. The army had no proven weapons to combat typhus or any other contagious disease.

For a time the emperor seemed to have settled on a break in the advance. He met with his advisers and unstrapped his sword, clattering it down on a table covered with maps. "The campaign of 1812 is finished," he told them. "The campaign of 1813 will do the rest." But soon his mood changed and he lashed out at his coterie, bitterly accusing them of wanting to avoid battle and return to their mistresses in Paris. Napoleon seemed to change his mind by the hour. During one bath, he decided that he must advance at that very moment and dashed out of the water stark naked to give an order. But soon he went back to his maps for further study, countermanding the order.

The emperor took a tour of the hospitals, talking with the sick and wounded, awarding medals and handing out small gifts to the soldiers. Dr. Larrey was close at hand, but Napoleon didn't speak a word to him as he walked through the wards, an ominous sign. Napoleon kept up a cheerful banter with his men; still, he was clearly appalled at the conditions and the lack of supplies that forced the surgeons to tear up their own shirts for bandages. At the end of the tour, Napoleon erupted in rage at the doctors. "I shall send you back to Paris to care for the inhabitants of the Palais Royal," he threatened. "You, whom I have charged with tending to the needs of our soldiers, you want to sleep in white sheets!" He even rounded on Larrey and chastised him for the lack of medical supplies. The surgeon in chief took the abuse, but when he finally spoke up to defend himself, Napoleon turned and left. Larrey was furious. He wrote Napoleon a passionate letter detailing the failures of his own supply administration to get bandages and medicine to the front, and the two soon reconciled.

But the strain of the huge sick lists was clearly showing. The surplus of men Napoleon had brought with him had provided a kind of insulation against disaster, but the excess was being burned away. He needed a decisive battle and a surrender soon.

Trying to decide on his next move, Napoleon paced hour after hour, singing snatches of French songs, chatting absentmindedly about the weather, and mumbling questions to aides who happened into his tent. "Well, what are we going to do? . . . Shall we stay here? . . . Shall we advance? . . . How can we stop now on the

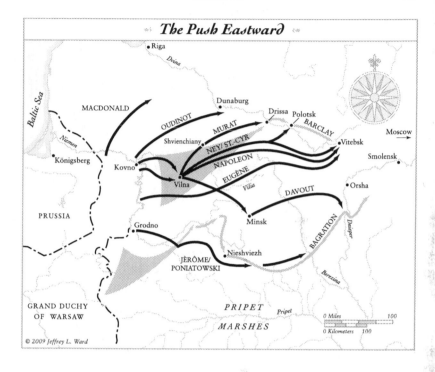

The Push Eastward

road to glory?" He was in a dialogue with himself, and one senses that the outcome was never really in doubt. When he finally announced the advance, it was with a sense of fatalism. "The danger pushes us toward Moscow," he wrote. "The die is cast. Victory will vindicate us."

His nature, his career, his philosophy all favored boldness. Napoleon decided to pursue.

CHAPTER 7

The Sound of Flames

THERE WAS A DRENCHING SERIES OF THUNDERSTORMS ON
August 11 as the army marched out of Vitebsk, providing
the soldiers with an extra source for drinking water. The
supply trains had caught up to the main body of troops in the city,
so the men had been able to eat their fill and even stuff a full seven
days of rations into their knapsacks for the days ahead. Thirst and
hunger fluctuated, but disease had become a constant. One hospital even had a "dying chamber," where hopeless cases were left on
the straw to expire in peace. By mid-August, typhus was exploding
in the ranks. "The number of sick people increased overwhelm-
ingly," wrote de Kerckhove, the Belgian doctor. "They were crawling along on the roads, where many of them died."

Caulaincourt, the former Russian ambassador, was sent to inspect the hospitals and pass out money to the wounded. He was
genuinely appalled at what he found. "Never was there such a situation more deplorable," he wrote, "or a spectacle more heartrend-
ing for those who could think, and who hadn't been dazzled by the
false glamour of Glory and ambition." He found most medical and
supply officials indifferent to the suffering around them, governed
by a "spirit of inexplicable and unpardonable meanness." Caulaincourt found the emperor was only intermittently in touch with the

looming disaster. He would acknowledge the problems and fly into a rage at an official from the commissariat, then be distracted by some report of a minor battle or the arrival of a fresh supply of ammunition, instantly reverting to his "old illusions" of conquering Russia, throwing the tsar out, pushing on to India, and crippling Britain's mercantile trade. The diplomat had never seen a wider gap between unfolding reality and Napoleon's grasp of it.

BUT THE SITUATION on the Russian side was hardly ideal, either. In the face of a seemingly endless retreat, Alexander resorted to propaganda to placate his subjects, churning out a steady stream of bulletins trumpeting imaginary victories against the French and instructing the leaders of the Orthodox Church to rally the faithful to the cause. But news of the French advance got out via soldiers' letters sent home, from gossip passed east from peasants who had watched the Grande Armée march by unimpeded, and with the arrival of refugees, all of which spread "fear and despair." The mood of the country darkened whenever the actual facts of the war escaped.

Finally, on August 2, the Russian First and Second armies met in Smolensk. "This news filled everyone with extraordinary joy," wrote Nikolai Mitarevsky, a young Russian artillery officer. "We thought there would be no more retreating and the war would take on a different character." Pressure was by now intense on General Barclay and on the tsar to confront Napoleon. Alexander's high command, the soldiers themselves, and average Russian citizens were growing impatient and increasingly suspicious of Alexander's motives. And rumors about the German-speaking Barclay were already beginning to spread—why didn't he turn and fight?

Smolensk was a small town of 12,600 citizens, a site without great strategic interest, but it had acquired a significance for Russians out of proportion to its size, due to the presence of the revered icon of Hodegetria (literally, "she who shows the way"), supposedly painted by Saint Luke in the eleventh century. The miraculous portrait of the Virgin Mary and Jesus made Smolensk one of Russia's "holy" cities, and the legacy of several battles between the Poles and Russians in the seventeenth century gave the place a nationalist pedigree as well. It was a maxim of Russian military history that "he who has Smolensk also has Moscow." The city was, all in all, a fitting arena for a showdown with the invader.

Napoleon, of course, wanted nothing more than a confrontation, and on August 7 he got exciting news. Cossacks had attacked Count Horace Sebastiani's 3,000 mounted troops at the town of Inkovo, halfway between Vitebsk and Smolensk, and dealt them a serious blow. Finally bowing to the political situation, Barclay sent three columns to attack Ney, "the Bravest of the Brave," and the dashing Murat, who were believed to be in advance of the main body of troops around the town of Rudnia. During the offensive, scouts reported that the French had been spotted to the north. Barclay turned his troops toward the French forces, but the new orders never got through to his cavalry. They continued advancing along the original lines and at Inkovo ran into the enemy cavalry, still in their tents. The Russians attacked at dawn, sweeping through the camp, spreading chaos, and capturing 200 prisoners.

The attack had acted as a trip wire. Now Napoleon knew where the Russians were, and he concluded that the main body of troops had gathered at Smolensk. He moved quickly to pin them down for a large-scale battle, moving his corps to the Dnieper River. Believing that the First and Second armies were southeast of him, he was engaging in a classic Napoleonic technique: he would circle around and get behind the Russians at Smolensk, cut off their line of retreat, and then crush them.

The hoped-for alliance between Bagration and Barclay had never materialized on the ground. Bagration, a Russian hawk to his highly excitable nerve endings, lobbied for a battle, while the

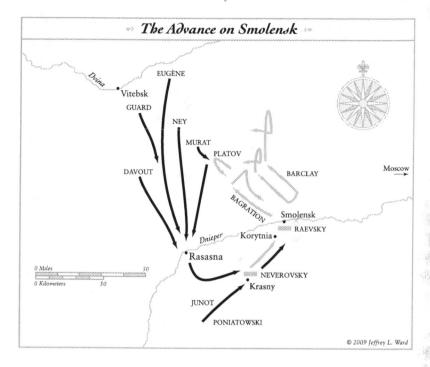

The Advance on Smolensk

Dvina

Vitebsk

EUGÈNE

GUARD

NEY

MURAT

PLATOV

DAVOUT

BARCLAY

Moscow →

BAGRATION

Smolensk

RAEVSKY

Dnieper   Korytnia

Rasasna

0 Miles   50

0 Kilometers   50

NEVEROVSKY

Krasny

JUNOT

PONIATOWSKI

© 2009 Jeffrey L. Ward

careful Barclay was still terrified of being crushed by one of Napoleon's surprise flank or rearguard attacks. Finally, Barclay agreed that a confrontation with Napoleon was necessary, and he marched northwest from Smolensk to find the French. But a confusing and contradictory series of orders was sent to Bagration, miles to the south, the last of which ordered him to a rendezvous. The Second Army's leader had grown exasperated by the blizzard of directives and now refused the command to turn around for another pointless march. Instead of joining forces with Barclay, his troops continued toward Smolensk. Barclay was forced to abandon his offensive and turned back toward the city. The rift in the Russian high command was now deep and wide.

Confusion—and Napoleon's own reputation—worked against Barclay, denying him the decisive battle he needed. Barclay didn't believe that his opponent's tactical skills had deteriorated. The Russians repeatedly suspected a Napoleonic strike would come wheeling in from some unexpected direction, and so they chose again and again to retreat away from the invisible presence they sensed over the next hill.

On August 14, Napoleon sent Davout rushing to Smolensk from the southwest, followed by Ney and Murat. "At last! I have them!" he cried when Marshal Ney reported back that he had the entire Russian army in sight. The emperor decided on a classic frontal assault against a fortified position, just the kind of warfare he had seemed to make obsolete in victories such as Austerlitz. The time for finesse was gone.

But now that Napoleon needed the kind of massive army he had assembled in Germany, his numbers were falling fast. He was down to 175,000 effective fighting troops, with 100,000 others on the sick or missing lists. Ney's corps had been reduced from 39,342 men at the start of the campaign to 16,053 troops fit enough for battle. The medical situation was grim.

The German foot soldier Jakob Walter saw his company dwindle to 25 men as they marched toward Smolensk. "One man after another stretched himself half-dead upon the ground," he wrote in his diary. "Most of them died a few hours later; several, however, suddenly fell to the ground dead." He attributes many of the casualties to thirst but reports no symptoms. It's likely that typhus and dysentery were killing as many as, if not more than, dehydration was.

As he approached Smolensk, Napoleon decided against sending an encircling force to block any Russian retreat, allowing the road to Moscow at the Russian forces' rear to remain clear. Some historians have theorized that he expected a decisive battle in which no retreat would be possible, but it's also likely that the emperor felt he needed every available man for the assault and couldn't spare a containment force. He could have bypassed the city and crossed the Dnieper farther down, and the German adviser Carl von Clausewitz for one was astonished and appalled when he failed to do so. But second-tier cities were less important to Napoleon than Russian casualties and prisoners—the key, he felt, to getting Alexander to the negotiating table.

Smolensk lies in an oval bowl, surrounded by hills in the south (which the French commanded) and the north (held by the Russians). Below their feet spread out thickets of birch and open spaces, slanting down to the dwellings that marked the city's outer suburbs, bisected by two streams that fed the Dnieper River. The city walls were whitewashed and studded with thirty bastion towers. It was a fortress, decrepit in places, but still a formidable target for a head-on attack. Inside the walls and arrayed through the suburbs were the 17,000 men of Nikolai Raevsky's VII Corps. Barclay and Bagration were rushing to reinforce them.

On August 15, the French soldiers cooked their meals and then gathered around their campfires, talking quietly. "The thought of the coming day alternated with fitful sleep," wrote Jakob Walter, "and in fantasy the many dead men and horses came as a world of spirits before the last judgment."

Early on August 16, Marshal Ney and his corps attacked the Russian cavalry, which retired in short order behind the walls. Napoleon rode up at nine in the morning and ordered a light bombardment of the city as he waited for the main body of his troops to arrive. In the meantime, the Second Army under Bagration streamed into the city, bolstering Raevsky's units and changing the face of the battle. Barclay, after an exhausting thirty-mile march, arrived with the First Army hours later.

The action resumed in earnest the next day. Napoleon had 140,000 men to throw against the Russians, with Eugène and Junot's corps still making their way to Smolensk. Ney took up the left position, Davout held the center, and General Józef Poniatowski, with his Polish troops, formed the right along with Murat. The Guard, as always, stood back to act as a reserve.

The two armies probed each other. French infantrymen went

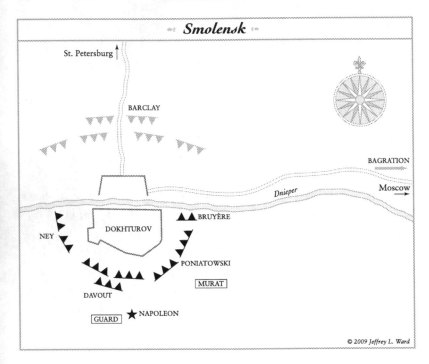

© 2009 Jeffrey L. Ward

streaming through the suburbs with bayonets fixed and ran
straight into the Russian infantry, who counterattacked and drove
them back with volleys of case shot, which "shattered great heaps
of them to the ground," leaving the French casualties "weltering
in their own blood." Townspeople, even Russian priests, one of
whom sighted an artillery piece, emerged out of the ramparts and
fought off the attackers.

Seeing the stiff resistance, Napoleon eagerly awaited an all-out
counteroffensive by the forces inside the city, but Barclay held
them back. The emperor stared and stared at the gates, willing the
Russians to emerge. Meanwhile, the French artillery was raining
shells into the fortress, hoping to kill as many enemy troops as
possible and drive the rest outside the forty-foot walls. The Russians fired back, their ball slamming into the French gun carriages,
sending shrapnel into the gunners, killing them. Wagons exploded,

deafening nearby troops and sending chunks of flesh from the dray horses spinning across the slope. As the Russian barrages rained down, the French noticed they were using a new variety— a triple-vented shell that spewed fire as it descended.

From the Russian side, Captain Eduard von Löwenstern watched line after line of French infantrymen charging the guns.

> A second earlier these poor victims of battle had advanced with fixed bayonets and pale faces. Now most of them lay dead or mutilated. Another column soon advanced and, with a hail of bullets, avenged the death of their comrades. Many of our artillerymen were shot.

By that afternoon, Napoleon knew that he wouldn't get his battle in open ground and ordered the entire front line of his forces to take the city. Two hundred guns erupted into a thunderous barrage, and three corps of troops—under Ney, Davout, and Poniatowski— went shouting toward the walls and their three gates, their peacock uniforms visible for everyone to see.

The topology of Smolensk forms a natural amphitheater, with the action centered between the feet of two facing slopes, as if on a stage. Workers from the Grande Armée's baggage trains came up to watch the action, calling out to units in danger below their feet and crying "Bravo!" at small acts of bravery. The regimental bands— made up of one piccolo, one high clarinet, sixteen clarinets, two trumpets, one bass trumpet, four bassoons, two military serpents (a distant and fantastically shaped ancestor of the tuba), four horns, three trombones, two snare drums, one bass drum, one triangle, and two pairs of cymbals—played their martial tunes at maximum volume, and observers on the rim of the bowl could hear snatches of the music between the cannon volleys, with the trumpeters playing flourishes and the drummers hoisting their instruments high into the air.

The cavalry moved first, charging at the Russian dragoons

and killing scores of them before the remainder fled in panic. The French infantry fell on the troops holding the suburbs and then pushed their way toward the fortress walls. The action was unusually close and vicious. The Russian soldiers seemed to be enraged, and officers had to beat them back with the flat of their swords to stop them from breaking ranks and charging at the enemy without orders.

Stabbing upward with their bayonets and picking off defenders at close range, the French troops marched relentlessly up the far bank. "The drums beat the attack," remembered one soldier from the 7th Light Infantry. "And everyone dashes forward at the double, driving everything before him." After three hours of exhausting combat, the French pushed the enemy back to the fortress wall, repelling ferocious counterattacks along the way. Over their heads arched round after round of artillery fire, their trails glowing in the darkening sky, while the Russians lobbed projectiles into the French battalions. One cannonball blasted at the flank of an advancing regiment smashed through the line, killing 22 men.

When the French troops reached the walls, many of the defenders dashed inside. "Everything which doesn't make haste to follow suit perishes," reported Captain Karl von Suckow. "Even so, our columns, in mounting to this assault, have left behind them a long broad trail of blood. . . ." The foot of the fortifications became a slaughterhouse, with men slashing at each other with bayonets and French soldiers climbing on top of one another's shoulders, attempting in vain to gain a hold on the ancient walls. But once they cleared the battlements of enemy troops, stalemate. The French had no ladders to climb the bulwark and no information from spies as to where the breaches and weak points were.

As nightfall approached, the guns on both sides fell silent. The soldiers panted for breath at the foot of the brick fortifications. Startled by the sudden silence, they looked around in wonder, then began to hear through the forty-foot-thick walls the sound of crackling wood. The city was in flames.

The wooden homes of Smolensk had caught fire from the constant shelling and were now burning out of control. The orange flames threw into silhouette the inhabitants searching desperately for shelter and the Russian soldiers rushing up to the walls to repel the latest charge as chunks of the brick wall crumbled and slammed to the ground. Unable to sleep, at two in the morning Caulaincourt was watching the conflagration and listening to its dull roar when a hand slapped him on the shoulder. He found Napoleon next to him, apparently invigorated by the spectacle. "An eruption of Vesuvius!" he cried. "Isn't that a fine sight?" The diplomat, horrified by the carnage in service of no strategic aim, replied, "Horrible, Sire." Napoleon waved his hand. "Remember the words of a Roman emperor: 'A dead enemy always smells sweet.' " He felt victory was near.

Surrounded by hills and open to bombardment, Smolensk wasn't defensible in the long term, and Barclay, as clear-sighted as ever, knew it. Once he had secured the road to Moscow late on the night of August 17, the Russian commander began shuttling troops out of the city. He wanted to initiate the retreat before Napoleon did the obvious and crossed the Dnieper, cutting off his escape route. With the city's famous icon placed on a gun carriage and the remaining structures and provisions inside the walls fired by the departing troops, the Russians made their exit. At the point that the armies broke off contact, the French had lost 19,000 men; the Russians, 14,000, including two generals.

The retreat caused a firestorm among the Russian command. Generals rushed up to Barclay and shouted that Smolensk must be defended to the last man. "You German, you sausage-maker, you traitor, you scoundrel, you are selling Russia," Count Levin August von Benningsen taunted him in one memorable sally that reflected the common soldiers' distrust of Barclay. But the general, correctly, refused to sacrifice his army for a point of pride and ordered the retreat to continue.

Bagration was beside himself with fury and helplessness. "It is painful and sad and the entire army is in despair, because they gave up the most dangerous place and all for nothing," he wrote a friend. "Barclay is irresolute, cowardly, senseless, and slow . . . the army weeps and curses him to death."

Smolensk's remaining wooden structures burned over the shoulders of the retreating Russians. "The flames became more intense," remembered the illustrator and soldier Christian Wilhelm von Faber du Faur, watching from the French side "forming a ball of fire that turned night to day and lit the countryside for miles around." The reflection of the flames turned the surface of the river orange and the light and shadows played along the surface of the brick walls. But inside the city was a burnt-over slaughterhouse.

It was hardly the smashing victory Napoleon had hoped for. "The mirage of victory," commented Comte Philippe-Paul de Ségur, the general who would go on to write a popular history of the campaign, "which lured him on, which he seemed so often on the point of grasping, had once more eluded him."

The French entered Smolensk the next day. Few were ready for what they encountered. One soldier told a friend: "Never can you form an adequate idea of the dreadful scene which the interior of Smolensk presented to my view, and never during the whole course of my life can I forget it. Every street, every square, was covered with the bodies of the Russians, dead or dying. The flames shed over them a horrible glare." About half of the city's structures had burned, their copper roofs lying rolled up on the ground. The fire had carbonized the corpses of the Russian soldiers and townspeople, shrinking them to the size of children. Men stepped over the corpses and even the old veterans vomited in the gutters. The dead were no longer recognizably human, the burnt flesh fusing with the iron of muskets and swords into grotesque black concretions. Others had been "literally grilled," the heat shriveling their lips and burning away their eyeballs until red sockets remained. The French had to step around the wailing survivors, just discovering their dead in the first light.

The memoirist Captain Roeder—sick with dysentery and the first signs of fever, he had missed the battle—toured the battle-fields outside the city and wrote almost the only benign thoughts recorded at the site. "And yet, maybe they did not really hate each other so much after all," he wrote in his diary, "for now French-man and Russian lie peacefully side by side." Nicholas Pisani, an Italian officer who passed through the town days after the battle, came across a French corpse with a book open in his hand. Pisani approached the body and found that the volume was a medical text on the treatment of wounds. The desperate soldier had carried the text with him hundreds of miles, but the instructions had failed to save him at the crucial moment.

The sick and wounded were herded into fifteen makeshift hospitals, many of them stone civic buildings that hadn't burned. "Here the wounded were lying often on top of each other, without any straw, food, or bandages, whimpering in terrible pain," wrote the medical historian Wilhelm Ebstein. To a miasmist, the reason for the spreading illness was clear: "terrible deprivations, the excessive heat, and the terrible smell from dead bodies" were the culprit. In fact, the hospitals should bear much of the blame. The wounded would have been better off staying where they were instead of being installed elbow-to-elbow with the infected.

Napoleon rode through the city at dawn, then camped out at one of the gates facing the Dnieper, where the black lines of retreating Russian troops were still visible. With his marshals, he sat on mats, intending to review the situation but instead launching into a diatribe against Barclay. "What a disgrace . . . to have given up without fighting, the key to Old Russia!" he cried. All the time, the bullets from the retreating Russian infantry whipped by the emperor's head as he stared down at the enemy.

Barclay wasn't out of danger yet. He still had to make good his escape east along the Moscow road. To do this, he held the northern bank of the Dnieper as long as possible, abandoning it only on August 19 and then sending his men north to avoid further bombardment from French artillery, which could sight anyone retreating along the thoroughfare and target them with ease. His army would then swing south to find the Moscow road again.

The French rushed to cut off the army they had failed to destroy in their best chance of the campaign. As the Russians retreated, the bulldog Ney had a chance to repair the major bridges at Smolensk and hurry his troops across to the Moscow road, followed by Murat and the cavalry. The star-crossed General Junot, who had yet to play a major part in the campaign, crossed the river ahead of him and set off in pursuit.

One column of Russians unfamiliar with the small roads they were forced to march along at night got lost and fell behind. Ney stumbled on them and the Russians turned and attacked. Both armies rushed in reinforcements. Napoleon galloped to the scene and, assuming this was simply a rearguard action designed to cover Barclay's retreat, ordered Davout to throw a division into the fight. Across the battlefield, Barclay himself appeared on the front lines and, in a rare moment of charismatic leadership, cried out "Victory or death!" and threatened to shoot any commander who retreated. Unlike Napoleon, he knew this was more than a delaying action. His army had struggled to move its artillery over the country roads north of the Moscow road and was now vulnerable to a breakthrough from the rear. Outnumbered two to one, the 20,000 troops fighting Ney had to hold or the army would never reach the capital. The two sides pushed each other up and down the thoroughfare, with neither able to achieve a decisive breakthrough.

The key became Junot, who had crept up behind the Russian forces and was poised to unleash a devastating offensive from a left-rear position. Napoleon sent the attack order, but Junot hesitated. Napoleon had first taken to the young commander because of his fearlessness and his devil-may-care wit. Junot was handsome, sarcastic, an aristocratic nihilist who nevertheless looked up to the Corsican leader as a demigod. But alcohol and cynicism had worn away Junot's dash, and now when called upon, he froze. Despite Napoleon's express order, the general simply stared down at the action unfolding in front of him while his Westphalian troops fumed and shouted for orders to march. Furious, the clearly unstable general threatened to have any protesters shot on sight. When the outraged Murat galloped up to find out what was delaying him, the two got into a spit-flying argument, with Junot claiming that he had no orders to attack and that his cavalry was too afraid to go on the offensive. "You are unworthy to be the last dragoon in Napoleon's army," Murat shouted at his fellow general, then turned his horse around and charged back into the battle, while Junot sallied off to a nearby house for breakfast. Some of his troops, in his absence, were called into action, but they didn't fall on the Russians with the devastating weight a unified attack would have carried. The moment passed. Fighting as if Russia itself depended on the outcome, the Russians held the French off and Barclay escaped.

The landscape told the story of the battle. "Amidst the stumps of trees," remembered the historian-general Ségur, "on ground trampled by the feet of the combatants, furrowed with balls, strewed with the fragments of weapons, tattered uniforms, overturned carriages, and scattered limbs." The Russians had lost 5,000 men; Napoleon, around 8,700.

Napoleon gave a rousing victory speech to his men and was unusually generous in bestowing decorations and promotions and small gifts of cash, which "rained down like hail." Wherever he went, Napoleon left deeply grateful troops eager to fight again, a talent he never lost. Men who hadn't dreamed of an officer's rank were quickly commissioned: with the dead from the battle and the rising epidemic, this was becoming an army in which one could advance rapidly.

It must be pointed out that the soldiers themselves often had a different attitude toward death—especially death in battle—than prevails today. The men of the Grande Armée felt themselves to be participants in something larger and much older than themselves: a living tradition of personal glory. "Death is nothing," Napoleon himself had written, in a phrase many of his men would have seconded. "But to live defeated and inglorious is to die daily." Battle swelled their difficult lives with possibility, with historical dimensions, with the possibility of immortal life in the memory of their nations and loved ones. "Even if one had to die, what did it matter?" wrote Alfred de Musset about the Napoleonic campaigns. "Death was beautiful in those days, so great, so splendid in its crimson cloak. It looked so much like hope . . . the very stuff of youth."

Were sentiments such as these fictions designed to shovel lower-class youths into the ranks of imperialistic armies? Certainly. Were men more expendable in the early 1800s, before the notion of individual rights and equality had fully taken hold? Yes. But much of the reverence for a courageous death was given freely by the men themselves. The notion that to die well was worthy of the highest effort was as palpable to the soldiers at Smolensk as it was to the Spartans over two thousand years before.

An aide watching Napoleon hand out medals thought he didn't do it in the old, hearty way, but out of an "imperative need . . . to react against melancholy thoughts." And away from the men, the emperor alternated between rage and depression. "Junot has let them escape," Napoleon screamed at his advisers. "He is losing the campaign for me." The inscrutable Junot would grow increasingly unstable and—some say haunted by his failure at Smolensk— would die a suicide a year later.

The strategist Clausewitz points to the failure to surround Barclay at Smolensk as Napoleon's greatest error in the campaign. It meant that everything would now escalate rapidly: the length of the supply and communication lines; the distance his reinforcements back in Germany had to travel; and, especially, the number of sick. The war before Smolensk was almost reasonable; it resembled other campaigns Napoleon had fought. Had the Russians stood and fought, Napoleon's strategy could have worked. After Smolensk, his approach became increasingly incoherent.

Napoleon's troop totals were being reworked by another number: the mortality rate of epidemic typhus. "The terrible deprivations," wrote Chamrey, a doctor on the Russian campaign, "the excessive heat, and the terrible smell from dead bodies everywhere around Smolensk causes an infectious disease which kills more men in a short time than the wounds of battle."

ALEXANDER CELEBRATED SMOLENSK as a great victory and ordered a Te Deum to be sung at a cathedral in St. Petersburg. Rumors spread through Moscow that the French had lost 30,000 men, including 13,000 taken prisoner. The idea of a despotic invader repulsed by a heroic resistance was increasingly effective, as the French troops could attest, since they were encountering increasingly bitter and violent peasants in their marches. Napoleon was disgusted. "They lie to God as well as to men," he remarked.

Post-Smolensk, a note of panic crept into a Napoleon communiqué. He dashed off a set of orders to his chief of staff Berthier, blaming the loss of men on problems with the supply line. He wasn't only worried, he was misinformed:

> Write to the generals in command of army corps, and tell them that we are losing numbers of men every day, owing to the disorderly way in which foraging is conducted; that it is urgent that they should concert measures with the various corps commanders for ending a state of things which threatens to be fatal to the army.... You must write to the King of Naples [Murat]... that it is indispensable for the cavalry to give adequate protection to

foragers and to secure the detachments on this duty from
the attacks of Cossacks and enemy cavalry. . . . Finally
you must inform the Duke of Elchingen [Ney] that he is
losing more men in a day than if a battle was in progress.

Cossacks and villagers were certainly attacking foraging parties,
but the main body of Russian troops was in full retreat and in no
position to mount operations. These minor skirmishes were in no
way as lethal to his men as sickness was, and one wonders at his information, or his interpretation of it. First Larrey had blamed rotten
cognac. Now Napoleon blamed marauders, who were certainly
killing his soldiers but not in the massive numbers that were actually
being lost. Miscommunication was masking the real problem. The
most virulent source of the unfolding tragedy was cloaked, invisible
to the eyes of the army's leaders.

The misdiagnosis was potentially significant. Mistakes in the
foragers' protection could be corrected: more squads sent out and
discipline enforced on the distribution of the provisions. But an
epidemic of typhus couldn't be stopped by his medical authorities.
Other armies in the past faced with the pathogen had retired from
the field whenever possible and taken up the campaign when the
epidemic had passed. Had Napoleon known (or acknowledged to
himself) the true reason for the astonishing casualty rate, he might
have considered a winter rest in Smolensk.

Considered and then probably plunged ahead anyway. There is
little in Napoleon's record to indicate he would have interrupted
the invasion and then resumed the campaign the next year. Allowing disease to stop a campaign would have been particularly
galling to him, as the experience of Egypt showed. To the emperor,
it would have been succumbing to an unforgivable weakness. But,
in Haiti when yellow fever had proved too lethal for his army, he
withdrew and then promptly sold off the Louisiana Territory, believing it to be infected with the same microbe. And he did seriously consider the wintering option along the road to Moscow, a

move Caulaincourt and others backed. A correct estimation of typhus's rising strength would have certainly argued against a long march (228 miles as the crow flies, 310 miles by road) to Moscow.

Napoleon again hesitated in his pursuit of Barclay, telling Caulaincourt that he would rest the army at Smolensk, firm up his supply and communication lines, bring the reserve units stationed back at the Dvina River under his own command, and raise additional regiments in Poland. In the spring, his army would be even more formidable and he could choose between taking Moscow or St. Petersburg as a prelude to negotiations. Caulaincourt, his former Russian ambassador, who should have known better than to believe in the emperor's cautious mood, was ecstatic. He told Napoleon that in stopping at Smolensk, he was refusing to play Alexander's game of drawing the French into the interior and letting the climate and the distance eat up his battalions.

A captured Russian officer was sent back to the enemy lines with a message for the tsar: Napoleon desired peace. As grateful as he was for the repatriation, the officer still gave the emperor the thoroughly unwelcome opinion that he doubted there would be a treaty with the French still occupying Russia. Once the messenger was sent off, the by now supremely irritable Napoleon began to waver. Smolensk hadn't changed anything in the strategic situation. The thousands of Russian dead would be replaced tenfold if he gave Alexander months to recover, and the tsar would very likely receive additional regiments from Moldavia and Finland. England could supply money and material to his enemy. The domestic situation back in Paris would grow more precarious without his presence, and the fragile chain of riders carrying his bulletins and orders to his ministers back home, so vital to a commander away from his seat of power, would become even more vulnerable.

Added to that, the infamous winter was only a matter of months away, and there were disturbing reports of Russian victories in the field. Throughout the advance, General Wittgenstein and his corps had been kept as an independent force able to attack the advancing Napoleon from the north, opening a second front. Napoleon had used his Bavarian corps to shield himself from those divisions. Now Wittgenstein and Count Alexander Tormasov had proved sharp adversaries in skirmishes and were toting up victories that worried the emperor.

Nevertheless, Napoleon snapped at anyone who spoke of retreating; when his long-suffering chief of staff, Berthier, mentioned the risks of advancing to Moscow, Napoleon lashed out, "Go back to France, I do not force anyone." The emperor grasped at any news that indicated that a quick end to the nightmare was at hand. When Murat reported that the Russians were conducting a disciplined retreat, instead of a pell-mell rush, and even stated that Barclay was already preparing fortifications at a site only a day's march away, he brightened. But the dashing Murat, eager for a fight, was as fanciful as his emperor. There were no fortifications. Still, Napoleon took the news to mean that Alexander was only searching for a more favorable spot for a climactic battle. "Once more the gauntlet was thrown down," wrote Caulaincourt. "And the emperor was not the man to turn back." Besides, the small momentum gained by Wittgenstein and Tormasov was reversed when the French dealt them quick defeats in the field. The emperor turned to the Russian lieutenant-general Nikolai Tuchkov, who had been captured after Smolensk, and asked him to write a letter to the tsar offering peace at almost any price. The letter went unanswered.

After wavering for days, Napoleon decided for Moscow. "The wine has been poured," he told his marshals. "It must now be drunk." The epigram was one of the fatalistic sayings he favored after having made a decision. It was as if he had exhausted his powers and now gave himself over to destiny. His reasoning mixed in fantasy with reckless optimism. "We have gone too far to turn back. Peace is in front of us; we are but ten days' march from it. So near the goal, there is nothing more to consider. Let us march on Moscow!"

He left Smolensk on August 25, rushing his troops out at one in the morning, as if the morning light might cause him to reconsider. Caulaincourt was drained. "Once again we set off in pursuit of the glory, or rather the fatality," he wrote, "which relentlessly prevented the Emperor from holding to his good intentions." Leaving the city, his army was down to 149,000 men, less than a third of his original frontline force. "The two armies converged toward the point of equalization," wrote the German tactician Clausewitz. Napoleon's bludgeon was gone, taken away by pathogens and hard Russian fighting.

IF NAPOLEON HAD NEVER encountered an opponent quite like typhus, the opposite was also true. Many leaders would have looked at their losses at this point in the campaign and called the retreat. It was the only reasonable decision. The contest with Napoleon was different from almost any other the disease had found itself in during its long history. Other armies, such as those under King Francis, had almost all disintegrated or retired from the field in the face of the pathogen. It was a tribute to the hold that Napoleon had on his men that despite the ravages of typhus, the Grande Armée not only fought on but remained the aggressor.

It would be overstating the case to say a microbe revealed the emperor's innermost drives. But the disease did expose how fanatical was Napoleon's devotion to his mission, to his own glorification through conquest. Without typhus, his losses would have been acceptable, in line with past wars, and his army would have been in no real danger of vanishing. With it, he was being tested in a new, macabre fashion. Would he really sacrifice an entire army larger than the population of Paris to a sense of his own rightful destiny?

The emperor marched on.

CHAPTER 8

Smoke

An autopsy conducted on a typhus victim in the late 1700s found the disease's work everywhere: ". . . the blood vessels, turgid to an extraordinary degree, give an appearance of commencing gangrene . . . [and] are found to contain little or no red blood, the ventricles and all of the interstices are full of water, and the whole substance appears pale, and as if it were macerated [softened by immersion in a liquid]. The lungs . . . appear to be suffocated or oppressed, resembling a sponge filled with black blood; they also appear in some cases to be irregularly inflamed . . . spotted in the back parts." The disease had run rampant through the vascular system, imploding the body's delivery systems as it went.

The doctors of the Grande Armée had no time to perform autopsies on the thousands of men lying all the way back to Poland. But beneath their blue tunics and their mottled skin, the same damage would have been evident. Typhus (from the Greek word *typhos,* meaning "smoke" or "stupor") was a highly consistent killer.

As the disease appears center stage in the invasion, it warrants a deeper biography. To call the disease ancient is to insult its pedigree. "Ancient" in epidemiological terms summons up images of the Black Death of the 1340s or the Plague of Athens in 430 BC (a devastating epidemic for which typhus remains a suspect, though recent studies have favored typhoid fever, a different disease, as the culprit). The microbe that causes typhus—called *Rickettsia prowazekii*—is older than our understanding of disease allows. When it was born, the Europe that Napoleon had conquered didn't exist as a landmass. To get a fix on its origins, one must think in terms of geological epochs.

Two billion years ago, the earth was cooling after its violent birth. Radioactive material had sunk and compressed to form the earth's heavy core, along with vast deposits of iron oxide, leaving only traces that would be mined to make the Grande Armée's muskets. Lighter material moved outward, forming layers of crust and mantle. Gases, in particular nitrogen and carbon dioxide, spewed from the hot core through the volcanoes that pocked the planet's surface. The water vapor that had most likely arrived in our atmosphere from comets that smashed into the planet hung above its surface, before condensing and falling to earth, forming the oceans. Cratons, the protocontinents that would merge and then split into the landmasses we know today as Asia, Africa, and so on, had begun rooting themselves into the deep mantle. And the earliest forms of life were spilling out near the deep oceanic vents.

Among them was a simple organism that would give us a pair of intriguing offspring. Scientists haven't yet identified this bacteria-like creature, but researchers know it existed because of its descendants. Sometime in the Proterozoic era, this microbe produced both the organelle known as the mitochondrion and the ancestor of the microbe we now call *Rickettsia prowazekii*. In terms of their effect on humankind, two more different progeny could hardly be imagined.

Mitochondria are often called the engines of cellular life; they use oxygen to produce the chemical energy called ATP (adenosine triphosphate), which allows cells to transfer energy during photosynthesis and cellular respiration. Without mitochondria, there would be no plant or animal life.

The other descendant of the mysterious organism was the tiny rod-shaped organism that causes epidemic typhus in humans. *Rickettsia* denotes the microbe's genus, placing it in the bacteria family in the planet's taxonomy; the name derives from the American pathologist Howard T. Ricketts, who studied—and succumbed to—typhus in 1910. *Prowazekii* pays tribute to the researcher Stanislaus von Prowazek, an Austrian bacteriologist who also died of typhus in 1915 while trying to unlock its secrets. The fact that the cellular power plant that generates life shares a common ancestor with the pathogen that has killed millions of humans points up how closely life and death are intertwined both in evolutionary history and in cellular biology.

Over time, *Rickettsia* came to rely on the host cells it invaded for most of the metabolic machinery necessary for life. The first scientists to look at its genome found it resembled "a molecular theater of war, with dead genes strewn among the living," full of "junk" (or noncoding) genes that had slowly atrophied as the *Rickettsia* came to depend on its cellular victim. Twenty-four percent of the microbe's genome consists of genes abandoned in favor of the host's DNA, the largest percentage found in any microbial genome to date. This is called "reductive evolution," and *Rickettsia* is one of its past masters.

Looking at the rickettsial genome, one of the most compact (meaning containing the fewest bits of DNA) known to science, one catches one's breath. Here is a predator millions of years in the making. Before our ancestors were using fire or learning to hunt, the organism had become a conqueror, not killing its prey, but invading and feeding off it. *Rickettsia* shaped itself to function *only* as a hunter; and not only a hunter, but a hunter that had to study and mimic life in order to live. The creatures it would inhabit in modern times were countless mutations away from being born, so the pathogen would have to survive almost the entire span of Darwinian evolution even to have a chance of altering history beginning that day in 1812.

To look at it alongside its evolutionary cousin the mitochondrion, one may be forgiven for anthropomorphizing the two and thinking of Cain and Abel. One "father" who ushered two progeny into a new world, two very different fates for humans coded in their genes.

THE FINAL TEST of a pathogen's power is the ability to go epidemic: to infect large numbers of humans in short, intense spurts, where it radiates from a small initial infection to spread its life force over an entire city, continent, or planet. Only a handful of diseases have achieved this capability: influenza, plague, and smallpox are among them. To go epidemic, typhus would need an effective vector: it couldn't "jump" from human to human by itself, and so it needed an agent to transport its genome.

It found its final vector in *Pediculus humanus corporis,* the six-legged common body louse. By choosing it, *Rickettsia* found a nearly universalized transport system. The mosquito that carried the yellow fever pathogen could only infect in its limited habitat. The rat, which transported bubonic plague, and the louse, which carried typhus, were despised but accepted presences in almost every human society, although the latter could travel places (such as the Arctic) where even the rat couldn't survive. The tiny parasite was so common that it was practically invisible, and so made a perfect agent for *Rickettsia*'s spread.

Lice have been with humankind from our earliest history. In Exodus 8:16–19, when Moses threatens Pharaoh should he refuse to free the Jewish people, the parasites are the third plague unleashed on the Egyptians:

> And the LORD said unto Moses, say unto Aaron, Stretch out thy rod, and smite the dust of the land, that it may become lice throughout all the land of Egypt.

And they did so; for Aaron stretched out his hand with his rod, and smote the dust of the earth, and it became lice in man, and in beast; all the dust of the land became lice throughout all the land of Egypt.

As repellent as the louse is, it is a miracle of perfect adaptation; it will starve to death before feeding on an unfamiliar host. Even its dislike of heat worked in *Rickettsia*'s favor. A rise of four or five degrees can be fatal to the louse, so when a patient infected with typhus runs a fever, lice move away from layers of clothing closest to the hot skin or migrate to men and women with cooler body temperatures. This exports *Rickettsia* to a fresh supply of carriers, a process that is repeated until all available human hosts are exhausted. The parasite even camouflages itself in the appropriate hue for world travel: the body louse in Africa is black, the North American Indian is bronzed, the Eskimo is a pale brown, and the European is gray-white. No other pest is as symbolic of humankind's dominion over the world as this infinitely adaptable creature.

The louse isn't a reservoir for *Rickettsia,* as the microbe is inevitably fatal to it. Lice become infected after feeding on a sick human, turn bright red, and then expire about five days later. *Rickettsia* thus has only 120 hours to transmit to humans or to another louse, but the fact that nineteenth-century humans often carried thousands of lice in their clothes, and only one infected one is needed to pass the pathogen on, made them highly effective carriers.

RICKETTSIA PROWAZEKII LIVES in the cytoplasm of the louse, the semitransparent fluid outside a cell's nucleus. Specifically, the microbe found a home in the epithelium that lines the stomach. Transmission to humans occurs in two ways. The first is through the louse feces, which can penetrate the skin, through an open wound. Or it can enter through scratching: when the louse bites (as a blood eater, it must feed several times a day) and the victim scrapes the skin, the infected contents of the louse's system spill out and are rubbed into the open wound, pouring *Rickettsia prowazekii* into the bloodstream.

Once it enters the human bloodstream, *Rickettsia* incubates for four to fifteen days, churning out millions of copies of its DNA, replicating and then invading the endothelial cells that line the veins and capillaries through the entire body, in the same way the microbe parasitized its original one-celled hosts. The host cells swell with the infection, fluid leaks out, and the blood vessels begin to spill their contents into the surrounding tissue. In the brain, the attack often leads to encephalitis, which results in the swelling of the brain and causes excruciating headache, as well as stranger effects. "These thunders, sudden noises; these eclipses," wrote the poet John Donne, who barely survived a bout of the illness in 1623, "this darkening of the senses; these blazing stars, sudden fiery exhalations; these rivers of blood." As the swelling and inflammation of blood vessels in the brain continue, typhus can induce hallucinations, stupor, and, finally, a deep coma. The blood pressure drops, as the ravaged veins can no longer carry the same volume of nourishment to the organs.

The decreased oxygen carried by the blood turns the face dusky. The massive infection of the blood vessels and arterioles in the hands and feet causes them to blacken and rot with gangrene. The tiny spots that are the most famous of typhus's symptoms are the outward markers of the vascular damage that riddles the patient's interior.

Death can come in different ways: *Rickettsia* devastates the small blood vessels of the lungs, filling air pockets with fluid, and the patient dies of rickettsial pneumonia, his blood starved of oxygen. Or the comatose patient loses his gag reflex, allowing saliva filled with deadly bacteria to flow into the lungs, triggering pneumonia. The sieve-like veins left after a rickettsial attack can lose so much blood volume that the patient goes into hypotensive shock:

the tissues and organs can't get enough of the nourishing plasma and shut down. Comatose patients left unattended can simply die of dehydration. Or the heart, trying to pump blood through vessels that are perforated by a million holes, simply exhausts itself and fails.

As a PATHOGEN, *Rickettsia* was attracted to great events: wars, migrations, and famines (due to the masses of people forced out of their homes in a search for food, giving infected lice a chance to spread). Throughout human history, it had a hundred faces and names reflecting the conditions during which it attacked. "Ship fever" attacked the men crowded onto unsanitary boats, and "jail fever" devastated prisons and courtrooms. "Hunger fever" struck when the crops failed; more Irish would die of typhus than of starvation during the Great Famine in 1845–49, earning the disease another name, "the Irish ague."

It was in the Middle Ages that typhus arrived in Europe. Recent evidence points toward the New World as the source: For decades, scientists had believed that the explorers carried the louse and *Rickettsia* to the Americas. But the discovery of lice in 1,000-year-old mummies recently found in Peru reverses that migration; typhus was most likely not the explorers' curse on the New World. Instead, it was America's revenge on the Old World.

There had been possible sightings of the disease, especially a description of an outbreak of a mysterious illness in 1083 in the Spanish monastery of La Cava. "There spread a severe fever with peticuli and parotid swellings," wrote a chronicler of the epidemic, remarking that the disease was "clearly different from the Pest," or plague. During the Middle Ages, typhus most likely lurked in the background of more-famous illnesses, contributing its power to epidemics led by plague and other diseases. It was often unrecognized as a separate illness and classed instead with other "pestilential fevers" that seeded the length and breadth of Europe.

Christian culture must bear some of the responsibility for its widespread success in those early centuries. The Catholic Church frowned upon bathing, which was considered "an indulgence, an invitation to illness, or even a sin." Female saints were praised for never washing, as being naked for even a moment in one's own private home was thought to be indecent. The poor could barely afford a change of clothing, and the close quarters that cold weather necessitated for the sharing of body heat gave the louse an ideal point of transfer. Even the aristocracy lived with the parasite all their lives. The death of Thomas à Becket gives an example of how completely the louse had infiltrated every corner of society. After his murder at the altar of Canterbury Cathedral in 1170 (on the orders of King Henry II), the body of the archbishop was prepared for burial. Layer upon layer of clothing was removed: a mantle, a surplice, a lamb's wool coat, another and then a third, the black Benedictine robe, a shirt, and then a haircloth. When the final garments were removed, the lice that had lived in the clothes near to the warmth and nutrition of the body "boiled over like water in a simmering cauldron, and the onlookers burst into alternate weeping and laughter."

As the typhus expert Hans Zinsser has pointed out, disease and Christian culture had a curiously symbiotic relationship: When epidemics struck, huge numbers of Europeans flocked to the local churches and converted. Priests pointed to calamities as an example of God's wrath for wickedness and disbelief, increasing the Church's rolls and spreading its message far and wide. For its part, Christian doctrine's aversion to basic hygiene gave diseases such as typhus a leg up in the race for their own converts. Each entity found a way to thrive in the other's culture.

ONE CONFLICT IN PARTICULAR, the Thirty Years' War (1618–48), seeded the road to Russia with disaster, and in fact spread *Rickettsia* throughout the length and breadth of Europe two hundred years before Napoleon marched on Alexander. This mammoth conflict at the beginning of the seventeenth century perhaps did more to seal Napoleon's fate than any stratagem he devised. Hans Zinsser called the conflict "the most gigantic natural experiment in epidemiology to which mankind has ever been subjected."

The armies marching to battle and then returning home to their far-flung lands carried *Rickettsia prowazekii* across Europe. Stragglers, hangers-on, deserters, and traders spread the pathogen to places that had no experience of typhus. Poland and Russia, where the disease had been well established since the mid-1500s, suffered from epidemics that entrenched the microbe even deeper into the native population. For the first time, the disease entered France with strength. Some 60,000 perished in Lyon alone, and even decades after the war ended, devastating epidemics would hit towns in Burgundy and elsewhere. It's unlikely that these were the first instances of typhus in France, but the pathogen was spread widely in the population, where it would remain until the time of Napoleon.

After typhus struck in the south of France in 1641, a poet described its impact and the confusion that followed in its wake:

> *Throughout all the people of Burgundy and the cities which the slow-floating river Araris irrigates, broke out an unusual fever, which attacked the bodies with red spots (sad and incredible to say) . . .*

> *That same fever ruined the people of Italy . . . and raged across the whole of Europe. Some people blame it on the rain waters, and the fall, extremely humid for the blowing of the wind, which corrupts the air with its marshy blow, and generates the contagions of the spreading plague.*

Some others believe that spoiled food had produced the
poison deadly to humans,
which caused the noxious humor in the rotten veins
with the attached disgrace.
From there came the diseases, from there the massive
devastation among the oppressed people and the
military camps.

This described the situation all over the Continent. Before the war, typhus was a minor regional power in several pockets of Europe, especially the Balkans. Afterward, it was an empire.

In those it didn't kill, *Rickettsia prowazekii* often lay dormant, occasionally flaring up in a mild condition known as Brill-Zinsser disease. This latent infection kept the pathogen alive, ready to pass from its host to a louse to fresh victims. If enough new hosts were available, the bacteria could spark a new epidemic—as was happening now in the Grande Armée.

FROM 1529 ON, typhus was present in some degree at almost every major European conflict. It hamstrung armies and stopped offensives during the English Civil War (1642–51). It killed tens of thousands of soldiers during the War of the Austrian Succession (1740–48), and it would keep its potency into the Crimean War (1853–56), which pitted Russia against France, England, and the Ottoman Empire, where it wreaked havoc on the French army and killed hundreds of thousands of soldiers and civilians.

The same agonizing symptoms that had attacked millions of Europeans for hundreds of years were being described in diary after diary of common soldiers and doctors marching toward Moscow. But Dr. Larrey and the upper reaches of the French military machine virtually ignored them as typhus swept through the ranks, killing wantonly. Now the cost was coming due.

CHAPTER 9

At Borodino

A S THE ARMY STREAMED PAST SMOLENSK AND ON TO AN uncertain future, the Hessian captain Roeder was sick but marching, every mile away from home increasing his ardor for lost things. He wrote in his diary to Mina, his dead wife: "Beloved, is it that I am soon to visit you among your airy clouds? Will our spirits soon fly to each other and embrace, or must we both dissolve forever? My body begins to waste away already." But the Russian campaign wasn't yet completely devoid of the pleasures of soldiering, not quite.

Roeder wrote with relish of camping after a long day's march, dropping onto the soft turf, wrapped in his warm cloak, and falling asleep under the stars to the sound of his horse contentedly munching on corn cut from nearby fields. He kissed a girl he met on the road and complimented her on her "fresh" appearance, recording the innocent encounter in his diary, which he sent to Sophie. She wasn't a veteran military wife used to such flirtations and responded angrily. Roeder wrote back, full of regrets, with eleven florins for her to buy a new hat. But the campaign was wearing him down; he felt the first touch of a fever at the end of August, and others were suffering, too. "My former Lieutenant, Bechstatt, and my present Lieutenant, Pfaff, have both been ill for several days," he reported. A major in the Württemberg corps told him that they had left home with 7,200 infantry soldiers but, although fighting just one engagement (Smolensk), were now down to 1,500. By September, according to typhus researcher Hans Zinsser, both typhus and dysentery were becoming "more and more intense."

The road to Moscow was broad. Artillery and supply wagons could ride two or three abreast, flanked on both sides by columns of infantry and, outside them, the cavalry. The fields they marched through were most often burned to the ground, and windstorms drove dust into their eyes. One soldier remarked that it seemed as if Mother Earth herself were rising up against the invaders. Some troops cut crude sunglasses out of bits of stained-glass window and wore them; others masked their faces with handkerchiefs or bits of cloth. The soldiers drank filthy water and horses' urine.

Many of the green youths who had signed up in Paris and elsewhere with such hopes of romance and glory, the boys who had caused the veterans to smile wanly, were now dead. The older campaigners, who were fitter and physically tougher, had survived in proportionately greater numbers. "You could make them out by the martial cast of their features and the way they talked," wrote the general and historian Ségur. "War was the only thing they remembered and it was all they could look forward to." Captain Roeder, who had nearly starved on a previous campaign, was eating less than he should have been on the way to Moscow, but he barely remarked on it in his journal.

Napoleon put the best possible face on the damage wrought by typhus and the other obstacles. "This poor army is sadly depleted," he told an aide-de-camp after Smolensk, "but what remains is good." The remark contained a hidden barb: Napoleon, with his moral idea of disease resistance, perhaps believed that the dead had not been good enough, not determined enough, to survive.

. . .

ON THE RUSSIAN SIDE, General Barclay sent reconnaissance squads ahead on the Moscow road to find a favorable spot for a battle. They reported back with two possibilities: one near the far bank of the Usha River, and the other close to the town of Gshatsk. Barclay arrived at the first spot on August 22 and ordered Bagration, whose Second Army had left Smolensk early to secure the Moscow road and had remained out in front of the First, to return for a climactic battle.

Bagration, close to open mutiny, again refused. He got into a heated argument with Colonel Karl Friedrich von Toll, who had chosen the site for battle and threatened to put "a musket across your shoulders," that is, have him demoted to a common infantry soldier. Clausewitz, the war strategist, wrote that Bagration was simply unhappy with the defensive possibilities of the position, but there may have been other, darker forces at work. Barclay knew that his constant retreating was interpreted as a slow treason by his fellow generals and a majority of the officers and troops, but he couldn't know how deep the rancor went. The fervent nationalist Bagration may have been avoiding battle to increase the pressure on Alexander to dismiss his commander and replace him with a "true" Russian. Bagration and his cohorts had been sending missives back to the tsar emphasizing the desire of the men to fight and the "foreign" plot led by Barclay that was preventing them from a glorious battle.

With dissension clouding every decision, the same pantomime unfolded at the second position chosen by Colonel Toll. The Russians stopped, started digging in, and then fell backward.

Finally, the two generals agreed on a battle position: Tsarevo-Zaimishche, a swamp only a hundred miles from the gates of Moscow. The two armies began to dig trenches and build fortifications on August 29, but politics intervened. A new general had arrived to take charge of the campaign, a true Slav, as the people demanded. General Mikhail Kutuzov would conduct the final showdown with Napoleon.

Alexander possessed a gut dislike for the charismatic, lazy Kutuzov, a dislike complicated by history. Kutuzov had dined with the tsar's father the night he was murdered, and the guilt-ridden Alexander suspected the general knew the truth of his own tacit involvement in his father's assassination. And Austerlitz, where Kutuzov had acted as a military strategist for Alexander, still stung deeply. "I was young and inexperienced," he told others. "Kutuzov should have advised me." The general *had* advised him, to retreat, but the tsar pursued the opposite strategy and lost.

The battle-scarred general had been elected by his genes more than anything else. Ensconced at his summer home on Kamenny Island, Alexander had done everything he could to avoid the general's appointment. Like Lincoln before finding Ulysses S. Grant, the tsar needed for domestic political reasons as much as anything else to find a commander who would fight. Bagration, he felt, "has no idea" of military strategy, and Barclay, whom he had thought the lesser of two evils at the beginning, had forfeited command by "committing one stupidity after another at Smolensk." The arrival in Moscow of refugees from that battle, which terrified the population, the letters from his brother Constantine, which vilified Barclay at every turn, and the "unanimous clamor" from the higher reaches of the Russian command down to the gossip in the street forced his hand. "I had no other course than to yield," he wrote his sister.

Kutuzov's roots were deep in the Russian aristocracy; no other general could rival his claim to being a native son or his popularity with the people. His ancestors had served in the army of Alexander Nevsky, and his father had fought for Peter the Great. Kutuzov had the common touch, whored alongside his troops, and grew fat on endless meals. Russians put off by Barclay's German reserve saw

Kutuzov as everything their former commander wasn't: a hedonist, suspicious of official bureaucracy, instinctual, charming but often deliberately coarse. An English diplomat once sketched the milieu he had emerged from:

> The nobility . . . live in the voluptuous magnificence of eastern satraps; after dinner they frequently retire to a vast rotunda, and sip their coffee, during a battle of dogs, wild bears, and wolves; from whence they go to their private theaters, where great dramatic skill is frequently displayed by their slaves. . . . The aristocracy enjoyed Molière and Racine in these private theaters, yet the best households would also keep dwarfs and cretins on their staff for knockabout amusements.

A prejudiced portrait, but it speaks to the complexities that Kutuzov lived out. He was also far more practiced in conspiracy and subterfuge than was Barclay, skills that a Russian army career practically demanded.

His daughter asked the general if he hoped to defeat Napoleon. "No," he replied. "But I hope to deceive him." Cunning had other uses than advancement through the ranks.

IT WAS KUTUZOV'S PERFORMANCE during the Turkish wars in 1806–12 that had made his name. The commander had received a message from his general congratulating him on taking the fortress of Ismail, which stood at the top of a steep bank on the Danube River. It was a perverse incentive; in fact, the citadel was still held by the Turks and Kutuzov's men were exhausted and terror-struck after wave after wave of assaults had left the fortress intact, producing horrendous casualties. Instead of correcting the messenger, Kutuzov had crossed himself, muttered "God help us!" and led a final charge on the bastion. His men smashed into the enemy lines, fighting a series of brutal close-range engagements. They finally overtopped the walls and bayoneted their Muslim enemies in a show of suicidal bravado. That is the kind of man the Russian soldier would follow to the death.

When this native paragon became their leader, the troops were, in general, overjoyed. "The day was cloudy, but our hearts filled with light," wrote one Russian soldier, A. A. Shcherbinin. His peers were less enthusiastic. General Benningsen, Bagration's chief of staff, called Kutuzov "old, broken, and ill." He and other staff officers considered Kutuzov to be gifted but incorrigibly lazy (Benningsen went so far as to say that the general was "disgusted" by hard work). His victories were attributed to his officers, while he was considered passive and timid when left to his own devices. Sir Robert Wilson, the British adviser to the Russian high command, saw him as a bon vivant more interested in diplomatic solutions than in fighting battles, especially now that he was sixty-seven years old. "Shrewd as a Greek" was Wilson's estimation, who felt the general was the wrong man to drive Napoleon back over the Niemen River. Alexander himself never wavered in his opinion of Kutuzov as "a hatcher of intrigues and an immoral and thoroughly dangerous character," hardly a vote of confidence in the man whom he had picked to save the motherland. Still, it hardly mattered. "The evil genius of the foreigners was exorcised by a true Russian," noted Clausewitz dryly.

Kutuzov didn't disappoint his followers. Immediately after receiving command on August 20 in St. Petersburg, the general told his driver to head to Our Lady of Kazan Cathedral, an imposing stone cathedral in the shape of the Latin cross, designed by Russian architects and finished just the year before. Inside the church, he took the medals and decorations from his long career from around his neck and set them in front of the cathedral's icon, a family heirloom of the Romanovs themselves, which was believed to work miracles. Fat and out of breath, he knelt on the marble flags, closed his eyes, and prayed for victory as the candles flickered and illuminated his bowed head. Word spread quickly to the nearby neighborhoods and Russians came running to see the nation's last hope. When he finally got up, grunting from the effort, and made his way out of the church, the crowds raised their hands in the air in supplication and solidarity and cried out "Save us! Save us!" The general wept. It was an iconic moment, and so ingrained itself in the Russian memory that the church would become a repository for mementos and captured trophies of the 1812 campaign, a fitting monument to the union of faith in God and motherland that the war represented.

Meanwhile, things were less sanguine in Moscow. Muscovites had been cheering along the Russian troops in their imaginary victories, but once the truth about the battle of Smolensk became widely known, the citizens panicked. Wagons and carriages appeared at front doors of mansions and servants began loading trunk after trunk into them. Those without vehicles to carry them began streaming out of the city on foot. Cash was king, as merchants and noble families sold jewelry and fine furnishings at fire-sale prices, fearing that whatever remained would be burned or pillaged by the French. Paranoia blossomed, and men clustered on the streets talked darkly of plots to sell Russia out. Anyone perceived as supporting the invasion stood in danger of losing his or her life: A Russian laborer who spoke of Napoleon as a liberator was beaten and then thrown in jail. Two months earlier such sentiments had been fairly common; now they were treasonous.

On hearing the news from Smolensk, Fyodor Rostopchin, the military governor of Moscow, was "plunged in grief." His fourteen-year-old daughter, Natalya, recalled finding the volatile count, his head bowed, considering the fate of his city. He stared gloomily at her, then directed her to take a dispatch from Barclay to his wife. "Smolensk has fallen," he told her. "We shall soon have the enemy at the gates of Moscow."

The nobles led the way out of the city, fleeing to their country dachas or to relatives farther east, taking with them carts heaped with tapestries, ancestral portraits, fine furniture, and other rarities. People began to hoard food and plan escape routes in case the enemy stormed the city. Neighborhoods filled with wooden structures were abandoned as the fear of a conflagration spread, and people took refuge in stone palaces that offered a fireproof sanctuary. Men escaping the city dressed up as women to avoid the insults of residents who had sworn to stay and fight, or who had nowhere to go and were venting their rage on the lucky rich. Governor Rostopchin organized a civic rescue project, carting off the city's icons, gold scepters, rare manuscripts, and other cultural treasures from the city's churches, museums, and convents. The distance between the tsar's propaganda and the reports from eyewitnesses only increased the terror. Now every wild rumor had the feel of believability.

NAPOLEON LEARNED OF Kutuzov's appointment from a captured Cossack officer, and he was thrilled with the news. Not only did he know his nemesis from Austerlitz, he felt that the general was overrated: Kutuzov had led the "finest army the Russians had ever had on the Danube" but had failed to force a treaty from the Turks. Now, in Napoleon's eyes, Kutuzov led a much less able and less motivated body of troops, completely discounting the almost fanatical Russian nationalism that stoked the common soldier. But the emperor was even more encouraged by the change at the top because he knew the firing of General Barclay was a sign that Alexander knew he had to turn and fight. Napoleon would get his all-out battle, and soon.

Kutuzov had learned war at the knee of Peter Alexander Rumyantsev, a brilliant commander in the 1768 Russo-Turkish War (and rumored to be a bastard son of Peter the Great) who had advanced all the way to Bucharest and occupied it, becoming the foremost war hero of his time. He wrote three books of military strategy, which deeply influenced Russian martial thought in the decades to come, and shaped Kutuzov as a battlefield thinker. What Rumyantsev preached was force preservation: never fight a battle unless the odds of victory were high, never sacrifice troops for territory, and keep the army intact. "The objective," he wrote, "isn't the occupation of a geographical position but the destruction of enemy forces." It was a military maxim suited to an immense country, but it was rapidly being made politically untenable by Napoleon's march through the heart of the nation.

On taking command, Kutuzov immediately began assessing potential sites for battle. Tsarevo-Zaimishche was favorable, but he felt that the army didn't yet have enough men to face Napoleon, especially as deserters had left many regiments understrength. They would have to move closer to Moscow and await reinforcements that were said to be en route. Bagration's chief of staff, General Benningsen, sent Colonel Toll out again to search for a defensive position, a tall order in a flat landscape without hills or valleys that would offer a natural redoubt.

The best of a bad assortment of positions was just outside the village of Borodino, only seventy miles west of Moscow. There was a crescent of high ground here that in the north ran along the banks of the Kolocha River and was topped with small thickets of pine and birch, with the ground rolling slowly down to a plain that was clearly visible from the elevations where Kutuzov could spread his regiments. The location's appeal was enhanced by the fact that the new Smolensk road led straight toward it. If Napoleon took the bait, the broad avenue would feed French troops directly into the heart of the Russian defenses.

Kutuzov ratified the choice on September 3 and began placing the bulk of his defenses: four corps, or half his men, were arrayed around the new Smolensk road, on the northern half of the line. "I hope that the enemy will attack us in this position," Kutuzov wrote Alexander, "and if he does I have great hopes of victory." But the topography on the southern half of the line was less favorable: a flat area dotted with hazelnut and juniper bushes that lacked any natural defensive terrain. Kutuzov would give up slightly higher ground to the French, who could use the old Smolensk road, which ran straight past the Russian left flank, to bring up forces. He acknowledged to Alexander that if Napoleon chose this route of attack, all bets were off. But there was very little else between here and Moscow with even these modest topographical features, and Kutuzov resolved to plan for battle at Borodino.

The Russian army went to work, chopping down trees, digging massive earthworks, and building two fortifications, the first in the middle of the line, known as the Raevsky Redoubt, two straight walls on each side with a half circle in the middle. Thousands of troops worked furiously to build a trench twenty-five feet wide by five feet deep to delay any attack on the bulwark and give the soldiers targets to hit. A hundred paces forward of the redoubt they also dug "wolf pits" to snap the legs of horses on a cavalry charge. A battery of 8- and 12-pound artillery guns was wheeled in and earthworks were dug, reinforced with thick logs, to protect them, while two sets of wooden palisades covered the rear of the redoubt. At 420 feet long, the bulwark was the heavy anchor in the Russian center.

Farther south the Russians built the octagonal Shevardino Redoubt far out in advance of the left side of Kutuzov's line. In addition, three flèches were built in front of III Corps under Bagration on the banks of a small stream, to firm up the defenses and allow the troops some protection from cavalry and infantry charges. (A flèche is a thick wooden wall, or redan, in the shape of a shallow V pointed at the enemy and open at the back, a less formidable structure than the massive redoubts.) On the right side of the line, four batteries of artillery were dug in behind earthworks. The entire defensive line stretched 11,000 yards.

Artillery would play a central part in the drama to come, as it did in most Napoleonic battles. The guns were very similar to the replicas that tourists pose atop at forts in America and Europe: blackened brass barrels supported by wooden carriages with two wooden wheels at the side and maneuvered from the rear by a wooden tail. The various models were identified by the ball they shot: a 4-pounder lofted a 4-pound cast-iron ball; the formidable 12-pounders used a 12-pound ball. The ball was for long-distance work, arcing over one's own ranks and the neutral ground into the body of the enemy. There it acted like a gigantic circular bullet, clipping off heads or legs as it shot through the ranks, often wounding or killing multiple victims. The alternative short-range option was the canister round: a cylinder of thin metal packed with musket balls. When fired, the cylinder would split open and release its deadly charge in a V-shaped fusillade that could stop a cavalry charge or shred a company of onrushing troops.

At Borodino, the Russians held the upper hand in terms of firepower. They could array 640 artillery pieces against Napoleon's 584. In addition, the Russians were stronger in the battalion pieces—8- and 12-pounders, which could do far more damage at longer ranges than the 4- or 6-pounders, which traveled with their assigned units and were used for short-range cannonades during infantry charges. Many of the French battalion pieces lay rusting all the way back to Poland, abandoned by the side of the road when the carriage horses died or the mud roads proved impassable.

As he waited for the French, Kutuzov assumed he would face a force of 165,000 men. The estimate was high. Napoleon was now down to 134,000 men, having lost more than 200,000 men in just ten weeks. His stepson, Prince Eugène, had 18,000 from an original 52,000. The forces under the "Bravest," Ney, had gone from 35,000 to 10,000. The cavalry under the beau ideal Murat had been cut in half, to 20,000.

Still, the Russians scrambled for every man and artillery piece they could borrow or commandeer. On August 30–31, 15,600 reinforcements arrived after only the most rudimentary training, and on September 3, 16,000 more marched into Kutuzov's camps. These recruits were even greener than most, ex-serfs dressed in peasant blouses and leather belts, with crosses sewn into the caps that covered their newly shaved heads, the mark of the Russian recruit. They looked more like farmers on a pilgrimage than capable soldiers, but Kutuzov put them to work constructing the entrenchments and wooden bulwarks.

The Russian commander even requested a secret weapon that was to have been deployed early in the war: a gigantic balloon designed to float over the approaching French and detonate, vaporizing the enemy in one blinding flash. (Another report that reached Napoleon stated that the balloon was going to be used to assassinate him in "a rain of fire and steel.") Rostopchin, the military governor of Moscow, was an enthusiastic supporter of the death zeppelin and met with its inventor, a German named Franz Leppich. "This invention will render the military arts obsolete," he wrote Alexander. "Free mankind of its internal destroyer, make you the arbiter of kings and empires and the benefactor of mankind." The device, however, had trouble getting into the air, as its wings kept breaking off during tests, plunging the balloon to the ground. It never saw action in the campaign.

Despite the other positions that the Russians had taken, only to quickly abandon, Napoleon believed that Kutuzov would have to fight. Bloodshed was necessary in order to silence the nobility, which was clamoring for a battle—not necessarily a victory, but a *battle*. "In a fortnight," the former Russian ambassador Caulaincourt wrote, relating the emperor's thinking, "the Tsar would have neither a capital nor an army." Napoleon had come to believe that annihilating the Russian First and Second armies and taking Moscow was the only way to force Alexander into a treaty; his plans had subtly taken on the rhetoric of total war. The emperor even floated the suggestion that Alexander was engineering a battle he couldn't win, so that he could claim he defended Moscow with honor, and then quickly make peace without being reproached by his various constituencies. The analysis completely misread the depth of Alexander's anger and his commitment to the war.

The French hurried forward, with Napoleon so anxious to catch up to the Russians that he ordered the destruction of any vehicles that were slowing the artillery train. When he spotted several officers' carriages, he ordered his bodyguards to chase them down and burn the leading vehicle. The owner objected, saying that it could ferry any officers who lost a leg in the coming battle. Napoleon snorted. "It will lose me a lot more than that if I have no artillery," he shot back, and ordered straw and wood to get the fire going. After seeing the blaze was lit, he sped off.

THE ADVANCE GUARD of the Grande Armée under Murat arrived in front of the Russian positions on the morning of September 5. The marshal set up temporary headquarters at a monastery at Kolotskoie and called Napoleon to inspect the enemy fortifications. Humming an "insignificant tune," the emperor arrived and began scouring the topography in front of him with his telescope, like a master jeweler examining a diamond with his loupe. The flaw was soon clear: the southern line.

As a preliminary to an all-out attack, the "Iron Marshal" Davout was ordered to smash the 18,000 troops from the 27th Infantry Division clustered around the Shevardino Redoubt, left out in advance of the main line—mostly cavalry and light-infantry jaegers valued for their marksmanship at close range. Davout sent the Polish V Corps in a sweeping movement through the lightly forested terrain to the south of the Russian line and sent a division to attack the redoubt head-on. As at Smolensk, the two armies looked on as the first act of the drama unfolded. The French marched forward in battalion columns under a setting sun and then waded into the fight, pushing the Russian infantry back with salvos of musket fire and barrages of chain shot from their 4- and 6-pound guns. The Russians held, then relented, but Kutuzov wasn't ready to concede the poorly sited fortification. Reinforcements rushed up to the battle and, firing their guns at point-blank range, managed to evict Davout's regiments from the battery.

As day turned to night, the momentum shifted back and forth, with soldiers in the blackness judging the strength of approaching cavalry by their hoofbeats, a terrifying way to face the onrushing enemy. The Russians, as always, proved to be formidable with a fortification at their backs, but soon the Polish corps had cut through their flanks and were advancing. A retreat was called. The soldiers of the 61st Line Regiment reentered the wooden walls of the redoubt and found that "gunners, horses, every living thing had been destroyed by the fire of our *voltigeurs* [light infantry]." The French began stripping the Russian corpses of their flasks. Inside was peppered brandy.

Finally, around eleven o'clock, the redoubt was secured. The Russians had lost 5,000 badly needed men in a pointless engagement. The French had lost 2,000 troops. When Napoleon rode up to the bulwark after it had been cleared of the enemy, he asked the location of the Third Battalion, who had led the initial charge. "In the redoubt," he was told. None had emerged alive.

The encounter pointed out the weakness in Kutuzov's strategy. The Russian commander had weighted his northern position heavily along the banks of the Kolocha and left his southern line and left flank lightly manned. It was an exercise in wishful thinking: Kutuzov planned for an attack ideally suited to his own strategy, which would have been dangerous against any general, let alone Napoleon, who was renowned for searching defects in defensive tactics, exploiting them to break his opponent's forces into their component parts, then isolating and annihilating them. Kutuzov seems to have fallen victim to the kind of reckless optimism that had plagued Napoleon's entire Russian expedition. One artillery officer, after surveying the two armies, made a bleak prediction. "Mark my words," he said, indicating the southern line. "Napoleon will throw all his forces on this flank and drive us into the Moskva River." Even a mildly competent junior officer could have devised a devastating battle plan for the positions Kutuzov had taken, which were no secret to the French. The "innumerable" campfires that the Russian troops lit on the night of September 5 gave Napoleon a white-on-black map of troop allotments in different areas.

Now Napoleon knew he would have his battle. And the strain was clear. His doctor reported that he was "eminently nervous" on the eve of battle, "tormented" and subject to psychosomatic twitches and spasms. Perhaps his body sensed what so far his mind had refused to admit: that he needed a complete victory or his army and his reign would be in mortal danger.

ON SEPTEMBER 6, the preliminaries over, the two armies finally stood face-to-face. As the Russians dug the last pits in front of their flèches and soldiers of both armies cleaned their guns, they could observe each other closely. Napoleon had ordered his troops into full dress. The resplendent colors of the regiments were spread across the rolling hills like layers of fabric laid out in a store window. "Our outposts were barely a pistol-shot distant from the enemy's," wrote Colonel Louis-François Lejeune, an aide-de-camp to Berthier. Napoleon ordered five bridges built over the Kolocha north of Borodino and sited the artillery batteries, then had his topographical experts prepare a final map of the battlefield, with the French and Russian units marked with red- and black-headed pins. The emperor stretched out full-length on the huge maps to study a streambed or a battery more closely, sometimes bumping heads with one of his experts. The day passed in a flurry of adjustments and last-minute directives.

The night before the battle, Napoleon sat in his tent issuing a stream of orders. He was ill with dysuria, an agonizing infection that causes difficulty while urinating. The pain had become so intense at points during the campaign that the emperor found it impossible to ride and had to step down from his horse. Now a cold and fever flared up, muddling his thoughts at the worst possible time.

A portrait of his young son, an infant already named as king of Rome, had arrived from Paris, and Napoleon delightedly set it up on an easel for the Imperial Guard to admire. Then, changing his mind, he ordered his aides to take it away. "He is too young to look upon a field of battle!" he told them. The emperor alternated between optimistic banter and the dark epigrams that so often came to him on the eve of great battles. "Fortune is a shameless courtesan," he told one general, "I have often said it, and I am beginning to experience it." That night, his asides were peppered with these gloomy mutterings.

Night fell. The emperor retired to his tent but got very little sleep. Obsessed with the possibility that the Russians would use the cover of night to slip away once more, he got up repeatedly to check reports from his outposts. The Russians hadn't moved. The historian-general Ségur would later write that it became clear the Russians were "determined to root themselves to the soil and defend it; in short, there to conquer or die." It was exactly what the emperor wanted. His army was melting away; every excess ounce of power had been drained away by mismanagement and *Rickettsia*. He had to stun the Russians with an overwhelming defeat whose aftershocks would be felt deeply in Moscow and St. Petersburg.

The men of the Grande Armée were cold, hungry, and wet, but they were ready. They had suffered and bled and starved for the kind of epoch-making battle that was now straight in front of them. One French officer, Eugène Labaume, remembered the night well:

> There were many among us, so eager of glory, and so flushed with the hope of the morrow's success, that they

were absolutely incapable of repose. . . . They gave themselves up to profound meditation. They reflected on the wonderful events of our extraordinary expedition; they mused on the result of a battle which was to decide the fate of two powerful empires; they compared the stillness of the night with the tumult of the morrow; they fancied that death was now hovering over their crowded ranks, but total darkness prevented them from distinguishing who would be the unhappy victims; they then thought of their parents, their country, and the uncertainty of whether they should ever see these beloved objects again plunged them into the deepest melancholy.

As Napoleon fretted and honed his plan of attack, Kutuzov and his staff walked slowly through the camp along with Orthodox priests carrying the Smolensk icon, which had been carted to Borodino on a gun carriage. The procession wove its way from campfire to redoubt to artillery battery as the priests swung their censers, sending out tendrils of bittersweet smoke, and blessed the men with holy water. After sharpening their bayonets and having a full dinner of buckwheat gruel (unlike many of their French counterparts, who went hungry), the men gathered around their campfires wrapped in their long coats against the cold drizzling rain and singing the "monotonous, melancholy, dirge-like yet not unpleasing" national songs that each remembered from home. Other soldiers discussed in low voices the ominous names of the towns and streams that surrounded Borodino: Ognik ("Fire"), Stonets ("Groans"), Voya ("War"), and Kolocha ("Stab").

ON SEPTEMBER 7, a cold dawn broke. The final Russian positions came clear through the mist. The enemy were arrayed in four ranks: First, the jaegers, or light skirmishers, spread along the Kolocha embankment and throughout the brushwood (as tall as a man in many places) that covered much of the ground. The infantry were behind them, in two rows of battalion columns, followed by the cavalry pinned up close to the infantry's rear. The modest reserves were also tightly packed in behind the cavalry. It was a powerful formation, allowing for quick reinforcements and for massed strength against attack, but it left the Russians open to artillery barrages that could destroy entire units at a time. It was also a remarkably straightforward alignment; Kutuzov presented the French with the entirety of his army, with no battalions hidden away for surprise counterattacks or flanking maneuvers.

The one attempt at deception was quickly undone. Kutuzov ordered a single corps to conceal themselves in a heavily wooded thicket near General Bagration's left flank, at the southernmost end of the Russian position. Thinking Napoleon would try to turn the flank and roll it northward, compressing the Russian forces in order to rake them with artillery and destroy them, the Russian commander planned to unleash the corps on the French and smash the flanking maneuver. But General Benningsen, chief of staff to Bagration, responded to the concerns of the jaegers, who had been left without close infantry support, and ordered the corps out of the woods and back onto open ground behind the skirmishers. Benningsen argued that only a tight, deep order of battle could repel Napoleon's fondness for concentrating huge numbers of troops on perceived points of weakness and breaking through. So the Russians revealed their hand to the French commander before the battle had even begun.

In fact, Marshal Davout had suggested just such a flanking maneuver with a force combining his I Corps and the Polish V Corps under Poniatowski. The night before the battle they would use the darkness to enter the thick woods to the south of General Bagration, steal around the left flank and rear, attack northward in the morning, and put an end to "the Russian army, the battle, and the whole war!"

Ten years before, Napoleon might have suggested the maneuver himself, or perhaps an even more involved and ambitious one. But Borodino, he felt, was different. He couldn't afford to let the Russians slip away again, and Davout's sleight of hand could have sent Kutuzov retreating toward Moscow. He could also lose the Polish regiments as a fighting force if the rough, wooded terrain and darkness caused them to lose their way. Some 1,500 miles from Paris, he was a far more cautious general than he had been at any time in his career.

But the deeper truth was that Napoleon no longer had enough troops. The French had about 126,000 men in the field, packed together at 42,000 per mile. But one has to subtract from this the 25,000 men of the Imperial Guard, which Napoleon held in reserve. Taking into consideration the habit of unit commanders to inflate their numbers, Napoleon had only about 100,000 troops to throw into action without risking the Guard. Facing him, Kutuzov had 155,000 men, or about 51,700 men per mile. In the climactic battle of a campaign he had begun just ten weeks before with the largest army ever assembled, an army that outnumbered its enemy three to one, Napoleon was now outmanned by a ratio of three to two.

Battalion strength was down across the board. If the emperor had back the 125,000-plus men that disease had pilfered from his ranks, he could have afforded to let Davout gamble with 40,000 of them and still have enough troops to smash into the Russian line head-on with hopes of breaking it. But *Rickettsia* had produced an army that was much smaller than it should have been for this kind of battle, and many of the remaining men were already sick.

Attacking a partially dug-in enemy on elevated ground with fewer cannon at one's disposal than the enemy had was accepting inferior odds, but with the troops he had left, Napoleon clearly felt it was his only option. Typhus hadn't only killed Napoleon's men outright in the tens of thousands, it had hamstrung him into fighting a very un-Napoleonic battle. General Ségur, in his memoir of the campaign, thought Napoleon was worried about the condition of his remaining men. "Weak and starved as they are," he wrote, "how could they stand up to a prolonged and violent encounter?"

Kutuzov, too, was violating his most deeply held tactical belief: force preservation. "The voice of the court, of the army, of all Russia forced his hand," wrote German theorist of war Clausewitz. The Russian commander was propping his entire army in front of the French and inviting them to wade into it, knowing that even in victory his army would be shattered.

The compromises both men made to reality, and the terrain the Russians had chosen to defend, led to a compact battlefield where most of the men were in range of the enemy's artillery. There were 250,000 men and more than 1,000 artillery pieces crowded into a small area. The Russian line was three miles across, and the main action would take place across only two miles.

It was a formula for mass slaughter.

CHAPTER 10

Clash

NAPOLEON EMERGED FROM HIS TENT AROUND THREE IN the morning, worked with his chief of staff Berthier on last-minute details, then rode with some of his staff across the Kolocha and made his way to the Shevardino Redoubt. He had taken the temperature of the ranks and found them "strangely quiet—the kind of silence you associate with a state of great expectation or tension." He issued a proclamation trimmed toward the pragmatic: "Soldiers! Here is the battle you have so much desired. Now victory depends on you; we need it. Victory will give us abundant supplies, good winter quarters, and a prompt return to our native land. Conduct yourself as you did at Austerlitz, at Friedland, at Vitebsk, at Smolensk, and may the most distant generations cite your conduct on this day with pride; may it be said of each one of you: 'He fought in that great battle under the walls of Moscow!' " It was a pedestrian effort, but he knew the men were exhausted by the campaign and each would be fighting for a return to his own hearth and loved ones. The men cheered him as he rode slowly along, and he responded, crying out "March on! We are going to break open the gates of Moscow!"

When the emperor arrived at the redoubt, a chair was brought to him and he turned it around, sat, and placed his arms on the backrest. He took his telescope and checked the Russian lines, still not completely convinced Alexander's forces would stand and fight. He remarked on the cold and mentioned how the sun resembled the one at Austerlitz. That place had been a constant theme of the past few days; Napoleon dearly hoped for a repeat of his victory there.

Kutuzov rose early as well and issued a proclamation to the men that was wonderfully stark in its simplicity and its sheer Russianness. "Trusting in God, we shall either win or die," he told his men. "Napoleon is His enemy. He will desecrate His churches. Think of your wives and children, who rely on your protection. Think of your Emperor, who is watching you. Before the sun has set tomorrow, you will have written on this field the record of your faith and patriotism in the blood of your enemy."

Like Napoleon, Kutuzov sat in a folding chair to observe the battlefield. He appeared more relaxed than his counterpart and chatted easily with his commanders and soldiers. He had at least chosen the best site for a defense of Moscow: when Soviet generals prepared to repel Hitler's forces in 1941, they built their fortifications in the exact same spot that the old general had chosen one hundred and thirty years earlier. Kutuzov also had an abiding faith in the individual Russian soldier, as neglected and abused and badly led as he often was.

The French plan of battle called for a main thrust led by the Iron Marshal, Davout, against the Russian center, held by Bagration, who would finally get the battle he so desired, behind the three flèches (Napoleon, unable to see the enemy position clearly through his telescope, believed there were only two of them). To Davout's left, Ney would lead his III Corps, supplemented with Junot's VIII Corps against the Russians' northern positions; Napoleon didn't want to risk letting his erratic general go unsupervised after the debacle at Smolensk. Meanwhile, a drastically modified flanking maneuver by Poniatowski against the left flank would

hope to turn the southern end of the Russian line and begin pushing those troops into the center, where Davout and Ney could finish them off. The maneuver would have to be done in daylight,
without enough soldiers for a shock victory, but the 5,000 Poles
were eager for battle and Napoleon hoped they could make up for
the lost troops with their ardor.

On the left side of the French position, Napoleon's stepson,
Prince Eugène, would smash through the Russian line, occupy the
town of Borodino, then proceed to neutralize the Raevsky Redoubt. Taking it would eliminate a hefty portion of Russian firepower and break the enemy line in the center. If one diagrammed
the attack, it would consist of the arrows along the French line
pointing almost directly east, with Prince Eugène's forces at the
top tilted slightly southward. A head-on charge, with no niceties.

"Here we touched bottom," wrote Ségur. "Here was the end,
here everything would be decided."

THE THREE FRENCH BATTERIES opened up at six in the morning,
followed immediately by the Russian guns. The staccato reports
built to a crescendo in which individual cannons couldn't be distinguished, merging into one deep-throated roar and accompanied
by billows of black smoke that "darkened the sun, which seemed
to veil itself in a blood-red shroud." Men likened the sound to
hundreds of drums beating rapidly, to the cliché of constant thun-
der, or to nautical broadsides at close distance. Not only could the
sound be heard over a mile away, it was, even at that distance,
enough to temporarily deafen the soldiers.

Although Napoleon had massed most of his troops on the center and right, it was the left that made first contact. One division
of Prince Eugène's IV Corps drove straight at the village of
Borodino, marching "with unbelievable speed" and catching the
Russians off-guard. The jaegers who held the thinly manned line
fell back, retreating across a bridge over the Kolocha River. Their

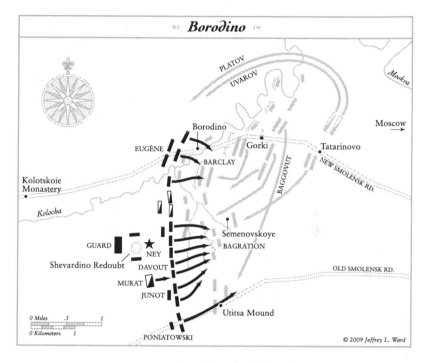

ranks were so compressed that the French sharpshooters began rapidly picking them off, with two more divisions supporting them from behind. Within fifteen minutes, the jaeger regiment had lost half its men and thirty of its officers. The Russians counter-attacked and drove the French back over the river, then returned to their main line, burning the bridge behind them. When they were done, bodies were layered at the smoldering pilings of the structure three and four deep.

In the south, Davout marched forward with two divisions, aiming directly at the flèches. The Russians waited until the French were in range and then opened up with their regimental guns, spewing canister shot that sliced through the enemy ranks, ripping off arms and legs and disemboweling the onrushing troops. The French came on relentlessly and finally stormed one of the wooden fortifications,

diving over the log walls as nearby Russian skirmishers poured fire
on the French from the cover of nearby juniper brush.

At one of the flèches, the 61st Line Regiment advanced and
threw the Russians back. As the enemy line retreated, one corporal
named Dumont, wounded in the arm, was looking for an ambulance when he caught sight of the Spanish girl who traveled with
the supply wagon. She was frantically looking for her friends in
the regiment.

> When she caught sight of all the drums of the regiment
> strewn on the ground she became like a madwoman.
> "Here, my friend, here!" she screamed. "They're here!"
> And so they were, lying with broken limbs, their bodies
> torn with grapeshot. Mad with grief, she went from one to
> the other, speaking softly to them. But none of them heard.

Among the dead and wounded, the pair found the Spaniard's father, but before she could help him, a musket round struck the
crouching girl, knocking her unconscious.

Lieutenant Roth von Schreckenstein surged forward with the
4th Cavalry, fighting in a mixed unit of Saxons, Poles, and West-
phalians. Pursuing mounted Russian troops, he was stunned when
his horse suddenly went down after a barrage of case shot from his
left, throwing him to the ground.

Von Schreckenstein found himself in no-man's-land: Russian infantrymen were firing on the enemy cavalry as they shot past, and
his own unit, intoxicated by the success of their charge, quickly left
him behind. The lieutenant watched the enemy troops move closer;
there was no sign of the four cuirassier regiments that were supposed to follow in the cavalry's wake. As panic rose in his throat,
the German officer felt his grasp on what was a linear battlefield—
the French to the west, the Russians to the east—slip. "Owing either
to an illusion stemming from fear, or else because they were really

there, I could see enemies on all sides," he remembered. He scanned the field for another horse to get him out of danger and found a Russian mount standing untended. Von Schreckenstein jumped in the saddle and whipped the reins around, but the horse refused to move. The German dug his spurs into the animal's flanks; still, it stood as still as a monument, clearly terrified by the noise of gunfire. The officer jumped down and unholstered his pistol, thinking he would have to navigate his way off the battlefield on foot. But with Russians seemingly approaching from every direction, he no longer knew in which direction the French lines lay. The artillery barrages and musket fire from both sides filled his ears with a constant roar of unintelligible noise.

There are few things as frightening for a soldier as feeling lost in enemy territory without a clear route to safety, especially after one has heard stories of stomach-turning enemy atrocities for weeks. "The thought of being captured and ill-treated over-whelmed me," von Shreckenstein wrote, "and I gripped my pistol in much the same way as a person who is drowning clutches at the nearest straw." Even as basic a battlefield as Borodino, with two huge armies ramming straight at each other in straight lines, could quickly descend into blurred chaos.

Just then a regiment of the Grande Armée's mounted troops came flashing by, their white jerkins and white leather breeches and billowing white wool cloaks a shock against the dun-colored landscape and the billows of smoke and dust. Among their outsize black and brown horses the lieutenant spotted a riderless mount. He ran after it and managed to catch the horse before the regiment sailed past. Running alongside, he gripped its bridle and with a deep breath vaulted into the saddle in midstride. He rode with the Lifeguards toward the Russian lines, safe for the moment.

As the day wore on, the lines of battle became increasingly confused. The troops' rushing forward and falling back through the curtains of smoke inevitably led to the kind of disorientation von Schreckenstein experienced. When French troops crossing behind the attacks on the flèches saw other units rushing out at them from the pall of smoke, they mistook them for Russians and fired, reloaded, and fired again.

As the early morning went on, Napoleon was waiting anxiously to hear the reports of gunfire from Poniatowski's Polish unit to the south, which had found the terrain more difficult than they had imagined and didn't encounter the Russian lines until eight in the morning. A fierce battle ensued, with the Poles driving the first line of Russian grenadiers back and taking the town of Utitsa, which marked the southernmost extreme of the battlefield. Napoleon sent units from General Junot's forces to firm up the line, where fierce Russian charges had brought the two armies within arm's length, battling hand to hand, stabbing with their bayonets and sabers. At the flèches, the French drove their way inside, but the Russians quickly brought up reinforcements and launched a counterattack.

The Poles were rewarding Napoleon's confidence in them. If they forced their way through the second Russian line, they could then turn north and begin rolling up the enemy flank, forcing their opponents to fight on two compact fronts simultaneously. Kutuzov, finally realizing that the main brunt of the French attack would be in the south, ordered units guarding the Kolocha River at the northernmost end of his line to turn and march toward the musket fire. When their commander asked an officer from the besieged jaeger units how the battle was proceeding, he was told, "We are finished if you don't hurry up." The units sneaked behind the Russian line and rushed toward the sound of battle.

NAPOLEON WATCHED THE BATTLE unfold from his chair, uncharacteristically silent and still. His aides stared at him with amazement and growing anger. The emperor was usually in constant motion during battle, riding on his horse to see engagements more clearly, looking for the weak spot in a line where a breakthrough might change the momentum, rallying or abusing his troops—Napoleon's paint-peeling tirades against a commander or unit he felt wasn't performing up to expectations could motivate as well as any call to glory. In effect, the emperor sought to understand the kinetic battlefield so that he might master it at the right time.

But now he sat, "sluggish, apathetic, and inactive." Officers would ride in, dismount, and run to report to him the latest change on the ground, and Napoleon would listen to them impassively and then dismiss them without a word. He studied the battlefield through his telescope, although the smoke and dust kicked up by horses and troops obscured the most important parts of the terrain; stood up to pace for a few moments; and then sat again. He was clearly ill, but the officers resented his passivity when many of his men in the field were sick, hungry, or already wounded.

The emperor's armies had always been things of speed. But now Napoleon stalled, complaining he had to "see more clearly on this chessboard." No issue was more critical than that of reinforcements: specifically, committing the Young Guard, the cream of that year's conscripts, and Imperial Guard, now massed behind Napoleon, to the battlefield. Marshal Ney was furious when Napoleon told him to wait for any supporting units. "What's the Emperor doing behind the Army?" he erupted at the messenger. "There he is within reach only of reverses, not of successes."

The first call for reinforcements came at the flèches. The Russians had counterattacked and thrown the French out of the southernmost earthwork. The general leading the charge was quickly wounded four times in rapid succession, two spent balls bruising him before dropping to the ground, a third shot tearing up his sleeve and grazing his arm, and a fourth smashing into his hip, dropping him from the saddle, the twenty-second time he had been wounded in battle. The Russian 7th Combined Grenadier Division, waiting on reinforcements themselves for the dead that were piling up inside the flèche, charged the oncoming troops and were swept by volleys of shot from the mobile French guns. The leader of the grenadiers reported that his defense of the flèches ended only when his division "ceased to exist." The 4,000-strong unit had suffered a 90 percent casualty rate.

When Napoleon saw his wounded general from the battle being carried back to his headquarters, he cried out, "What is going on up there?" The commander told him of the desperate fight the Russians were putting up and said that the only way to take the flèches was to send in the Young Guard: fresh men to overwhelm the enemy defenses.

But Napoleon felt the thinness of the forces between him and Paris keenly. He not only needed to win the war with Alexander with what typhus and the other diseases had left him, but he also had to keep control at home and intimidate his many enemies waiting to see the outcome of the Russian campaign. "No!" he told the general. "I will take good care to see that the Guard is not used. I will not have them knocked to bits. I'll win the battle without them." It would become a theme of the day: field commanders rushing to the emperor to request the troops standing at Napoleon's back, to put them over the top in some part of the battlefield, only to be told they were too precious to commit.

Instead, Napoleon moved units from other parts of the line to the flèches, throwing units from Davout's corps at the fortifications, along with three divisions of Ney's troops, Junot's entire corps, and elements of Murat's troops. This one feature of the battlefield would eventually absorb 40,000 French troops and 30,000 Russians.

Had Napoleon committed the Guard, giving the French a one-time boost in manpower and firepower, they would have most likely been able to take the flèches, drive through to the second line of reinforcements that was feeding the constant Russian counterattacks, and neutralize them in one climactic battle. Instead the three fortifications became slow-motion meat grinders, each side committing just enough troops to take the trio of defenses, but not enough to hold them permanently or to end the battle. The flèches were taken and then given up to the enemy seven times on the morning of September 7, costing Napoleon thousands of soldiers.

Inside the earthworks, the scene was bestial. Troops were packed inside the walls, being raked by canister fire and attacking each other with bayonets, swords, musket butts, and even ramrods. When Murat, arrayed in his battlefield finery, led the First Württemburg Jaeger Battalion and the 72nd French Infantry to the southernmost flèche to retake it, the Russians mounted a fierce counterattack. The marshal was quickly surrounded by cavalry troops. Just as Russian soldiers closed in to capture him, Murat managed to jump over the earthen walls to the flèche's interior. He was shocked by what he found: many of the men inside had been cut down, and only a few were left "completely out of control and racing wildly around the parapet." Equal to the moment, Murat grabbed a weapon, took his signature plumed hat off his head, and held it aloft as a sign that he was in charge. He began calling out in broken German for the men to hold. The dapper marshal mangled the unfamiliar language so badly that the Germans merely laughed at his words, but his high-spirited gesture kept the soldiers focused on holding the flèche until Murat could be rescued.

The marshal was at his finest during Borodino. Standing tall in the saddle and dressed in his customary outrageous colors (dominated by a pale blue jacket crossed by a gold sash), he dashed from sector to sector leading cavalry attacks and rallying exhausted soldiers. "With his thundering artillery and the immense cloud of smoke into which he disappeared entirely . . . ," wrote his aide-de-camp, "he resembled one of those terrible gods of Olympus." When one of his officers, seeing his men being cut down by grapeshot and shells, ordered a retreat, Murat rode up to him, grabbed him by the collar, and shouted "What are you doing?" over the deafening roar of artillery. Shocked that it even needed explaining, the colonel gestured to the landscape around them covered with his dead and dying, a full half of his contingent. "Surely you can see we can't hold out here any longer," the officer shouted back. Murat looked at the carnage and announced that he was staying put. As his men waited for his answer, the colonel stared at Murat bitterly, then turned and shouted to his retreating men, "All right, soldiers, about face! Let's go get ourselves killed!"

ALTHOUGH THE SOUTHERN END of the battlefield had erupted in every kind of encounter—cavalry charges, canister barrages, musket fire, and bayonet assaults—most of the soldiers on both sides were, at eight thirty that morning, enthralled observers. Having received no orders to march, they lived in fear of the cannonballs that were raining down on both lines.

As the action in each sector escalated or died away, cannon rounds from both sides never let up. "The shells burst in the air as well as on the ground," wrote one Russian soldier, "while the solid shot came buzzing from every side, ploughing the ground with their ricochets and smashing into pieces every object they encountered in their flight." The most conservative estimate of the number of French artillery shells of all descriptions fired on the enemy is 60,000, 10,000 more than the Russians, who had the advantage in artillery pieces—a tribute to the efficiency of the French gunners under Napoleon, the ex-artilleryman. The total cartridges fired was about 1.4 million musket shots. That equals about 3 cannon shots and 38 musket rounds per second on a crowded battlefield.

Leading his troops in the center of the battlefield, the volatile General Bagration was hit by shrapnel, shattering his shinbone. He tried to disguise the wound, but he slumped forward and toppled off his horse. His officers carried the general to a medical tent, where doctors tended to his wound. "Tell General Barclay that the fate and salvation of the army depends on him," he told an officer, in what must have been a bitter moment. Rumors immediately began circulating that in fact the charismatic general was dead, and the morale of the men plummeted. Barclay, expecting a French attack on his line at any moment, couldn't send reinforcements or take personal command of the Second Army, as Bagration had requested, but he sent two generals to direct the troops.

The Russian infantry fought heroically to hold the flèches and, behind it, the town of Semeonovskoie, under assault from the main French thrust in the center. When their muskets were shattered by French shot, they used the stocks as bludgeons, then took out their swords. But it was a lost cause. By noon, the French had taken the fortifications and the shattered town and held them.

Ney and Murat again called for reinforcements to finish off the left side of the Russian line. They could see the demoralized units of the enemy's second and final line through the burning huts of Semeonovskoie. But again Napoleon refused to send the Imperial Guard. "And if there is a second battle tomorrow, what shall I fight it with?" he asked.

It has to be emphasized that Napoleon had never considered the Guard to be untouchable before the devastation of the march to Moscow. At Austerlitz, at a key moment, with his center line in danger of being overwhelmed by oncoming Russian infantry, Napoleon had ordered Murat's cavalry to rush through the hole, followed by the mounted divisions of the Imperial Guard. The maneuver had saved the day, allowing the infantry units of the center to hold long enough for Davout's corps to storm in and repel the Russians. But at Austerlitz, he hadn't lost a third of his army to disease.

IN THIS NEW, stationary combat involving huge numbers of troops fighting over the same ground that would so accurately foretell the set pieces of the Somme, there were only glimpses of the past, of King Francis and knightly warfare that Napoleon still saw himself as part of. Each side spoke with awe of the sheer relentlessness of the other. The French compared the Russians to "moving fortresses that gave out flashes of steel and flame-bursts." For his part, Bagration, a Russian nationalist to the core, was sufficiently moved by the French troops forming and re-forming as barrage after barrage of canister fire cut through the ranks that he began applauding and calling out "Bravo! Bravo!" But the sheer numbers of troops engaged in a small area and the heavy use of field artillery ensured that the action more resembled large-scale butchery than it did any romantic ideal of combat.

There were a few instances of mercy in a savage day. Franz Ludwig August von Meerheimb, a colonel with the Saxon Guard cavalry, was knocked unconscious during hand-to-hand fighting on the battlefield and woke up to find his pockets being rifled by a number of Russian cuirassiers. He might not have survived if it hadn't been for an older soldier who chased the robbers away, bandaged the saber wound that had punctured a vein beneath von Meerheimb's jawline, found him a horse, and lifted him into the saddle. Walking his captive back through the Russian rear, the cuirassier passed peasant vigilante groups looking for French soldiers to "escort" (their actual fate, the soldier implied, would have been much darker) and soldiers with beards so thick he could see only their noses and eyes. Von Meerheimb must have felt he had traveled back in time, but the old man soon found a sympathetic Swiss medic, taking with him only his gold-colored helmet, which he might have thought was made of real bullion. The cavalryman was eventually transported to Moscow and received excellent care for his numerous wounds, in all probability better care than he would have received behind French lines.

As the French fought to control the northern line, without having the numbers to smash through and annihilate the Russian reserves, the action in the center was intensifying. Prince Eugène had reorganized his units after the attack on the village of Boro-dino, which he had finally taken after fierce opposition. Now Napoleon ordered him to advance to the earthworks, anchored by the eighteen heavy guns that looked down over the slope.

Opposing him was the Russian general Raevsky, after whom the central redoubt was named. Wounded in a freak accident (gashing himself badly on a bayonet left carelessly lying on the back of a cart), he was quickly learning that being the last position to be attacked presented its own challenges: requests to send his men as reinforcements to the south were constant. His forces were already spread thinly behind the redoubt and to the plains to the south, and he had lost four regiments sent to hot zones on the battlefield before repelling a single enemy soldier.

Prince Eugène softened up the position with an artillery barrage beginning around nine thirty. The Russians could only hold their ground and wait. Half an hour later, they saw the first units sweeping up from the ravine at the foot of the rolling slope. They waited until the French had crossed it before opening up with their regimental guns filled with grapeshot. The veteran Captain Charles François of the 30th of the Line jumped into the air with his men to avoid the cannonballs that followed. "Whole files, half-platoons even, went down under the enemy's fire and left huge gaps," he recalled. The captain was hit in the leg but, kept upright by will and adrenaline, charged ahead with his men. Russian infantrymen had come from behind the redoubt to form a line; at thirty yards, the French took aim with their muskets and broke through, running toward the earthworks. The wolf pits, hidden by the smoke, caught a number of the soldiers, who tumbled atop Russian jaegers snagged in their own traps.

When the French reached the redoubt, they poured through the embrasures cut into the structure. The redoubt itself was packed with the enormous cannon and their gunners; the artillery took up so much room that there was no space for infantry. Blackened by

the powder and smoke, the gunners had no muskets to defend themselves and were doomed the moment the redoubt was breached. But
instead of surrendering, they attacked the onrushing troops with
rammers and handspikes. Captain François cut down one after the
other with his sword. "I had been through more than one campaign," he remembered, "but I had never found myself in such a
bloody melee with such tenacious soldiers as the Russians."

The captain ended up fainting from loss of blood and was carried to one of the few field ambulances as the French finally took the
redoubt. But the first push had exhausted the French attack: as in
the south, there were no units following the front line to drive
through and complete the victory by smashing the Russian reserves.
Raevsky, unrecognized, managed to limp out of the fortification on
his bad leg and found himself among panicked troops from the
18th, 19th, and 40th jaeger units, who were "putting up no resistance at all." The Russian general later remarked that had that original charge been backed by a significant force, the center would
have collapsed and the battle would have been over by midmorning.
But all over the battlefield, the French were finding they had the
men to take and retake positions but not to do the one thing that
might force Alexander to capitulate: destroy the Russian army.

If Napoleon was passive and uncertain in the early stages of
the battle, he was at least following a tactical plan in his head,
even if he refused to reveal it to his aides. In contrast, now that his
hope that the French would base their assault on the new Smolensk road clearly hadn't come true, Kutuzov struggled and failed
to come up with a defensive strategy other than patching the
holes in his line. Clausewitz, the strategist attached to the imperial staff, was appalled. "He appeared destitute of inward activity," he wrote, "of any clear view of surrounding occurrences, of
any liveliness of perception, or independence of action." The Russian leader allowed his generals free rein to implement their own
tactics, without integrating the maneuvers into an evolving plan

of battle. Sketchy reports from the front lines, which implied that the flèches had been stoutly defended and the French repelled—along with a wild rumor that Marshal Murat had been captured—led the general's staff's morale "to blaze up like lighted straw." Kutuzov celebrated the news with a hearty picnic lunch. Clausewitz began to see the Russian not as a general in any traditional sense of the word but as a kind of impresario, a confidence man, who went around proclaiming victory, instilling the Russians with hope after the long retreat by proclaiming one thing: "the bad condition of the French army."

General Barclay and Kutuzov's other generals stepped in to fill the leadership gap as best they could. The pattern of the flèches repeated itself at the redoubt. The chief of staff for the First Army had been rushing past the rear of the central fortification to take the injured Bagration's men in hand, but he was shocked by how thoroughly the Russian line had been broken at the center. Ignoring Kutuzov's orders, he rallied a battalion of infantrymen, took the jaegers under his command, and, along with elements from the 12th and 26th divisions, turned to counterattack, marching in line to the beat of a drummer. The French had suffered heavy casualties on the attack, particularly from grape- and canister shot, and couldn't hold off the Russian attack. Some of them turned and ran, and the only sustained fire the advancing troops experienced was from the regimental gunners. The Russians took the redoubt back in ten minutes. The French had lost 3,850 men in the failed attempt to secure it.

When the primitive fort was retaken around midday, there was a lull in the French forays against the Russian line. Even with his galvanizing battlefield leadership, Marshal Murat couldn't push forward in the center without fresh troops, and his position was being raked with fire from the elevations of Semeonovskoie, which was constantly receiving fresh supplies of troops from Kutuzov's right. Napoleon again agonized over whether to send in the Imperial

Guard. He finally gave permission for the Young Guard's artillery to move forward and begin shelling the village, and even agreed to send the elite troops themselves to join the battle, giving the French a chance to regroup and push toward the Russian reserves. But just as the units began to march toward the action, the emperor suddenly changed his mind, claiming that the existing troops were sufficient to hold the French line at Semeonovskoie. The Young Guard returned to its place behind the emperor.

In the south, starved of reinforcements, the French slowly began to give way to the bulging Russian line pushing down from the village. Murat sent another emissary to Napoleon, begging for troops. The officer pointed out the clouds of dust on the ridge at Semeonovskoie, under which the Russian cavalry was advancing. But just as the Young Guard prepared to move out, Napoleon reversed himself once more and halted their advance. Perhaps Napoleon was afraid that the Poles on the extreme right would let the Russians past, where they could circle behind Ney and Murat and annihilate those corps. Or perhaps Napoleon thought he could be outflanked on the left. Whatever the reasoning, he threw no more troops into the crucial engagement.

KUTUZOV DID ATTEMPT one daring foray against the French lines. Alerted that morning by the commander of the Cossacks that his horsemen had managed to ford the Kolocha River north of the French position, the Russian commander had sent a contingent of 8,000 hussars, Cossacks, and dragoons on a flanking maneuver against Napoleon's left. General Barclay, delighted with the idea of outmaneuvering the French genius, had called the attack a "decisive blow." But the Cossacks, known for their brilliance in harrying small groups of enemy soldiers, were going up against deployed lines of experienced soldiers, against which they were notoriously useless.

The mounted soldiers managed to panic the Bavarians holding

the flank and cause a pell-mell retreat, news of which quickly made its way to Napoleon. But the attack ended up as more of a feint than a serious attempt to roll back the left flank. Without infantry to support the cavalry charges, the Russians satisfied themselves with scaring off the Bavarian horses and making a few passes at the 13th Infantry Division near Borodino, which formed up in squares and refused to wilt. With riders being dropped right and left by grapeshot and musket fire, the Cossacks and cavalrymen turned and raced back to their lines. The raid reinforced the idea that the Russians were past masters at defense but lacked the confidence or skills (especially the Cossacks) to press home an audacious offensive strike. What Napoleon lacked in men, the Russians lacked in tradition and mind-set.

The probing startled Napoleon, and clearly contributed to his decision to hold his reserves back. Marooned at the Shevardino Redoubt, he wasn't convinced he knew what the Russians were up to. "My battle hasn't begun yet," he told his aides.

Most of the Grande Armée was held in suspended animation as Napoleon debated the endgame, alternately pacing and peering through his telescope. During the lull, however, men continued to die. The most outrageous waste came in Murat's cavalry, which had been moved up around noon to fill the gaping hole in the line that opened up when Prince Eugène turned north to deal with the Cossack feint. The change in position had put these elite horsemen in range of the Russian 12-pounders at the Raevsky Redoubt.

The results were gruesome. The men sat in their saddles for several hours, serving as gorgeously dressed targets for the enemy gunners. Lieutenant von Schreckenstein, back with his Saxon cavalry brigade, watched as his comrades dropped amid the exploding shells. "For strong, healthy, well-mounted men a cavalry battle is nothing compared with what Napoleon made his cavalry put up with at Borodino . . . ," he wrote. "There can have been scarcely a man in those ranks and files whose neighbor did not crash to earth with his horse, or die from horrible wounds while screaming for help." Shattered bits of helmet and iron breastplates came hurtling through the rows of horsemen, along with bits of bone and flesh. One cuirassier remembered that they could actually see the Russian artillerymen sighting their guns at their units. The troops had to remain unmoving as the guns were primed, loaded with ball, and then fired.

Captain Jean Bréaut des Marlots stood under the barrage with his men. "On every side one saw nothing but the dying and the dead," he wrote. Twice during the three hours des Marlots reviewed his men, giving them encouragement and trying to judge who was holding up under the strain and who was slowly losing his nerve. He was chatting with one young officer who said all he wanted was a glass of water when the man was cut in two by a cannonball. Des Marlots turned to another officer and had just finished saying how awful it was that their comrade had been killed when the man's horse was hit by a cannonball, knocking him to the ground. Writing an account for his sister, the captain told her how such random deaths from above gave him a deep sense of fatalism that carried him through. "I said to myself: 'It is a lottery whether you survive or not. One has to die sometime.'" He vowed to be killed with honor rather than run from the field.

TRYING TO REGAIN the initiative, Napoleon ordered the artillery of the Guard to be wheeled from their positions forward to the edge of the plateau above Semeonovskoie. He would commit guns, but not the reserve itself. The 12-pounders added their reports to the unceasing roar.

A few minutes after two o'clock, Napoleon gave the order for a fresh assault against the Raevsky Redoubt in the center, which had become the Russians' stronghold on the battlefield. He directed a three-pronged assault: three divisions of infantry would attack the structure head-on. From the French left, the III Corps of cavalry would move against the northern end and rear of the fortifications;

from the right would come II and IV Corps, attacking the southern end and veering into the rear as well. Napoleon's orders to General Auguste de Caulaincourt, the younger brother of his former Russian ambassador, were "Do what you did at Arzobispo!," the 1809 battle where Caulaincourt had executed perfectly a daring encircling maneuver that won the day for the French. Now the general galloped off to lead his cavalry in a very different assignment: a frontal assault into withering artillery fire. Before the general left, he told his brother, "The fighting has become so hot that I don't suppose I shall see you again. We will win, or I'll get myself killed." The elder Caulaincourt, knowing that his brother's old war wounds caused him so much pain that he often wished for death, was shaken by the words.

Across the battlefield, General Barclay watched the enemy

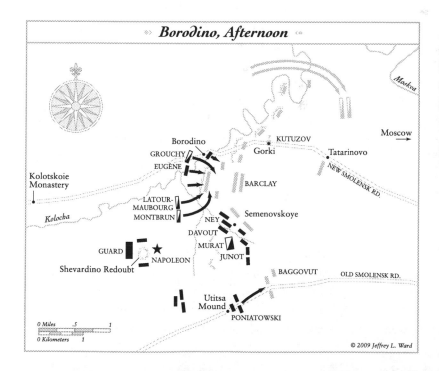

© 2009 Jeffrey L. Ward

forces assemble. "I saw they were going to launch a ferocious attack," he remembered. He called for the 1st Cuirassier Division to be brought up from the second line, a unit he had "intended to hoard for a decisive blow." But his messenger returned to report that the division had been ordered (by whom, no one knew) to the extreme left flank to support the troops battling Poniatowski. It was symptomatic of a command structure where generals grabbed regiments whenever they could find them and stuck them in to fill holes, without coordination by Kutuzov. All Barclay could find were two regiments of cuirassiers, which he felt would be slaughtered in the first few moments of battle. He held them back until more units could be found.

As the clock ticked toward three o'clock, the Russians were forced to stand under a ferocious bombardment from the batteries around Semeonovskoie. Finally, the French infantry marched out, but the cavalry swept past them and reached the redoubt first. A squad of Polish and Saxon cuirassiers had been trotting from sector to sector all morning, avoiding the Russian guns and waiting impatiently to be called to action. Now they charged up the steep slope toward the battered earthworks and slipped their horses through the slots cut for the cannon, or wheeled their horses around the palisades and entered from behind, followed by the 5th Cuirassiers. Leading the 5th, General Caulaincourt was killed as he charged the walls, a musket shot cutting through his jugular. The Saxons and Poles smashed through the Russian defenses first, leaping over the bayonets of the defenders and chopping at the gunners with their sabers.

The first horsemen over the wall were met by musket fire but plunged into the enemy ranks regardless, and were met by bayonets, which the infantrymen stabbed up into the riders, breaking the blades on their iron breastplates or cutting blindly into thighs and groins. A roar went up from the French soldiers watching the action from the rear as they saw the sun wink off the cuirassiers' helmets inside the distant redoubt. "It would be difficult to convey our feelings as we watched this brilliant feat of arms," wrote Colonel Charles Griois, a cavalry officer, "perhaps without equal in the military annals of nations." The Russians cut down the vanguard of cavalry, but more and more mounted troops poured in every available entryway and rushed in from behind, slashing at the enemy with their swords. Hopelessly outnumbered, the Russians fought to the death.

The body of one Russian gunner was decorated by three medals. "In one hand he held a broken sword, and with the other he was convulsively grasping the carriage of the gun he'd so valiantly fought with," remembered one of his adversaries. But most of the dead were horribly chopped up and contorted, piled at the entrances, in the wolf pits outside the palisade walls, and trampled by horses or mixed in with dying mounts cut by bayonets and unable to stand. The fort was an abattoir in which the piles of dead told the story of the day like alternating layers of sedimentary soil. One soldier described the action inside as a "frenzy of slaughter," with men slashing at each other or bludgeoning the enemy with musket stocks.

Barclay watched the action, rushing troops to fill the gaps the French were gashing in his front line. As the French attack progressed, he was conferring with another general when he looked up to see an enormous cloud of dust rolling over the turf toward the redoubt from the north. The Russians formed squares, with Barclay inside one, and waited for the cuirassiers to come within range. When the French appeared, the Russians fired and then advanced. One Russian general remembered what happened next:

> It was a march into hell. In front of us was a mass of indeterminate depth, even as its front was impressive enough. To the left, a battery . . . and everywhere, French cavalry, waiting to cut off our way back. . . . We went

straight for the enemy mass, while the huge battery hurled
its ball at us.

The redoubt was taken by three thirty in the afternoon. General Caulaincourt was carried out on a white cloak clotted with blood, soon to be one of the heroes of Borodino. When word reached his brother, the diplomat began to weep silently and Napoleon offered to let him retire from the field. Caulaincourt said nothing but touched his hat in acknowledgment of the gesture.

The small number of Russian prisoners, only 800, testified to the implacable nature of the defense. Prince Eugène gathered up the remnants of the different cavalry units and sent them at the Russian reserves that Barclay had formed into a line. But again, a lack of manpower doomed the effort and the Russians retreated in good order, managing to take a number of the Raevsky guns with them.

Napoleon was incredulous that so few prisoners had been taken, even sending orderlies to the redoubts to make sure none were being held there. "These Russians let themselves be killed like automatons," he complained. The prisoners would suffer terribly in the hands of the French. "Taken to Smolensk," the illustrator Faber du Faur recalled. "They were dragged toward the Prussian frontier, tormented by hunger and deprived of even the most basic necessities." Few of the captives would ever see Russia again.

The last push for a breakthrough occurred on the right. Spurred by the attack on the redoubt, Poniatowski and his Polish regiments renewed their assault on the town of Utitsa, which marked the southernmost point of the advancing French line, pushing around the sides of the hill with combined cavalry and infantry attacks. The Russians, seeing their position grow untenable, retreated from the hill and left it to the triumphant Poles. A last-ditch counterattack of 650 men was cut to pieces by the French and the battle on the extreme left was over. The Poles had managed to expel the Russians from a stronghold but failed again to break through the line or turn the flank.

The artillery on both sides continued to fire, but when Poniatowski broke off contact with the enemy, the action at Borodino ceased. Finally, at six o'clock, the guns too fell silent.

THE FIELD OF BATTLE was now a landscape gashed and cratered by artillery shells and covered from nearly one end to the other by corpses, body parts, dead or dying horses, regimental flags, the immense detritus of war. The Würrtemburg lieutenant H. A. Vossler walked across the field and saw men and horses "gashed and maimed in every conceivable way." Studying the faces, he wrote that one could see the last emotions to pass over their faces before dying. For the French, "desperation, defiance, cold, unbearable pain." Among the Russians, "passionate fury, apathy, and stupor."

Napoleon, too, rode out to survey the landscape and witnessed the carnage firsthand. The men cried out, "In the name of God, take care of the wounded," but there was little that could be done for the catastrophic injuries that characterized Borodino. One of his officers' horses stepped on a dying Russian soldier: it was almost impossible to avoid on grounds tightly packed with casualties and body parts. Napoleon erupted in rage, to which one of his staff replied that it was only a Russian. "There are no enemies after a victory, but only men!" he shouted, a reversal of his remark to Caulaincourt at Smolensk. He ordered his men to fan out and assist the wounded in any way they could.

"They lay one on top of the other," wrote one Captain von Kurz, "swimming in pools of their own blood, moaning and cursing as they begged for death." The scene at the Raevsky Redoubt was indelible. "It was horrible to see that enormous mass of riddled soldiers," wrote the Prussian baron Wolzogen when he came across it. "French and Russians were cast together, and there were many wounded men who were incapable of moving and lay in that wild chaos intermingled with the bodies of horses and the wreckage of shattered cannon." Even the men who had escaped the Russian bullets looked spectral: their uniforms were ripped here and there by bullets and bayonets; their faces were ashen from the black powder used in their muskets. As miserable as they were, the men called out to the emperor, congratulating him. But the victory was only half-achieved. The Russian army was still visible, massed within musket shot, and the droves of prisoners that usually signaled a great triumph were nowhere to be seen.

The worst places were near the bottom of the ravines that snaked across the battlefield. Soldiers had been hurled back from cavalry charges or blasted by canister shot and ended up in the streambeds. Others had come crawling in search of water. One soldier, horribly mutilated, whose legs and one arm had been blown away, looked so "full of hope, even gaiety" that officers were moved to try to save him. As they carried him off, he complained of pain in the missing limbs. There is no record of his fate, but it would have been a miracle if he had survived his wounds, especially in the fetid "hospitals" that sprang up after the battle. Men were found living in the shelter of stacked corpses, and one legend of Borodino is that a single Russian soldier crawled into the still-warm carcass of a disemboweled horse and survived by eating its raw flesh.

The emperor returned to his tent dejected and in physical pain. At ten o'clock, Murat, his gaily colored tunic torn and dirtied by powder and dirt, barged in to request the Imperial Guard once more, claiming that a disorganized and vulnerable Russian army was retreating across the Moskva and that a surprise attack would finish them as a fighting force. Napoleon sharply reprimanded him and never seriously considered the pursuit.

The German strategist Clausewitz was surprised that Napoleon, having shredded the Russians' front lines and pushed their reserves into a compact, vulnerable mass against the Moskva River, didn't deliver the coup de grâce. "It is another question whether Bonaparte, who had time and fresh troops sufficient, should not have made greater exertions on the 7th, and have raised his success to the pitch of a complete victory," he wrote. "He might have . . . achieved the utter destruction of the enemy." The fact that Napoleon had in the past thrown in the reserves and attained dazzling victories made the decision at Borodino even more inscrutable to Clausewitz. He attributed it to the "consumption, rapid beyond all expectation" of the Grande Armée.

Barclay, too, expected the final blow to fall at any moment: Napoleon had taken the major fortifications and the Russian army was exhausted, its reserves depleted and many of its key officers—from generals down to the regimental commanders—out of action, dead or badly wounded. Murat estimated that he needed only 10,000 infantry soldiers to break the Russian center.

Napoleon knew that his officers, and historians a hundred years later, would focus on the question of the Imperial Guard. After dinner, he chatted with an officer and his secretary of state. Napoleon asked about medical facilities for the wounded, attended to some other minor matters, and then fell asleep after an exhausting day. Then, suddenly, twenty minutes later, as if prodded by a dream, he woke up and began defending his rationing of the Guard. "People will be surprised that I did not commit my reserves in order to obtain greater results, but I had to keep them for striking a decisive blow in the great battle which the enemy will fight in front of Moscow," he told his startled aides. "The success of the day was assured, and I had to consider the success of the campaign as a whole."

As a chilly night settled on Borodino, and the wounded crawled on their elbows and knees toward the campfires or resigned themselves to a lonely death, the French and Russians began to count their dead. The French had lost 28,000 men, including 49 generals;

the Russians, about 45,000, roughly half of their entire frontline troops, including 29 generals. It was the deadliest engagement in the annals of warfare to that date. It would take a hundred years, until the Battle of the Somme, for the totals to be exceeded.

Neither side at the Somme was hampered by a lack of men; each had millions to throw into a futile confrontation. But typhus had stolen precious thousands of troops from Napoleon, and with them, the battle, the war, and the future of his empire. If he'd had the tens of thousands of men who had fallen to *Rickettsia*, he would most likely have broken the Russian army as a fighting force and put immense pressure on Alexander to reach a settlement—or inspired a pro-peace party to unseat the tsar and negotiate in his stead. Even if he hadn't gotten a treaty, he would have marched out of Russia at the head of a significant army, by a far more tenable route than he eventually took, and may well have fended off the swarming attacks on his regime that were soon to follow. The pathogen destroyed any chances for that.

The emperor, fatally wounded, limped away from Borodino toward an utterly different future for himself and for Europe.

CHAPTER 11

The Hospital

THE WOUNDED ON BOTH SIDES WERE LEFT IN A DESPERATE situation. Dr. Larrey had ordered five of the six light ambulance divisions to remain at Smolensk to care for the thousands of ill and wounded, leaving only a rudimentary medical staff to care for the thousands of patients at Borodino. "There was virtually no sanitary service or activity," one officer remembered.

All the villages and houses close to the Moscow road were packed full with wounded in an utterly helpless state. The villages were destroyed by endless fires which ravaged the regions occupied or traversed by the French army. Those wounded who managed to save themselves from the flames crawled in their thousands along the high road seeking some way to prolong their pitiful existence.

The Russian soldiers were remarkably stoic. A French colonel who walked through the battlefield after the last guns had fallen silent was surprised to find the enemy troops, even those with terrible wounds, mostly quiet, avoiding the hooves of passing horses. They took the religious medals from their necks and held them in their hands, sometimes praying to them. The most popular was

Saint Nicholas, the Miracle Worker of the Orthodox Church, protector of the poor and powerless. The Russian saying "If anything happens to God, we've always got Saint Nicholas" was particularly appropriate to the men's situation as night closed in.

If one was a soldier unlucky enough to find himself sick or wounded the morning of September 8, he was at the beginning of a searing, uncertain journey. Doctors were scarce, patients uncountable. The dawn was cold, wet, and violently windy, the sun obscured by heavy fog as soldiers picked their way through the battlefield, the heavy mist cloaking most of the carnage but revealing here and there a shattered ammunition wagon, a dead horse with an enormous, bloated stomach, abandoned pistols and muskets, sabers twisted or impaled in the dirt, and the corpses of soldiers missing heads or entrails, pieces of men and animals seemingly thrown violently against the ground, their blood smeared in the dirt. Each small tableau was uncovered and then obscured by the fog.

The injured soldiers walked toward the field hospitals rumored to have been set up in houses and stone buildings nearby; the medical services were already a shambles and reliable information was hard to come by. The men fell in line with the parade of wounded and healthy trudging on the rutted lanes, their faces blackened by powder and mud, their tunics ripped by ball or streaked with mud and gore. If they had a friend willing to help them, they slung an arm around the other man's neck. Solitary figures used shattered musket stocks as canes or rifles as crutches.

On the side of the road, men who had begun the journey but were unable to go on cried out. "Mercy, please!" they shouted or called out their unit number looking for a mate. There were attempts at humor. One man called out to a soldier whose lower leg was mangled, "If thy foot offend thee, cast it away!" But mostly men cried for water, doctors, and their mothers in a half dozen languages.

The surest way to find a doctor would have been to follow

one's nose: a putrid smell meant bodies, and bodies meant hospitals. The odor carried for hundreds of yards, a mix of the smell of clotted blood, of putrefying flesh, of feces and the musty stench of filthy dressings. The flying ambulances from the battlefields, which looked like large coffins fixed to the back of two-horse wagons, could guide the soldiers but they rushed ahead, too fast for anyone to keep up with. Every house on the road to Moscow, no matter how ramshackle, were filled with wounded. But only a few had doctors.

Imagine the journey of a wounded soldier staggering from the battlefield on September 8 and coming upon one of these hospitals. When at last the destination came into view, it would most likely have been a local nobleman's house or a church, the most substantial structures around, taken over by the army to house the wounded. Men clustered around the entrance, begging to be let in. Corpses littered the yard in front; some of their shirts had been torn off to use as bandages. Others were naked and dogs had gotten to their exposed flesh. Horses lay disemboweled in the mud, pieces of their flanks cut away for food. There was shouting and cries of pain coming from inside the building. Orderlies carried in men with their heads drooping off the ends of the stretchers.

There was a standing order in the Grande Armée stating that any man with serious wounds was to be saluted—a remnant of the original Revolution's fervor for the common man. It had long fallen into disuse; the numbers were too overwhelming. And the decree that stated that enemy soldiers were to be given equal treatment, which was symbolized in the doctors' uniforms with the word "Humanité" inscribed on the buttons, was also void. Around the back of the hospital, Russian patients had been dumped into the garden to die.

If you were an officer, you would have stood a better chance of making it inside the typical hospital. Rank and birth, whatever Napoleonic rhetoric stated, still mattered. The men stumbled through the lines of patients littering the floor. Some lay on filthy straw taken from nearby barns, others used corpses as pillows; in places men had toppled on unconscious soldiers and lay there, too exhausted or sick to move.

Those sick with typhus would have desperately looked for a place to lie down. The energy had been sucked out of their muscles and they felt faint, their heads splitting with headache that made it difficult to open their eyes. They collapsed anywhere they could. But after a battle, the wounded took precedence over the ill when it came to medical attention. Typhus patients would be among the last to be seen, and the grunts and cries from the next room told them that the surgeon was busy with casualties from Borodino.

The surgery would have been the center of the typical hospital. Pale men still in shock, their limbs sometimes hanging from a ribbon of flesh or muscle, flowed toward it in a steady stream, and bandaged or dead men flowed out. At the center of the room was a stout wooden table surrounded by assistants. Amputations were almost the only thing on offer. Some leading doctors advocated waiting a day or two before operating on a damaged limb, but Dr. Larrey and his staff were firm believers in amputating quickly. The patient was often already in shock from the wound and would feel less pain, and the impact of the wound actually lowered the blood pressure, meaning he would bleed less during the operation. The risk of gangrene—deadlier to the soldier than the bullet itself—would be minimized if the limb was gotten off quickly. Speed was highly prized.

The table would have been covered in blood, bits of tissue, and uniforms. The surgeon didn't wash his hands between operations, or clean his instruments; perhaps he dipped them in a bowl of bloody water between procedures, but that was it. Beside him on the table were his tools. The typical traveling surgeon's case of the early nineteenth century would have contained everything from scalpels to elevators used to lift bones in skull fractures to trepanning braces and drills for penetrating into the skull to spreaders for peeling back the rib cage, encompassing twenty to thirty instruments in all. But the French doctors, prodded to be quick, had reduced it to the bare minimum: On the table lay different-size knives for cutting through skin and major muscles, a large bone saw made of steel and horn with a stout solid blade for cutting through femurs and humeri, and a smaller version for tibiae, fingers, and more delicate work.

The soldier's friends would have hoisted the injured man onto the table and held him down. The doctor then examined the wound, sometimes probing the hole with his filthy finger to see if the bullet was close to the surface. If the wound was to an arm or a leg and the patient was conscious, the doctor rattled off a quick diagnosis, usually recommending the limb come off. Officers were typically given the choice of amputation or a patching-over of the wound. In counseling one general whose arm had been shattered by a musket round, Dr. Larrey spelled out the options: "Doubtless we might have some chance of success if we tried to save your arm," he explained. "But . . . numberless fatigues and privations still await you and you're running the risk of fateful accidents." Namely, infection. (The general refused the amputation.) Average soldiers, however, could find their limb removed without any kind of consultation. If the soldier insisted on keeping his limb, the doctor simply shrugged, patched the wound with a bit of linen, and nodded for the man's friends to take him to nearby rooms, where he was lowered into a bed or, more likely, a bit of straw on the floor. When the soldier agreed to an amputation, a leather tourniquet was tied around the top of the limb, cinching off the major blood vessels, and the other end was tied to a leg of the table. The man was given a bullet or a bit of wood to bite on; officers were offered a quick shot of liquor if any was available.

Growling for the friends to grip the man tight, the surgeon would have cut down to the muscle with one of the knives, making the incision all around the circumference of the limb. Then he grasped the larger knife and, leaning into the patient's body, began sawing to the bone. Some patients cursed and bucked from the pain, but others, tensed and stoic, only stared up at the ceiling. It was considered bad form to scream.

The amputation of a leg at the thigh would have taken around four minutes, but if one got to the operating table late in the day after the surgeon had worked on dozens of men, the bone saw would have been perceptibly dulled and the operation would have taken much longer. Unconscious men came to in the middle of the procedures and began screaming. One British officer whose arm was amputated during the Napoleonic Wars raged at the surgeon as the blunted blade of the saw took twenty minutes to cut through the bone. Many of the heavy Russian balls had not only cut through muscle and broken bones but also shattered them, sending shards into the tissue. The doctors had to probe the wounds for these pieces. "The muscles were lacerated and reduced to the consistency of jelly," Dr. Larrey observed in a typical patient suffering from a wound from a musket ball.

Once the limb was off, the surgeon would have sewn the flaps of skin together with black thread to give the man a stump that stood a fair chance of healing. Then a piece of linen or cloth dipped in water was wrapped around the stump and the man was lifted off the table and sent out of the room. The limb he left behind was tossed into a pile with the others: by the end of the day, the jumble of arms and legs would reach the ceiling.

The propensity of the artillery balls to bounce waist-high through a regiment resulted in countless disembowelments, and men would have been brought into the hospitals holding their intestines in their hands. The bloody mess was simply cleaned off as best as possible and stuffed back in the body cavity, then covered with a wrap of linen. In a torso injury, any wound where the bullet had penetrated deeper than the length of the doctor's finger was deemed inoperable. An injury caused by a ball to the chest, the lungs, or the intestines was often waved away as being too dangerous for surgery. The hopeless cases—"horribly disemboweled or mutilated . . . motionless, with hanging heads, drenching the ground with their blood"—were left to die.

Surgeons worked nonstop as more patients were brought in. Dr. Larrey himself performed 200 amputations in twenty-four hours after Borodino, an average of 8 per hour, but he would have been examining patients, triaging, and supervising the field hospital at the same time, and a good surgeon working steadily could have easily doubled that number. Larrey recorded some exceptional cases in his memoirs, including one Russian colonel who had his nose cut off by a musket ball and a soldier who had a piece of mortar shrapnel hit him in the right calf, ricochet and travel upward through the thigh muscles, and then shoot out of the top of the leg, having sheared the man's calf muscle off and shattered both bones of the leg. But the vast majority of what a surgeon did at Borodino was butcher's work.

As evening fell, wax tapers would have been lit in the dark rooms. Men's faces were thrown into sudden illumination by the flickering candles and then covered by darkness again. The stench was overpowering: the fetid, rotting-meat smell of gangrene, the sickly odor of suppurating wounds, and the coppery tang of fresh blood, as well as the smell of feces and urine. The rooms were so dark that when orderlies came through with the evening meal, unconscious men lying in the straw were sometimes missed and died from thirst or simple inattention.

As the night progressed, some typhus patients would have entered their own worlds. Long-dead friends appeared and the patients struck up conversations with them, or they screamed at phantoms only they could see, or stared unblinking at sights or visions that, even after they recovered, they found impossible to put into words. Sometimes the patients had never before seen the fever-people that visited them and couldn't account for how they had pictured them so vividly. Typhus patients had been known to reenact scenes from their past lives: a young cowherd imagined that the other patients were his cattle and called to them constantly with the cry used to move cows into their pens; thieves bragged again and again of the same accomplices, the same heists. A thick noxious film covered their tongues and their teeth turned black; observers remarked on their resemblance to breathing cadavers. The rooms echoed with dry, urgent coughs. Sometimes a man's cheek flushed a deep red color and then, hours later, the color drained away and appeared in the other cheek. The men often gave off a peculiar odor that smelled like ammonia or "putrid animal matter," though that could have been an olfactory projection by observers, as it was widely believed that decaying plants and animals caused the infection in the first place.

As the night wore on, infected lice from the dead and dying would have crawled off the bodies and through the straw, seeking warmth. When they found a new host, they would feed almost immediately. *Rickettsia* feasted on the wounded.

If the doctor had run out of amputations and surgeries to perform, he would have made his rounds and done what he could for the men suffering from typhus. The Belgian surgeon de Kerckhove described what it was like to move among these men who seemed only half alive. "The face was sometimes red," he wrote, "sometimes pale, the eyes dark and sad, often lifeless or tearful. Their ideas were incoherent, their smell and hearing was weakening, deafness at intervals." Some of the patients shivered uncontrollably, others tried to tear off their clothing for relief from fever. Men stared, their eyes gleaming in the candlelight, their chests pumping up and down in fast, shallow breaths. "Tendon jolts" sent arms and legs snapping into the air, while other men, overcome by sudden terror attacks, tried to make it to the door, stumbling over bodies and being cursed in guttural voices. Patients cried out for someone to blow their brains out.

The hospital doctor would have moved among them, administering cool drinks where he could, herbs known as "vomitories" to those who seemed strong enough to bring up what were believed to be noxious substances in their stomach. Doctors on the march often veered into the forest searching for tonics, certain barks and plants such as elder blossom and mint. If the doctor had managed to hoard some of his primitive anesthesia such as tincture of opium or Hoffman's drops (a combination of alcohol and ether), he gave it to the patients raving with pain. The supplies simply hadn't arrived from Paris, so the surgeons were forced to scavenge what they could. Some of the doctors at Borodino made futile attempts to separate the typhus patients from the wounded. "If it was possible, I put the men suffering from typhus in spacious rooms, well-aerated and cool," wrote de Kerckhove. But the ancient preventive remedy of quarantine was impossible in mass-casualty situations.

Quarantine had been used throughout history to stop an advancing microbe such as *Rickettsia*. The practice goes back at least to Justinian's Plague in 541–2, when the Roman ruler instituted a new law to stop travelers from plague-infected areas from entering unscathed towns. Lepers were regularly isolated from the healthy by societies around the world. In times of plague, vessels from infected regions weren't allowed to dock in "clean" harbors. Guards were posted on roads twenty miles from town and forced unhealthy-looking peddlers and workers to turn around. Those who tried to skirt the blockade could be executed. Quarantine hospitals were built on the outskirts of cities to house people suspected of having the disease, who were watched carefully for any symptoms for forty days.

Other doctors in the Grande Armée tried to get as far from the infected men as possible. Among them were the hated *chirurgiens de pacotille* ("junk doctors"), cowards from the medical service who grabbed the first lightly wounded man they saw on the battlefield and dragged him to a hospital, their ticket to survival. There was, theoretically, a stiff penalty for cowardice under fire. Napoleon at the beginning of his career had ordered that any health officer caught abandoning a first-aid station in battle or refusing to care for a patient suffering from a contagious illness was to be court-martialed. "Whatever his station," wrote the emperor, in an edict dripping with contempt for doctors, "no Frenchman shall fear death." One surgeon who had refused to treat plague patients in Alexandria had been arrested, stripped of his citizenship, and then dressed in women's clothes and paraded on a donkey through the city streets, with a sign on his back that read "Afraid to die, unworthy of being a Frenchman."

As he tended to the ill patients, the Belgian doctor de Kerckhove had no doubt what was killing them. He described how the disease appeared among the troops and found it "generally the same as other typhus epidemics that affect armies in wartime." The symptoms began with a general malaise, then a state of "languidness," a slow pulse, and then a puffy and affectless visage (what the doctor called "a deterioration of facial features"). The patient became unable to move—the men called this stage of the illness "broken limbs"—and total exhaustion set in. Appetite disappeared, the subject became giddy, a whitish coat covered the tongue, and fever began shaking the patient's body with pulses of strong heat, followed by the chills; thirst became "inextinguishable" and the brain became "congested." The vision began to suffer as the disease spilled blood into the brain; the eyes became "dark and sad," and then simply lifeless. Hearing and even the sense of smell weakened, with some patients going completely deaf. As the days passed, the men became shadows of their former selves. They would whisper in nearly inaudible voices; they became indifferent to their condition or their futures; their breathing speeded up and they suffered from "absolute insomnia." Giddiness turned to full-blown hallucination and delirium, alternating with sudden fits of panic. Three days after the fever appeared, the men would become completely prostrate, unable to rise or walk. The small purplish spots appeared and spread over the body, along with what de Kerckhove called "black rusts and passive hemorrhages," bleeding beneath the skin that he half-accurately diagnosed as being "caused by the decrease of vital energy of the vascular system." In fact, that system was beginning to break down, threatening the heart, lungs, and brain. He found that the disease was most contagious in the fourth to tenth day.

In the final stage, the burning skin became cooler, the patients appeared better in the mornings but deteriorated at night, and "the eyes were turning off and sinking into eye-sockets." The face became "deeply altered," pale with exhaustion. The body began to stink, as if it were decomposing while the man was still alive; indeed, de Kerckhove wrote that the men's figures had a "dead-body look and seemed ready to dissolve themselves." The limbs blackened with gangrene, especially where vests or tight clothes prevented blood from circulating.

The physician found that the typhus epidemic, rooted in the "reeking places" the men were forced to occupy, was almost weirdly potent. "Here," he wrote, "it often happened that men died in a lightning-fast way." For this, he blamed the exhaustion of the men and the conditions in the hospitals strung back to Poland like a filthy necklace. In a final burst, looking back on those days, he called the hospitals "plague-filled cloacae," diseased sewers. One feels the even-keeled de Kerckhove straining for vile effect, eager to fleck his reader's eyes and ears with the awfulness of what he had seen.

Often, those typhus patients in the typical hospital who were seen by a doctor would have been bled and cupped to draw noxious substances away from the vital organs. Bleeding was a classic Hippocratic approach to restoring humors that had gotten out of balance, but it was a particularly awful solution to typhus, where the veins are already having trouble delivering blood to the body. Bark was given when available, as well as water reddened with wine, but there was so little of that to go around that few patients would have received even a taste.

Of the several courses of treatment de Kerckhove administered, the one he called "the stimulating method" gave the best results. This consisted of administering herbs to get the patient to vomit (if de Kerckhove deemed him strong enough) and then administering stimulants "if the skin was not too dry or burning." He would give them water mixed with wine and lemonade, light tonics to cool their thirst.

It was a minimalist approach, to say the least. The doctors who tended to the poet John Donne two centuries before would have found it appallingly lacking in imagination and proactive measures; there were no split pigeons to apply to the skin, no bleeding to drain away the putrid blood, no complex formulas for balancing the humors. But de Kerckhove and his fellow physicians had few supplies, brutal conditions to work in, a largely indifferent medical administration, and patients worn out by epic marches. De Kerckhove was certain his men could stand little else besides a purging and a decent bed, if one could be found.

WHATEVER THE CONDITIONS of the specific hospital a wounded or sick soldier ended up in, the majority of them feared infectious diseases. The medical authorities might debate the idea of contagion, but the soldiers believed in it. "Typhus, sir," says one doctor to Count Rostov in Tolstoy's *War and Peace,* which chronicles the invasion of 1812, as he tries to enter a sick ward. "It's death to go in." It was an accurate reflection of what the soldiers felt.

The great difference between the French doctors struggling to come to grips with typhus at the hospital at Borodino and later researchers—or ourselves, watching them struggle blindly as thousands died—was the arrival of germ theory in the mid-1800s. In 1835, Agostino Bassi traced an epidemic killing Italian silkworms to infectious spores he observed under a microscope and became the first to formulate the idea of living, contagious agents as the cause of disease. John Snow's tracking of the source of the 1854 London cholera epidemic, ending with his identification of the famous Broad Street Pump as the source of the contaminated water, advanced the cause of contagion, and Louis Pasteur proved in the early 1860s that spontaneous generation was superstition. But it was Robert Koch in 1876 who connected a pathogen—in this case, *Bacillus anthracis*—and a disease, anthrax.

As the medical historian Charles-Edward Amory Winslow has pointed out, by 1812 the key elements for a germ theory of disease had been in place for almost two hundred years. Antoine Philips van Leeuwenhoek had used primitive microscopes to identify bacteria in the human mouth. Athanasius Kircher had originated the idea of living organisms capable of transporting disease. Francisco Redi had demonstrated that piles of rags and other inanimate objects didn't give rise to living things (there was no way, for example, that rats and insects could materialize from decomposing matter). As Winslow writes, "If an openminded and imaginative observer had put the work of these three pioneers together, the germ theory of disease could have been developed in the seventeenth century instead of the nineteenth."

The great-man theory of medical history, the idea that progress against illness is one long string of discoveries by a series of geniuses, gains support not only from pioneers such as Pasteur or Curie but from absences such as the physician who with a flash of insight could have assembled the available evidence into an airtight case for contagion—the physician who, in the seventeenth and early eighteenth century, didn't exist.

Dr. James Lind, the British surgeon who had invented the blind test and drastically reduced the incidence of scurvy and typhus in the Royal Navy, wasn't that great mind. He had essentially skipped the "Eureka" moment and moved to a way of evaluating treatments and thereby found a remedy without knowing how it cured. Had that phantom genius been present to codify the work of others into germ theory, Lind could have contributed the method of proving it.

Rickettsia profited from the competition among theories of disease. In the hunt for the secret of typhus, a key element wasn't only an attempt to understand what caused the epidemics but to understand *how to understand* the evidence in front of one's eyes. The most important clues would remain in plain view for hundreds of years. Generation after generation of doctors and generals, swayed by culture, conflicting evidence, and a lack of systematic thought, would confront the same evidence with the same theories and make their gambits. Those who read the evidence correctly, and there were some, survived and often prospered, for the fact is that, centuries before Napoleon faced typhus, it had been stopped dead in its tracks more than once, only to reappear and outwit its next opponent. The case of typhus illustrates how difficult and hard-won knowledge truly is.

It was Napoleon's misfortune that the political evolution of warfare had outpaced medical thought. War had become total war, with Napoleon as its first great practitioner. But medicine lacked an equivalent genius who might have revolutionized disease theory the way that he had battlefield tactics.

THE MEN PACKED shoulder to shoulder in that hospital at Borodino knew nothing of the debates and missed opportunities that had left *Rickettsia* to strike freely as the wax tapers burned. They were certainly aware of how drastically Napoleon had cut back on the medical service, and now had a chance to bitterly regret it. But neither they nor their doctors knew that the lice soundlessly fleeing from the dead bodies in the middle of the night and climbing up the sleeves of uninfected men were the vectors for the blossoming epidemic. The cries of the grievously wounded and dying men they understood as part of the rigors of war. But the ranting men who gibbered to unseen faces in the fetid little hospital, or laughed uproariously for no reason, were no doubt odd and worrying.

Those who died were carted away and tossed in open graves or simply piled by the side of the road. The officers and the well-connected often received small gestures at their death. One soldier requested that his brother's heart be cut out and placed in a small beaker of wine, to bring back to France as a keepsake for his family. The body itself was then placed in a coffin, escorted by twenty-five gunners, and entombed in a stone wall in the nearby town of Mozhaisk with the notation "The body of Ferdinand Gaston de Lariboisière, lieutenant of Carabiniers, killed at the Battle of the Moscowa, Sept. 1812. His father recommends his remains to the public piety." But most corpses were left to molder.

The doctors would come again in the morning, and orderlies would bring food and water. In the hospitals at Borodino, one prayed to see the dawn.

CHAPTER 12

The Last City

T HE FRENCH SOLDIERS KNEW THEY HADN'T WON THE NEEDED victory. "We had never suffered such heavy losses," wrote Colonel Raymond de Montesquiou, who took charge of the 4th Regiment of the line after its commander had been killed. "Never had the Army's morale been so damaged. I no longer found the soldiers' old gaiety." Instead of the songs that usually echoed around the campfires after even the most bruising engagements, Montesquiou heard only "gloomy silence."

The Russian army was in perilous shape. On the night of September 7, Barclay sent Colonel Ludwig von Wolzogen to report to Kutuzov and receive any orders—in writing, as Kutuzov could be both wily and mentally lazy. On the way, Wolzogen met a lieutenant resting with 30 to 40 men behind the front line and ordered him to rejoin his regiment. "This *is* my regiment!" the man cried. He had lost approximately 1,250 men. Ironically, an almost identical exchange occurred on the other side of the lines, when Napoleon found an officer in charge of 60 to 80 men standing near the Schevardino Redoubt, well behind the front line. The emperor was annoyed that an officer was allowing his men to linger behind their unit. "Rejoin your regiment," the emperor called. "It is here," said the officer, pointing to the dead heaped around the fortifications.

Confused, Napoleon shouted at him to catch up to his men. The officer spat out the same reply, and a junior officer had to explain to the commander that the six dozen soldiers were all that remained of the unit.

Colonel Wolzogen found Kutuzov on the Moscow road miles from the frontline troops, surrounded by aides and aristocratic scions who hadn't come near the artillery barrages. He reported on the state of the battlefield: all the redoubts had been captured and the troops were "extremely tired and shattered." Kutuzov's reply showed how out of touch he had become during the course of the day.

> With which low bitch of a sutler have you been getting drunk, that you come giving me such an absurd report? I am in the best position to know how the battle went! The French attacks have been successfully repulsed everywhere, and tomorrow I shall put myself at the head of the army to drive the enemy without more ado from the sacred soil of Russia!

But Colonel Toll went out to survey the ranks and soon returned with bad news: Wolzogen's estimates had been accurate. In addition, the artillery was nearly out of shells and the guns themselves were battered, their carriages held together with rope. Kutuzov soon ordered a tactical retreat to a more defensible position. The fact that he could muster only 45,000 effective troops the next morning shows how badly the Russian forces had been mauled, and how close they were to breaking.

THE NEXT DAY, the sun rose on thousands of corpses still covering the field of battle. Napoleon's clerks were sent out to compile casualty reports. In one German regiment of the Grande Armée, they "used a dead horse as a writing table, and the orderlies even dragged up a few Russian corpses to act as chairs for the scribes." The cadavers would still be there weeks later when the artist-soldier Faber du Faur marched through with his artillery regiment and sketched the mournful scene.

Both Napoleon and Kutuzov wrote home to their wives, claiming victory. The Russian commander, who the night before had contemplated a morning attack on the enemy, also wrote Alexander a letter filled with half-truths, saying that he had inflicted greater losses on the French than they had on the Russian forces and that "the enemy did not gain a single yard of ground." Badly in need of reinforcements, he ordered a retreat of six miles to the town of Mozhaisk.

The Russians who had survived the battle were, on the whole, in high spirits. "Everyone was still in such a rapturous state of mind, they were all such recent witnesses of the bravery of our troops, that the thought of failure, or even only partial failure, would not enter our minds," remembered Prince Piotr Viazemsky. These men had a very modest definition of success when facing the great Napoleon. Simply to have stood up to his legendary army was enough. They'd banished the image of the French as supermen and proved themselves at least their equals in terms of courage. The order to fall back was a blow, but nothing could dampen the enthusiasm of the ordinary troops.

As the Russians retreated toward Moscow, Napoleon followed. At Mozhaisk, Napoleon's quartermasters found the emperor a just-built house, so new the doors hadn't been installed. Here they established the imperial headquarters. Napoleon went to work, but his cold had now completely robbed him of his voice and he could only furiously scribble order after order to his aides, who struggled to decipher his handwriting while he raced on to the next directive, banging on his desk for the orderlies to collect the latest batch.

When the Grande Armée reached Mozhaisk, it found the city packed with Russian casualties and its heights commanded by the

Russian rear guard and squads of Cossacks. The dashing Murat, now a favorite with the Cossacks because of his flamboyance and bravery, soon put the Russians to flight and the troops swarmed into the town. Bodies were stacked in the doorways of burned-out buildings or left lying in the ruins of collapsed buildings.

Many of the enemy wounded were tossed out of the makeshift hospitals to make room for the Grande Armée's casualties. When the food ran out, desperate Russians left behind by their comrades resorted to cannibalism. Alexandre Bellot de Kergorre, a French commissary, remembered: "Six hundred wounded Russians had fallen in the gardens and here they lived on cauliflower stalks and human flesh. Of this there was no shortage!"

French commissaries struggled to keep 3,000 wounded men fed. Foraging parties headed out into the countryside, bringing back grain and corn to be milled and made into bread. Even fleeing townspeople and soldiers were stopped on the Moscow road and ordered to give up part of their provisions for the wounded.

Napoleon lingered in the town while the army lumbered slowly after the Russians, who were moving toward Moscow. The emperor now expected, and prayed for, yet another "climactic battle" at the gates of Moscow. The very name of the city seemed to have acquired a talismanic power for the emperor, and he repeated it at every turn. When the names of the generals killed at Borodino were read out, Napoleon stopped the recitation and cried, "One week of Moscow, and this will not matter any more!" To him, the idea that the Russians would fail to defend their capital was as unimaginable as Frenchmen abandoning Paris. Moscow was the sum of Russia, and taking it would mean that Alexander could no longer deny him victory.

In the week after Borodino, Kutuzov was still maintaining that he would make a stand in front of the capital. He sent General Benningsen, Bagration's chief of staff, to survey the terrain for a suitable defensive position and, like Colonel Toll, the general found the available sites to be few and far between. He finally settled on Poklonnaya Hill, the two summits of which provide the highest elevation for miles around the capital. Barclay, who rose from his sickbed to survey the site, quickly saw that the uneven, fissured ground was a death trap for an army that might have to retreat quickly. The majority of Kutuzov's generals and advisers agreed with the levelheaded Barclay, but the question of whether Moscow would be actually defended still hung in the air.

Kutuzov met with the bombastic governor of Moscow, Rostopchin, who would soon come to despise the general as a schemer. The Russian commander boasted that he was preparing to give battle to Napoleon on the ground under their feet. Rostopchin was astonished. He pointed out that the terrain was unfavorable, and that any breakthrough of the first line would leave nothing at the army's back but a rolling slope into the streets of Moscow, precipitating a disastrous retreat. Even a military novice could see the speciousness of Kutuzov's claims. On his way out of army headquarters, Rostopchin encountered Barclay, who did nothing to allay his fears. "You see what they want to do," Barclay told him. "The only thing I desire is to be killed if we are mad enough to fight where we are." The governor warned the generals that if the army abandoned Moscow, he would set it ablaze.

On September 13, Kutuzov called his commanders together to decide whether or not to make a stand. In a shabby peasant hut, the generals gathered around a table covered with maps. Kutuzov framed the matter in a way that told the others what he was thinking: "Is it proper to await the enemy's attack in this disadvantageous position or to abandon Moscow to the enemy?" The staff was split, with Barclay, Toll, and others favoring retreat and General Benningsen putting forth the idea that the Russian army shouldn't only turn and face Napoleon but attack his right flank, where Poniatowski's Polish regiments had been decimated. It was an audacious proposal, indicative of how keen the Russian fighting spirit remained.

The debate was, as one might expect, heated. Kutuzov was most likely looking for political cover for the decision to abandon Moscow than real options for defending it. But the generals strained to change his mind. Benningsen argued that the sacrifices of Borodino would be meaningless if they didn't defend the capital. Barclay, ever the voice of reason, pointed out the hard facts: the regiment-level leaders needed to lead an attack on the French lines were lying in the fields near the Raevsky Redoubt, as were many of the men needed to execute it.

Kutuzov dismissed his generals and mulled over the options. When he made his decision on the night of September 13, he phrased it in the best possible light. "Napoleon is like a torrent which we are still too weak to stem" was his famous justification. "Moscow is the sponge which will suck him in." The order for a retreat went out, startling citizens and enraging the army. Kutuzov decided to head south, toward the rich farmlands around Kolmna, where his troops would find plenty of food. With a typical flourish, he presented the abandonment of the nation's capital as an unorthodox offensive tactic, but he couldn't disguise the fact that Russia was unable to protect its jeweled city.

Alexander, now ensconced in St. Petersburg, was oblivious to the unfolding debacle. He'd reacted to Kutuzov's bulletin from Borodino and a second that claimed the Cossacks had pushed Napoleon's rear guard seven miles from the battlefield—a complete lie—with an outpouring of honors: the general was awarded a marshal's baton and 100,000 rubles. St. Petersburg was swept up in a patriotic ecstasy: the city echoed with the ringing of church bells, strangers embraced on the streets, residents pressed for a glimpse of the tsar at a celebratory mass at St. Alexander Nevsky and cried thanks to God for delivering them from the Antichrist.

Governor Rostopchin reacted to the final edict with despair. "The blood boils in my veins," he wrote his wife. "I think I shall die of grief." But he delayed only a few moments before issuing a blizzard of directives. The Muscovite police went through the taverns, puncturing the vats of vodka and spirits; the city's 2,100 firemen prepared the city's fire pumps for evacuation, so that the French wouldn't be able to use them; wagons were arranged for the wounded who could be safely transported; and a stream of notables with a dizzying list of requests—to find a lost relative or for an escort through the mobs—were seen to.

The governor also assembled a crew of policemen, nationalists, and street thugs for committing mass arson once the French had occupied the city. Ironically, one of Kutuzov's pet devices, the dirigible that was to fly over the Grande Armée and incinerate it in a massive fireball, figured in the plan. The unused fuses and combustibles that the builders had left behind would be used to set Moscow alight.

The residents who had stayed in Moscow and vowed to fight were horrified by the order to abandon the city. Rostopchin had pledged that Muscovites would form citizens' brigades armed with pitchforks and old muskets at the back of the Russian army, but now burghers and peasants alike raced for the city gates.

The city's population during peacetime fluctuated between 250,000 and 350,000 people, the latter number accounting for the aristocrats and their households returning to the city after their summers in the countryside. Now entire blocks emptied within hours. Soldiers weeping from shame and anger marched through the streets, abandoning the half-dug entrenchments they had been constructing to meet the French, while families rushed from sector to sector looking for loved ones who had been off on an errand when the news arrived. Criminals, easily recognizable by their half-shaven heads, were let out of their prison cells and joined the crowds, and the walking wounded streamed out of the hospitals, leaving their bedridden comrades behind, while inmates of the local insane asylums wandered about or gibbered on street corners. Looters broke the locks on basements and cellars and got drunk on the wine and vodka inside, even going as far as licking the paving stones dry of the liquor that had spilled from the vats. All joined in a roiling scrum, vengeful, despairing, and as eager for scapegoats as they were to reach safety.

Louise Fusil, a French actress and performer, was holed up with a collection of artists in a palace belonging to a prince on the eastern edge of the city. "We kept on climbing to the top of the house," she remembered, "where we could get a long view, and one evening we spotted bivouac fires. Our servants came into our rooms in great alarm to announce that the police had been knocking at every door to urge the occupants to leave, as the city was going to be set on fire, and the fire-pumps had been taken away."

It was dangerous to be French, rich, or insufficiently patriotic in the city now. The poor threw stones at gaudy carriages as they flew by, and nativist mobs roamed the boulevards looking for traitors. One political agitator released from prison was quickly surrounded by an enraged crowd and literally torn limb from limb.

The memoirist and general Philippe Ségur records one scene from the lower depths of Moscow. A French citizen who called Moscow home had gone into hiding as Napoleon approached. Early in September, she'd come out of her sanctuary and wandered through the empty streets, puzzled as to where everyone had gone. Then a "far-off mournful wailing fell on her terrified ears." Frozen with fear, she watched as a great wave of poor men and women approached, dragging whatever of their ragged possessions they could carry. They held up icons to bless their escape and led their children away, following the priests who headed the procession. The rich had contacts and mansions in other towns, salable treasures. But it was these poor people on whom the burden of Napoleon's invasion fell. The woman watched as this biblical river of misery passed her by, pausing only to look back once "and seeming to bid farewell to their holy city."

Hidden in various quarters of the metropolis, the firebugs waited for word to begin their work. Napoleon would be allowed to occupy the city, but Rostopchin hoped the city walls would become a trap in which to consume him.

To give the Russian army and the remaining citizens time to traverse the approximately six-mile breadth of the city, General Mikhail Miloradovich, who was in charge of the rear guard, sent a messenger to Murat under a white flag. He asked for twenty-four hours to arrange his troops for surrender and threatened stiff resistance if he didn't get it. Murat agreed; he could use the time to rest his men and bring up any available matériel, as his men's pouches contained only enough musket cartridges for one day's fighting. The temporary truce granted, Murat waited for the peaceable surrender to be finished. No one among Napoleon's marshals could yet imagine the lengths that the enemy were willing to go to defend the homeland.

Two of Kutuzov's battalions decided to play their way out of the city, marching past the Kremlin with their band in full voice. General Miloradovich, an unflappable soldier known for his dry wit under the direst conditions, rode up and snapped at their commander, "What blackguard gave you orders that the band should play?" The lieutenant general replied that it was tradition since the time of Peter the Great that a garrison surrendering a fortress marched out with accompaniment. "But where in the regulations of Peter the Great," Miloradovich replied acidly, "does it say anything about the surrender of Moscow?"

Nearly four hundred miles away, Alexander got the news from Moscow in small, agonizing doses. With Kutuzov having mysteriously cut off communication, Rostopchin dashed off a note to the tsar on September 13 announcing the plans for the abandonment of the capital. "Moscow has been taken," it read. "There are some things beyond comprehension."

The ordinary Russian soldier left his capital full of bitterness and regret. Cries of "Where are we being led?" and "Where has he brought us?" murmured in the ranks. The savior's glow around Kutuzov had dissipated in the minds of his men, and soldiers pestered by fleeing civilians about the military state of affairs could only shrug. They knew nothing except that they were retreating and that mother Russia had again been betrayed by a coterie of rich generals. Rostopchin told his son, age sixteen, who had seen action at Borodino, "Salute Moscow for the last time. Within an hour it will be in flames."

NAPOLEON REMAINED AT MOZHAISK, still unable to speak and racked by fever. (Although it's possible that the emperor had caught a light case of typhus, there were many types of fever present in the Grande Armée, and he developed no other symptoms of the disease.) The emperor kept seven secretaries busy with his orders and dispatches. His main concern at this point was manpower. He instructed his chief of staff to write urgently to the duke of Belluno, who was stationed in Poland with reinforcements guarding against any Russian attack on the territory. "The enemy, struck to the heart, no longer busy themselves with extremities. . . . Tell the Duke to send everything, battalions, squadrons, artillery, and detached men to Smolensk, whence they can come to Moscow." Regiments were called up from all over Europe: 140,000 from France, 30,000 from Italy, and more from Poland, Bavaria, Lithuania, and Prussia. "Not only do I want to have reinforcements sent from all quarters," Napoleon wrote, "I also want those reinforcements to be exaggerated, I want the various sovereigns sending me reinforcements to publish the fact in the papers, doubling the numbers they are sending." He ordered the French, German, and Polish troops of IX Corps from Germany to

Moscow and sent dispatches to many of the detachments strung out behind him to make their way to the front line. Knowing that the Russians had almost inexhaustible resources of men to draw from, the emperor was desperate to get as many bodies as possible.

On September 12, he set out to catch up with the leading elements of his army. He rode slowly toward the city, still anticipating a fierce battle. Napoleon could see evidence of abandoned earthworks, and as he approached his advance units he expected to find the Russian army around each turn. Scouts and guards combed through the forest ahead of him, looking for the first line of jaegers that would signal the Russian position. But they passed through without encountering a single enemy soldier.

Finally, on September 14, his entourage came to Poklonnaya Hill, the same outcropping where Kutuzov had proposed to site a last defense of the city. Riding up, Napoleon and his men crested the top and pulled up to find Moscow spread out before them like a gleaming carpet embroidered with gold and silver. It wasn't the slate- and brick-colored cities of Germany or even the darkly romantic skyline of Paris. It was a riot of colors and shapes, a city of turrets and steeples and cupolas in shades of blood red, sky blue, and the dominant jade green. The men had marched for months through raw provinces and filthy little villages, but here was a great city, delighting the men with its richness and alien forms. They ran forward and broke out in spontaneous applause, calling out "Moscow! Moscow!"

"It was two o'clock," wrote General Ségur, the soldier-memoirist. "And the sun made the magnificent city twinkle and shine with a thousand colors. . . . At the sight of this gilded city, this brilliant capital uniting Europe and Asia, this majestic meeting place of the opulent, the customs, and the arts of the two fairest divisions of the earth, we stood still in proud contemplation." Napoleon rode up and the men swarmed around him. The capture of this place, many felt, made their sacrifice worthwhile. For a moment, before the pillaging began, the soldiers of the Grande Armée felt that the bestial campaign had been transformed by this exquisite prize.

Napoleon was expecting a procession of the city's notables to greet him with the keys to the city and the opening gambits of a peace negotiation. He scanned the city's gates for signs of them, and scoffed at reports from scouts who said that the mansions and streets were empty. They couldn't find a single Russian official to bring to the emperor. The troops *had* seen graffiti scribbled on the walls that made them wonder: "Good-bye," and "Farewell, delightful haunts that I leave with so much sadness!" The emperor studied a large map laid out on the grass as he questioned each returning scout or prisoner and interrogated them about what they had witnessed and in which sector: the bazaar district, Chinatown (where the long caravans from the Orient deposited their exotic wares for sale), the white town, the German suburb, and the "earth town" (named for the earthworks built there in the late 1500s). Only the French expatriates who had hidden from the mobs came out to greet them, eager to tell stories of terror and the city's rapid abandonment.

The men looking down on the capital grew increasingly nervous. "They will wait a long time," said one soldier. "All those Russians will emigrate to Siberia rather than surrender." Napoleon studied the streets through a telescope balanced on one of his aide's shoulders. "The barbarians!" he shouted. "They are leaving all of this to us! It isn't possible!" Finally, the emperor ordered Count Daru, the head of his commissariat, to search the city and bring him the boyars.

Meanwhile, Murat's cavalry penetrated farther into the city and found only silence. The men, spooked by the empty districts, rode quietly ahead, hearing only hoofbeats echoing back to them off the stone buildings. When they did find Russians, they were looters breaking into the Moscow arsenal or soldiers hurrying for the eastern gates. There was scattered resistance at the Kremlin walls, accompanied by drunken curses from the men and women who baited the French, but it was obviously unorganized and quickly put down with a cannonade.

Every scout returned with the same message: the Russian army had withdrawn under the cover of the truce, along with the city's notables and most of the citizenry, leaving only the lowest of the low. Napoleon was intensely frustrated. "It would be difficult to describe the impression made on the Emperor by this news," wrote the diplomat Caulaincourt. "Never have I seen him so deeply impressed. . . . His face, normally so impassive, showed instantly and unmistakably the mark of his bitter disappointment."

Napoleon appointed Édouard Mortier, commander of the Young Guards, governor of Moscow and told him if the army looted the capital, he would pay with his life. The emperor, now thoroughly depressed, settled for the night in a local inn outside the city's gold-colored walls. Squads of Young Guards were sent in to secure the city, and they were accosted by sad remnants of Rostopchin's citizen army: one old man with a flowing beard appeared on the Dorogomilov Bridge as the Guard marched over it, thrusting his pitchfork at a drum major, who avoided the prongs and sent the elderly defender tumbling into the river with a well-timed kick. There was no enemy worthy of the name to stop the French advance.

THE LOOTING BEGAN almost immediately, out of necessity. Some of the men hadn't eaten in days. Sergeant Adrien Bourgogne of the Imperial Guard, along with his squad mates, battered down the doors of the local mansions and helped themselves to whatever had been left behind: flour, vodka, jarred fruit, which they quickly consumed or bartered away. Once their hunger had been satisfied, the proper sack began, the kind of bacchanal that the men had dreamt of since first signing up. Silks, leather boots (a real find for many of the men who had been shoeless for weeks), paintings of boyars and their ancestors all started to come out of the homes and into the streets. Sergeant Bourgogne found "a small machine for gauging the force of powder," an obscure luxury that he pocketed anyway. Dressing as "Russian boyars, Chinamen, or French marquis," the men draped women's clothes across their chests to the laughter of their friends, but these capes and heavy cassocks made for the Russian winter would later become fiercely guarded valuables once the bitterly cold weather arrived. "Even the gallery slaves concealed their rags under the most splendid court dresses," remembered Eugène Labaume of IV Corps. Prostitutes, criminals, and serfs joined in the scramble for loot.

The strict hierarchy of Moscow housing—where mansions inhabited by counts and princes were surrounded by modest houses and hovels occupied by their servants—was re-created as the Grande Armée's officers took possession of the finer accommodations, the mansions with silk tapestries still on the wall, and the ordinary soldiers pitched their rucksacks in the homely coach houses and stables. There was, at last, plenty of food, both in the larders of the abandoned homes and in the fields surrounding the city. One soldier remembered finding beets "as round and large as bowling balls," but there were ample supplies of pork, mutton, and other meats as well. The Grande Armée hadn't been so well fed since leaving Germany.

As the French advance guard secured the main squares, the firebugs were prowling the outer districts. Led by the police superintendent, Voronenko, they began setting fire to shops and houses. The first sighting of flames came around noon, in the commercial district of Kitai-Gorod, and was confined to a few paint and upholstery stores. Hours later, more pillars of dark smoke appeared in the same district, and then in the early evening, near the governor's palace. Troops were sent to extinguish the flames.

Napoleon had been hearing stories of a coming conflagration from expatriates who had emerged from cellars and attics, but he had refused to believe them. Now as the night progressed, "sinister reports" flowed in: fires were sprouting at points around the city, and mobs of thugs had appeared on the streets, burning everything in their path. Near midnight, a tremendous boom echoed through the darkness as a munitions dump exploded in the east, near the Yaouza River. One Swiss officer was strolling through the dark city when a French officer charged at him. "Run for it!" the man shouted. "There's a band of brigands behind me." The Swiss soldier peeked around the next corner to find a terrifying sight: a gang of arsonists, 50 to 60 strong, flaming torches in their hands.

The emperor gave the order to shoot firebugs on sight. Sergeant Bourgogne and his unit nabbed one in the act, fired a bullet into his side, and left him to die. Hours later, some of his fellow troops reported that they had returned to the scene of the "dreadful execution" and found a young woman sitting beside the body, cradling the young man's head in her lap, gently stroking his face and kissing him. She told the French soldiers she planned to stay with the body for three days, supposedly fulfilling a Russian tradition.

Napoleon entered the city on September 15 and set up headquarters at the Kremlin. Buoyed by the sight of the Romanov throne and the cross of Ivan the Great, he sat down to write Alexander a peace proposal. But soon news of the fire overwhelmed everything. Dr. Larrey watched the flames sweep toward the Kremlin. "It [would be] difficult, under any circumstances whatever, to present to the eye a more horrific spectacle than that, which it was so melancholy to behold. . . . The flames, driven in all directions, and propelled by the violence of the winds, were accompanied, in their ascent and rapid progress, by an awful hissing sound and dreadful detonations, resulting from the combustion of powder, salt-petre, oil, resin, and brandy, with which the great part of the houses and shops were filled." Wooden houses caught fire, and the heat was so intense that beams of fir shot from the structures and set alight buildings several streets away.

The emperor rose from his desk and watched the city burn. To him, the blaze was a symbol of the utter foreignness of the Russian mind. "It was the most grand, the most sublime, and the most terrific sight the world ever beheld!" he would later write. Torching one's own capital was something no Frenchman, not even Napoleon, could imagine; it was outside their psychological reach. The fact that the Russians had dared to do it elicited a certain horrified respect.

The sparks from the fire fell on the exteriors and roofs of nearby houses and began to smolder while the buildings' contents were being systematically looted from inside. The pillaging had become frenzied. Thousands of men prowled the streets brandishing Turkish scimitars inside their leather belts or sporting enormous fur hats or bits of Tartar costume. Great heaps of swag made their appearance: a jewel-encrusted spittoon from a prince's palace, silver candlesticks and icons from the local churches, silk Persian shawls threaded with gold, bracelets thick with emeralds and diamonds, enormous rugs and even embroidered armchairs from the finest salons found their way to the impromptu markets that had sprung up and bartering was soon under way.

On the morning of September 16, the fires began to approach the Kremlin walls. Sparks and burning cinders floated in from the burning districts and landed on the roof of the apartments where Napoleon was staying. The heat pressed against the building until the windowpanes were hot to the touch. Napoleon was uncharacteristically agitated by the inferno, pacing frantically, throwing himself down in an armchair and then springing up to look at the flames again. The fire was no longer "the most sublime . . . sight" in the world but a threat to his future. When a Moscow police officer who had set the nearby arsenal tower ablaze was interrogated, Napoleon learned that the Kremlin had been targeted for destruction, another indication of Russian resolve. "He was extremely restless," remembered the Italian general Rossetti, "his gestures short and vehement revealed a cruel distress. He ran at every moment to the windows to observe the progress of the fire. Finally, abrupt and brief exclamations escaped from his overburdened heart: 'What a frightful sight! They did it to themselves. So many palaces! They are Scythians . . .' " Napoleon's staff and his marshals begged him to leave, but he was fixed to the spot.

The fire was now so close that its roar deafened them and the superheated air scorched their faces and lungs. Furious and despairing, Napoleon fled with his staff. Breathing in the ashes, they found the exit blocked by "an ocean of fire" and turned down a narrow passage that enabled them to escape from the golden walls. The conflagration had swept around the Kremlin, engulfing the streets around it. Houses imploded in showers of hot sparks, ceilings and floors collapsed inside the burning facades, and sheets of the metal facing and roofing bounced off the streets. "The flames that were noisily consuming the buildings on both sides of the street rose high above the roofs and were caught by the wind and curled down over our heads," remembered the general and historian Ségur. "Thus we were walking on a floor of fire, under a sky of fire, between walls of fire." Finally, the imperial party came across some soldiers pillaging nearby buildings before the fires could claim them, and the looters led them to safety.

The realization that it was "wild-looking women and men in rags with hideous faces" and Russian policemen who had initiated the blaze was a relief to the marshals, who had originally suspected their own troops of starting the fires. But for Napoleon, it was the thing that tipped him into blazing anger and then depression. People who would burn their own city to the ground were clearly not prepared to negotiate. "This forbodes great misfortune for us!" he said while watching the fires burn on September 17 from the safety of the Petrovskie Palace. There would be no delegation of nobles knocking at his door.

The fire raged through the night of the 16th and into the 17th, so bright that it was said one could read a book five miles from Moscow by the light of the flames. Finally, on the 18th, the inferno subsided and Napoleon made his way back to the Kremlin. The four days since they had first looked down on the unearthly city had transformed it utterly: from an Eastern masterpiece of gold turrets and centuries-old wealth to a burned-out, blackened shell where everything and everyone was covered with soot and mud.

THERE WERE A VARIETY of options open to Napoleon at this point: Leave a strong garrison in Moscow and march north toward St. Petersburg to storm the seat of Russian government, freeing the serfs along the route to bring added pressure down on Alexander. Head southwest and confront Kutuzov once again in hopes of demolishing his army, and take the famous arsenal and munitions factories of Tula, near where the Russian army was now positioned. Winter in Moscow and prepare for a spring campaign. Retreat.

Crucial to any offensive plans were the reinforcements pushing across the Moscow road, which should have bolstered the Grande Armée's strength. But many of them were shirkers, deserters pressed back into the ranks and men marking time until they could make their way back home. And a great many of them were sick. *Rickettsia* fell on the fresh troops as a fire would on old wood. It was now raging out of control. In Moscow's Foundling Hospital, which had been turned into a sick ward for officers, 40 of the 45 patients died from typhus. Later, during the withdrawal, a contingent of 10,000 German reinforcements joined the main body of troops, only to be infected. Some 3,000 of them died on the return. "Want, sickness, and an enraged peasantry inflicted terrible reprisals and caused a daily fearful reduction of numbers," wrote

Sir Robert Wilson, the British mercenary attached to the Russian imperial staff. "Which successive reinforcements could not adequately meet and replace." The 6th Chasseurs were an extreme example. They received a contingent of 250 reinforcements from northern Italy, but not a single one of the new men would survive the war. The troops who had been on the campaign from the start and had survived cases of typhus had developed immunity to the disease, but the new recruits had no defenses in their bloodstream to protect them from the pathogen.

The sudden availability of food and decent housing would seem to have held out the promise of better health for the Grande Armée, but the field doctor de Kerckhove reported differently. "During our first days in Moscow," he wrote, "we observed how harmful it is for health to change physical conditions suddenly. . . . Typhus and dysentery were very strong within our ranks." And according to Ebstein, typhus "ripped into" the army at Moscow, at times so intense that it exhibited a "plague-like character."

As he debated his next move, the emperor was fast drawing new victims into an epidemiological tempest. In Moscow, although the troops were well fed, the hospitals were packed with victims of typhus, "slow fever," and diarrhea. "Thousands of sick soldiers took refuge in gutted houses," reported de Kerckhove. "And many of the big buildings that didn't burn were turned into hospitals." Convoys of sick arrived from the units along the route of march and the men were carried into whatever domicile had a space available on the floor.

The diseases awakened by the war had by now spread to the Russian troops and villagers. The partisan leader Denis Davidov met a peasant named Theodore from the town of Tsarevo who left his wife and children hiding in the forest to fight against the French. When he returned two years later to look up his comrade, Davidov found he had died "from contagion, along with many other people who had sought refuge in the woods during the hostilities." Davidov never identifies the epidemic, and one can never rule out a local, unreported bout of a different illness, but typhus has to be a leading contender.

As for the army, exact numbers are contested, with some authors arguing that Kutuzov's ranks were only lightly touched by the epidemic. One report detailing casualties between October 20 and December 14 specified that of the 61,964 men missing from the ranks, 48,335 were sick in military hospitals with typhus, and few of those survived. "In 45 days," writes Bernhardy, "three-fifths of Kutuzov's army perished." There was certainly disease in the ranks. Carl von Clausewitz, the strategist attached to the imperial staff, referred to the Russian army in November and December as "decimated by sickness," and the army melting away in Kutuzov's hands.

Even though they fought only one major engagement with the French, the Russians lost half their effective troops between Tarutino and the army camps south of Smolensk. Only the fact that he was being constantly reinforced saved Kutuzov from mirroring Napoleon's fate.

CHAPTER 13

Decision

ALEXANDER WAS SHATTERED BY THE NEWS OF WHAT HAD happened in Moscow. On September 20 came the overdue letter from Kutuzov, which confirmed the handover of the city to the French, and added news of the fires that had engulfed the capital. Despite his horror, he sent Kutuzov's messenger back to the commander with a message of defiance, swearing that even if every soldier was to be killed, he would organize a citizens' army of nobles and serfs and march to meet the Grande Armée. In St. Petersburg, the tsar issued a proclamation in which he admitted what the nation already knew: Moscow had been surrendered to the "haughty destroyer of kingdoms." He called on Russians to redouble their efforts to expel Napoleon and make Moscow a tomb. And he mocked the remnants of the Grande Armée. "Look at the condition of this enemy," he wrote. "He entered Russia at the head of more than three hundred thousand men, but . . . half the army is destroyed by Russian valour, by desertion, by want of discipline, by sickness and hunger!"

In the days before Napoleon had entered Moscow, according to General Baron de Marbot, the Cossacks had captured 100 sick French troops, who had been sent to Moscow for treatment. Instead, Governor Rostopchin had paraded them through the city streets, where some of the prisoners had collapsed and died on the spot. As they lay on the pavement, Russian policemen read out a proclamation from the mayor claiming that the entire Grande Armée was as weak and disease-ridden as these pathetic men. As despicable as the gesture was, General de Marbot acknowledged that "our strength diminished daily owing to sickness and the increasing cold."

Kutuzov ordered a new call-up and men as old as seventy joined the ranks. His devastated units were quickly replenished. In one month, the Russian army had added over 48,000 troops to the 40,000 who had escaped Borodino alive.

Rage at the loss of the capital and the lies told by the tsar's propaganda machine began to bubble to the surface in St. Petersburg. The Council of Ministers took the unprecedented step of demanding a full accounting of Kutuzov's decisions, beginning with the sketchy and often inaccurate communiqués that declared victory, only to be followed by reports from other sources of huge losses and retreats. These nobles were simply vocalizing the whispers from the streets and drawing rooms: How could Borodino have been a victory if it had led to the destruction of Moscow?

Napoleon, too, kept a steady stream of cheerful news flowing back to Paris in the famous Bulletins—war dispatches sent under the emperor's name—packing them with staccato accounts of French victories and Russian weakness. But, unlike Frenchmen 1,500 miles away, the Russian people could see and hear evidence that contradicted their leaders' rosy visions.

Napoleon's hope—that Alexander would be dethroned—became for the first time a hotly debated topic. The loss of Moscow convinced many of the ambassadors and foreign observers resident in St. Petersburg that a treaty with Napoleon was inevitable, and they had their counterparts within the Russian nobility. The "French party" counted among its members Alexander's tempestuous brother, the Grand Duke Constantine, who had for years been an appeaser when it came to Napoleon. After the

Battle of Preussisch-Eylau in 1807, Constantine had screamed at Alexander: "If you do not wish to make peace with France, then give a loaded pistol to each of your soldiers and ask them to blow their brains out!" He had warned that antagonizing the emperor would inevitably result in an invasion of Russia by an army "trained for battle and always victorious." Constantine, an inveterate schemer, had changed sides after the Battle of Smolensk and pushed for a to-the-death battle with the French, but now the burning of Moscow had convinced him that Napoleon was indeed unstoppable. Many others agreed.

Quietly, the same early signals that had forecast the arrival of the Grande Armée at Moscow's gates began to be seen in St. Petersburg. Carts and wagons were seen at the entrances to the finest mansions, being loaded with trunks filled with silk dressing gowns and fine china. Mansions, libraries, and archives holding the nation's treasures were slowly emptied of their paintings; anyone looking through the nearly 2,000 windows of Catherine the Great's Hermitage Palace would have seen empty spaces where the Titians and Raphaels had hung, the masterpieces now packed up and heading north on barges. The glittering nightlife of the capital, the banquets and soirees attended by counts and foreign diplomats, went dark. Those without connections were left to wonder about the strange happenings in their city and to stew in their own anxiety.

As the tension escalated, the neurotic Alexander even began to feel that he might follow in his murdered father's footsteps. When the anniversary of his coronation arrived, the tsar's coterie strongly urged him to abandon his plans for arriving at Kazan Cathedral on horseback, something he had always done, and instead suggested the safer confines of the empress's carriage. Alexander heeded their advice. One noblewoman who was part of the procession to the cathedral remembered the sullen, silent faces of the men and women arrayed along the streets, so different from the usual cheering crowds that had promised Alexander they would die for him. "One could have heard the sound of our footsteps," wrote Mademoiselle Stourdza, "and I have never doubted that one spark would have been enough, at that moment, to produce a general conflagration." When she looked over at the anxious face of Alexander, she felt her knees start to give way.

Even the tsar's own sister chastised him for the loss of Moscow. "It is not just one class that is blaming you," she wrote him, "but all of them together." Alexander became so concerned by the change in the people's mood that he had the police arrest anyone caught spreading rumors about the invincibility of Napoleon or the coming abandonment of St. Petersburg.

Kutuzov kept up a stream of optimistic dispatches, writing the tsar that he was rebuilding the army and keeping watch on Napoleon. "I have taken my stand on the flank of the enemy's long line of operation, holding it blocked by my detachments. From here I can keep an eye on their movements, protect the resources of the empire, and reform my army." Alexander no longer trusted the upbeat missives of his commander, and Rostopchin gave him ample reason for doubt: he reported that the army had dissolved into a brawling, drunken mass of thieves and murderers who were preying on the local peasants.

NAPOLEON SPENT HIS leisure hours assiduously reading Voltaire's history of Charles XII's disastrous invasion of Russia in 1708. The Swedish invader had chosen the coldest winter in living memory to take on his Slavic neighbor; for months, temperatures plunged so low that in the Nordic countries elks were found frozen to death standing in the fields and in Venice the canals were rimed with ice. But the deadly weather that spelled doom for Charles hadn't arrived until December, and now, as Napoleon waited for a response from Alexander, the air was practically balmy. He joked that Moscow was warmer than Fontainebleau.

Awaiting the emperor's decision, the French spent their days in a

strange holiday in the burned-out shell of a city. It was a grotesque
scene:

> At every step one trod on dead and scorched people, and
> the corpses of incendiaries hung from many half-burnt
> trees. Amid all this horror one could see the wretched in-
> habitants, who had come back and had no roof over
> their heads, collecting iron or lead which had once cov-
> ered the roofs of palaces. . . . They did this so as to build
> huts . . . and they stilled their pangs of hunger with raw
> vegetables which our soldiers had overlooked.

The soldiers spent their days scrounging for swag, gambling, brawling, robbing peasants who came in from the countryside to sell their
produce, and recovering from the rigors of the march. They whored
with girls from decent families who had been somehow left behind
and who sold their bodies out of sheer hunger. These freshly minted
prostitutes took over the mansions of families who had fled, wearing the fine clothing they found, accepting stolen silver baubles and
expensive dresses looted from homes down the block. The men slept
on altar cloths from the Orthodox churches and drank punch out of
porcelain china. The city was lit at night by enormous watch fires in
the middle of once elegant avenues, around which the French par-
tied and gossiped. Meanwhile, Muscovites cut strips of flesh from
the corpses of horses and even dived to the bottom of the Moskva
River to retrieve handfuls of the wheat dumped there by retreating
Russian forces.

Few soldiers or officers did anything to prepare for the approaching winter. A few caches of furs were found and men could be
seen parading through the blackened streets in the latest foxes and
minks—men's or women's, it didn't matter—and some enterprising
troops had new boots made up out of bearskin. But mass preparations (acquiring heavy winter clothing, reshoeing the remaining

horses for icy roads) were largely left for another day. "Nothing was done to guard against the rigors of winter," confirmed Labaume. Caulaincourt called it a time of "dreaming dreams." Napoleon quietly acknowledged that his gambit for a quick peace treaty had failed, and he admitted to his intimate advisers that his former enemies, the Austrian and Prussian troops, now forming the rear guard and directly in the line of any retreat, could be easily turned into fresh adversaries "if we met with the slightest reverse." As in Paris before the invasion, he delayed and delayed and hoped for the best. But days passed without any response to the peace proposal the emperor had sent to Alexander before the firebugs torched the capital.

THE LULL IN HOSTILITIES was broken on September 21. Pressed by his advisers and determined to reenergize his troops' morale, Kutuzov had turned west on the 16th, onto the road to Tula, the center of the firearms industry. He reached Podolsk, a town along that road, on the 18th. The maneuver was completed under the eyes of a complacent Murat, who had been sending Napoleon reports of the Russian army's deteriorating condition (when in fact it was gaining men and supplies on a daily basis) and even claimed that the Cossacks were amenable to changing sides and fighting under his banner. Instead, Kutuzov had maneuvered himself to a strong position to jab at Napoleon's rear guard and strike at his connections to Paris.

The Russians now began to utilize hit-and-run tactics, probing and harassing the outlying French units and communication lines. Cavalry units struck the Moscow-Smolensk road to disrupt Napoleon's famously efficient couriers, who could do the 1,500 miles of the Paris-Moscow run in an astonishing fourteen days. Supply caravans were attacked as well; a train of munitions wagons was hit outside Moscow and fifteen caissons were wrecked and 200 horses stolen. On September 24, Cossacks and regular troops clashed with 150 French dragoons and cut the key road completely. The major in charge of the dragoons was taken prisoner, along with some of his officers and men. "All certain communication with France was cut off," the ex-ambassador Caulaincourt noted. "Vilna, Warsaw, Mayence, Paris were no longer in daily receipt of their orders from the Sovereign of the Grand Empire." Napoleon was in the habit of pouncing on dispatches from his far-flung holdings, and the loss of communications frustrated him intensely. The mail line was soon reestablished, but it was clear Kutuzov had learned how to fight while rebuilding his forces.

As winter approached, Napoleon stirred. On October 3, he presented his marshals with a bold plan: a joint force consisting of four divisions from IX Corps, now garrisoned at Smolensk, and an attack force led by Napoleon departing out of Moscow would converge north of Vitebsk, smash into Kutuzov's forces (which he contemptuously numbered at around 32,000, when the real figure was tens of thousands higher), and then head north to take Novgorod on their way to the gates of St. Petersburg. The audacity of the plan, of putting the spear point to the administrative heart of Alexander's empire, excited Napoleon enormously.

After his stepson Prince Eugène read out the details of the plan, the emperor turned his eyes toward his marshals, who were sitting in what must have been shock at the news. "What?!" he cried. "You, you are not inflamed by this idea? Has there ever been a greater military exploit?!" Napoleon taunted them with the idea of capturing the two great northern capitals in the span of three months. Again, he was thinking in terms of places such as Austerlitz, of exploits to be emblazoned on a monument. It was as if he couldn't conceive of the dirty war of attrition he was now engaged in.

The counterarguments were obvious, and the generals made them. Winter was coming; the terrain was difficult and supplies for men and horses couldn't be guaranteed. Even if they did take St. Petersburg, there would be no guarantee of a Russian surrender, and the army would be stranded even farther from home than it was now.

Napoleon called Caulaincourt and informed him he was sending the diplomat to St. Petersburg with another proposal for ending the war, his second try at peace while in Moscow. Caulaincourt forcefully declined. "These overtures will be useless," he told Napoleon. The weather and the condition of the Grande Armée were turning to Russia's advantage. Napoleon dismissed him and pushed the mission on the Marquis de Lauriston, Caulaincourt's replacement as ambassador to Russia. He sent him off with a manic last few words: "I want peace, I must have peace, I want it absolutely!" Lauriston sped toward Kutuzov's camp for permission to proceed but was turned away.

Finally, Napoleon ordered his administrators to begin preparing for a possible retreat: troops started to gather every wagon, carriage, and cart to move the thousands of sick and wounded who were now packed into makeshift Moscow hospitals, and on October 8 a massive harvest began of all the locally available produce, mostly cabbages and potatoes, to sustain the Grande Armée on its way back to the friendlier terrain of Lithuania and Germany.

Napoleon whiled away the days, tortured by indecision. Although he was used to rushing through his meals and then turning back to work, he now stretched his dinners out, overeating and lingering silently at the table. When General Georges Mouton tallied the latest troop strengths for the various corps, Napoleon refused to believe he had lost so many soldiers since Borodino and claimed the counts were off. His ability to focus exclusively on a problem now tormented him. The problem had no solution, but the emperor couldn't stop turning it over in his mind.

There were frenetic bursts of activity. He wrote up a proclamation of freedom for the serfs early in October, though he never intended to actually enforce it. The edict was another probe into

Alexander's mind, as Napoleon hoped the threat of a social revolution would force him to the peace table. But St. Petersburg remained silent. On October 12, he suddenly decided on an excursion to Murat's advance guard, then changed his mind, then reconsidered again and announced he would go in a few days and initiate a new attack on the Russians. The impulse drained away, however, and Napoleon stayed put. The arrival of the first real snowstorm on October 13 dampened his enthusiasm for maneuvers. Sleet and rain had pelted the capital for weeks, but now winter moved in. On October 15, three inches of snow fell, making it clear that a decision on the army's plans had to be made and made quickly.

NAPOLEON HAD NEVER lost a major campaign central to his reign. Egypt and Haiti were peripheral battles in the scheme of Continental power. Now he felt the world watching him for a single slip, when they would unite to crush him. He agonized to Count Daru: "What a frightful succession of perilous conflicts will begin with my first backward step! In affairs of state one must never retreat, never retrace one's steps, never admit an error . . ."

The winter of 1812 would take on sinister forms in the French imagination, as a kind of Asiatic dervish. The French novelist Hilaire Belloc introduced the cold this way:

> A thick fog descended. The sentries felt for the first time no longer discomfort even of that acute and gnawing sort which seems to those who read of it under civilian conditions to be a hell; what they felt as the night advanced was a thing new to them, and perfectly intolerable to humankind—a thing no Westerner among them had yet known—the winter advancing from out of Asia, from the frozen steppes.

Finally, Napoleon called his advisers in to announce the withdrawal from Moscow. In the spring, he believed, a refreshed and reinforced army could then storm northward and conquer St. Petersburg. The emperor issued a stream of orders: Lauriston was sent back to Kutuzov's headquarters in the hopes that Alexander had agreed to receive him. General Baraguay d'Hilliers headed to Yelnya, fifty miles east of Smolensk, with directions to put together a supply base and garrison to support the retreat. The reinforcements heading toward Moscow on the Smolensk road were turned back to clear the route, and the sick and wounded in Mozhaisk were readied for travel. Those who couldn't be moved were gathered at the Foundling Hospital, and Russian casualties were mixed in with them to afford them some protection.

On October 16, the Grande Armée marched out of Moscow. Napoleon pointed to the bright sky and told his aides that the sun was his star, shining the way to fresh conquests.

TYPHUS HAD INITIATED a cascading series of events and decisions that had crippled the 1812 campaign. The offensive was finished, even if the emperor clung to his illusion of fighting in the spring. Now, with only his reputation and a shockingly reduced army to threaten his enemies, he was beginning the battle to save his throne.

Napoleon had done remarkably well against his human opponents. He had outfought the best generals of Europe, outthought the military strategists, charmed enemy princesses into his bed, and won over soldiers who likely would have revolted if another general had put them through his campaigns. But with natural opponents he had a mixed record, and they had slashed the size of his empire.

In the south, his 1798 invasion of Egypt and Syria had been an outright disaster. He had been unable to bring the two Ottoman strongholds to heel during a chaotic campaign that, had all the details been fully known back in France, would have left his military reputation in tatters. And in the West, he had lost his grip on Haiti, and through it, the New World, after a disastrous 1803 campaign plagued by a different pathogen.

In Egypt plague had swept through the ranks of his army of 38,000 men, killing thousands and blunting the army's effectiveness. The campaign was poorly planned, underequipped, and strategically incoherent, so the war would probably have failed without the microbe's intervention. But Napoleon had further stained his reputation when he ordered the euthanasia of hundreds of the most seriously ill patients before the French abandoned the campaign. And when the emperor tried to blame the disease for his defeat in Egypt, his chief doctor on the campaign had reacted furiously, citing the cover-up as an example of Napoleon's "oriental despotism" (the Chinese emperors being symbols of despotic rule in the French mind). The disease had hurried the Egyptian debacle to its close and almost buried Napoleon's career with his unfortunate men. Only the political failings of the Directory in Paris, which opened the way for a coup, saved him.

One gesture in Egypt belied his cruelty there. The French leader had shown great bravery by entering the plague hospital set up by his doctors and touching the dying men, even helping to carry out a corpse. Touching plague victims was simply not done, except by medical professionals, as the disease was suspected to be extremely infectious. The incident had become an essential part of the Napoleonic mythos. Antoine-Jean Gros's painting of the scene portrays Napoleon as a modern-day Jesus, with the ability to heal the sick with the touch of his finger.

In Haiti, the disease had been yellow fever and the effect was even more devastating. Spread by mosquitoes, yellow fever (also known as "yellow jack" and "the American plague") is an acute viral disease noted for its ability to inflict pain, especially in the back and abdomen. The pathogen attacked the French forces and was quickly putting 30 to 50 men into the sick ward every day. "The mortality continues and makes fearful ravages," wrote the twenty-nine-year-old commander to Bonaparte. The fact that the disease simultaneously hit units spread over different parts of the island, in different climates, and walking over different types of topographical features was especially terrifying. One staff officer wrote about the suspected causes. A soldier only had to:

> . . . expose oneself at length to the hot sunshine, be caught in a draught when perspiring, neglect to change one's rain-drenched clothes, undertake a taxing journey on foot or on horseback, breathe the burning air in churches during the great religious ceremonies, be bled needlessly, take excessive baths or drugs, be frightened, depressed, homesick, agitated by a passion such as rage or love or simply experience some strong stimulation . . .

In other words, one could get sick doing practically anything. One senses in the passage the paranoia that swept through the ranks as the fever vectored in from every direction.

The disease attacked the French from the beginning and grew in waves until it was said that troops went straight from their transport ships to the grave. Within a few months, 14,000 men were dead and the fighting had degenerated into terror on both sides. The French commander died of yellow fever in November 1802, and a year later the invasion had failed.

The defeat shocked Napoleon. Fearing that yellow fever was also endemic to the Mississippi Delta and surrounding regions, he sold France's holdings of 530 million acres of land to Thomas Jefferson at the fire-sale price of under 3 cents an acre. For $15 million, the fledgling republic got Missouri, Oklahoma, Arkansas, Iowa, Kansas, Nebraska, Minnesota south of the Mississippi, and the bulk of North and South Dakota, along with parts of New Mexico, Texas, Montana, Wyoming, Colorado, and all of Louisiana, including the city of New Orleans. America had become a behemoth, while Napoleon had forsaken his best hope for a westward empire, all because of an obscure pathogen.

By 1812, the map of Napoleon's ambitions had been circumscribed by disease: yellow fever in the far west, plague in the far south and now in the north, the most implacable sickness of all.

CHAPTER 14

Two Roads

BY THE BEGINNING OF NOVEMBER, NAPOLEON HAD ONLY 75,000 of his original 440,000 frontline troops—365,000 troops had died in a little over four months. He had lost an average of 3,000 men every day of his campaign. The majority of those deaths, perhaps as many as 200,000, were from disease, with typhus the lead killer. One doctor called it a dying-off that "had scarcely a parallel in the history of the world."

The Grande Armée didn't keep precise statistics of cause of death, so how can one be sure that typhus was responsible for so many casualties? By sifting through the various theories and comparing them with the descriptions given by the soldiers themselves, one can discern the main causes of death on the road to and from Moscow with some clarity.

The response from the top ranks of the medical corps was confusion. Dr. Larrey noticed the men stumbling out of the ranks and falling down dead in the road, but in his memoirs, he makes a startling claim about what was killing them: not disease, Larrey claimed, but exposure, constant rains, and hard drinking. "These unfavorable circumstances," Larrey wrote, "in conjunction with the immoderate use of chenaps (the brandy of the country), proved fatal to a large number of the conscripts of the junior guard." As the diagnosis of the chief French medical authority, it deserves some investigation.

There is no question that some young recruits were getting blind drunk on the corn brandy that Polish peasants had left behind or were relieved of by French troops. But Larrey makes no case that a bad or poisoned batch was making the rounds, simply writing that the "stupefying power" of liquor was killing men by the score. That is, the men were dying from liquor that the peasants drank without any apparent harm to themselves. The surgeon in chief recorded the symptoms: loss of muscular movements, vertigo, drowsiness, half-closed eyes, lethargy, and even "gangrenous spots on the feet and legs." All were consistent with late-stage typhus.

But perhaps there was a kernel of truth in Larrey's diagnosis. It's possible the brandy was interacting with disease to kill the men. A doctor on the campaign, Scherer, reported that three of his patients had found bottles of brandy in the hospital cellar and quickly downed them. Soon the men "fell down senseless" and began vomiting, crying nonstop, and suffering uncontrolled bowel movements. They were dead within six hours, and on their abdomens, necks and chests, and especially the feet there were gangrenous spots. Exactly as Larrey had reported. There is very little literature on the interaction of alcohol and typhus patients, but the liquor would most likely have worsened the condition of exhausted patients infected with *Rickettsia*. The rapid death of soldiers after drinking a pint of brandy might have suggested to onlookers that the liquor was the culprit, but the more likely explanation is that the alcohol only accelerated the progress of typhus or another disease.

Another theory mentioned in the accounts of several soldiers was exposure, or hypothermia. Hypothermia is caused by a drop in core body temperature, which renders the body unable to perform normal metabolic functions. The patient stumbles frequently and has trouble controlling his movement. Shaking becomes violent. The face, lips, toes, and fingers lose their natural color and may show tints of blue. The mind becomes clouded. In the final stages, the patient appears confused and drowsy; hallucinations and amnesia set in. The pulse drops, breathing slows dramatically, and the organs begin to fail. Death soon follows.

The staggering gait and blue skin match some of the descriptions of dying soldiers, but the conditions necessary for Stage 3 hypothermia simply didn't exist in the early stages of the campaign. Most of the soldiers had access to blazing campfires at night; they had warm cloaks and overcoats; and the nights were described as "chilly" or "cool" but not downright arctic. Hypothermia can occur in temperatures above freezing, but those cases usually involve people dressed in light garments, with their skin exposed to the cold air. Some of the soldiers who had imbibed enough brandy could have lain out during the chilly nights without their overcoats, but unit cohesion was still strong within the Grande Armée and it was highly unlikely that entire units were left sprawled out half-dressed away from their mates and campfires long enough to expire from advanced hypothermia.

By blaming rotten liquor and exposure, Larrey may have been protecting his reputation. Death by poisoned chenaps could be attributed to incorrigible soldiers out on a spree and not to failures by the medical staff. The doctor was undoubtedly courageous on the field of battle and deeply concerned about the health and lives of his men—there was probably no more beloved figure among the ranks of the common soldiers—but he was also famously tetchy about his reputation and prone to exaggerate his own accomplishments.

The historian Jean Morvan compared Larrey's surgical memoirs of various campaigns with the diaries of soldiers and found that the good doctor had consistently overlooked symptoms of illnesses racking the army and declared the men to be in good health when in fact many of them suffered from a variety of dangerous conditions. Throughout his career, Larrey regularly dismissed clear evidence of widespread illness.

· · ·

THE GERMAN ARTIST and soldier Faber du Faur would survive the holocaust to come, one of only 100 soldiers of the Kingdom of Württemberg to return out of an original contingent of 15,000. His portraits in the beginning noted the rough beauty of the countryside, and the occasional skirmish, but on July 31 the tenor of his work changed. *On the Road between Beschenkovitschi and Ostrovno* shows two bootless soldiers collapsed on the ground, while four others dig a grave. The commentary by Faber du Faur and his collaborator, the officer Frederich von Kausler, emphasizes how common such scenes were: "The two days of march . . . presented an unforgettable glimpse of the shocking state of the army . . . exhausted soldiers oblivious to exhortations, threats or punishment. At each halt, each camp, we noticed that the number of effective troops had diminished. The vast majority of these exhausted soldiers soon turned into corpses."

Laymen who recorded the deaths in their diaries and memoirs often attributed them to two causes: "want," or hunger, and exhaustion. Hunger is mentioned again and again in memoirs of 1812. But is it possible that young and relatively fit men were actually starving to death on the road to Moscow? How long does it in fact take for a healthy man to die of malnutrition? The answer varies according to the person's general health and reserves of body fat, but it would take several weeks before a reasonably fit and originally well-nourished soldier on the march would succumb.

Admittedly, food had become a pressing issue early in the campaign. The green, inexperienced troops gorged themselves on their rations; supplies meant to last four days were consumed in one. Again and again, the high command's preparations proved inadequate or based on faulty information: The barges loaded with provisions found the Vilia River too shallow to navigate. Corrupt officials in charge of food distribution often withheld supplies from troops to sell them on the side for astronomical profits. One Westphalian officer wrote home to his wife that he was passing a detachment from Davout's corps on July 29 when he saw soldiers execute a commissary who had been found selling off supplies meant for the troops. Fights broke out between commanders and their regiments competing for their daily rations, and carts full of wheat were dumped by the side of the road, as there were no horses or oxen to pull them.

This wasn't unprecedented. Napoleon's armies in Italy and Spain had never had adequate supplies pushed from Paris to fill their needs, and armies going back to Francis's in the sixteenth century and beyond had extracted what they needed from local peasants. They lived off the land, by the ancient code of pillage. But Poland along the Smolensk road presented a bleak picture to the scavenger. It was filled with forests, swamps, and marshes, with few cultivated fields, and small villages with tiny stores where the local populace lived just above subsistence level. This wasn't Italy, where family farmers tilled fields, raised cattle, and produced fresh cheese and wines. Invading that country, the emperor had promised his men "the most fertile plains on earth . . . rich provinces, wealthy towns." In Russia the troops encountered miles of swamp, forest, and poor villages of hovels the lowliest French peasant would find unlivable. Napoleon had been warned about the scarcity of food along the route, but he had brushed the advice aside. Now he was paying dearly for his self-delusion.

What crops and stores did exist along the Smolensk road often lay smoking in ruins by the time the Grande Armée arrived. Barclay and Bagration had ordered their troops to destroy everything that could sustain the French: crops were set alight, food depots were ransacked and burned; cattle and horses were slaughtered; entire villages were put to the torch to deny Napoleon's men basic shelter. The weather was so hot and the air so dry that Cossacks could ride by a hamlet, fire bullets into the thatched roofs, and start a blaze without even stopping.

The starving man goes through a long process of catabolism, where the body begins to break down the fat and muscle reserves and convert them to energy to keep the vital systems functioning. In the famous "starvation experiment" at the University of Minnesota in 1944–45, the food intake of the thirty-six volunteers (all fit young men, like the troops that made up most of Napoleon's army) was reduced to about 1,500 calories per day, roughly half of what was needed to keep the men's weight at preexperiment levels. The test subjects were slowly starved for twelve weeks. The volunteers lost fat and muscle, on average about 25 percent of their body weight. They became obsessed with food, highly irritable, and depressed (one volunteer, Number 20, even dropped a Packard on his hand and then amputated three fingers with the chop of an ax to get out of the study.) Their energy levels dropped precipitously. But none of them came close to dying, especially in the ways described in the memoirs: men stumbling and then suddenly keeling over dead, or never waking after a night's sleep.

What most of the soldiers who left records of the campaign report is scarcity, not starvation. On the stretches of the road where supplies had become hard to find or had been gorged on by the lead troops, some would go a few days without a solid meal—gnawing on a biscuit or a handful of rye through the day—before they were able to forage or pillage a substantial amount of food. By the time the Grande Armée reached the Smolensk road in late July, the landscape had changed once more to ripe fields of wheat dotted by flocks of cattle (though it is true that the frontline regiments often ransacked these and left little for their comrades). There are few passages relating a *complete* absence of any food for weeks at a time, or the physical wasting-away of the body, the emaciation of the face and body, the intense irritability, the slow descent into a coma-like state, and the hysteria that characterize true starvation and would have been clearly evident to the sufferer's comrades. Certainly men were weakened by the loss of a steady intake of protein, but there is almost no evidence of deaths purely from hunger on the advance to Moscow.

It's far more likely that the conditions and the pace Napoleon was setting weakened the men's constitution and gave an opening to disease. Typhus survivors had been known to succumb to even mild infections during their recovery, as their vascular systems and hearts had been so ravaged by the disease that they typically became susceptible to other "chronic disorders." Even those it didn't kill, typhus often fatally weakened.

Exhaustion is the other cause given by nonmedical men and physicians alike. But this diagnosis, too, fails to hold up to close scrutiny.

The recruits for the Grande Armée came from a mainly pastoral society, drawn from villages and farms, where outdoor work would have given most of them a vigorous, if occasionally malnourished, constitution, used to long days full of demanding work. As for the veterans, they were specimens: lean, rugged men who could march or ride for miles on end without complaint. Nor did those men who were suffering from hunger have to keep up with the intense marching that the army was experiencing; they could quite easily drop back to the mini-army of stragglers that had quite quickly appeared behind the main body of troops.

It is actually very hard to march men into their graves, even hungry, tired men, without complicating factors such as heatstroke, heart ailments, or extreme dehydration serving as the real cause of death. Dehydration would plague the troops later in the march, but as yet, it wasn't a major factor, and the days were certainly hot, but no hotter than the army had experienced during Italian or Spanish summers.

Fatigue could certainly have weakened men suffering from an

undiagnosed illness, but the assertion that large numbers of troops simply dropped dead from exhaustion is almost certainly false in the vast majority of cases. Something else was at work, something that would show up in the bones of the men who were lucky enough to reach Vilnius, 488 miles away.

THE ARMY LEFT Moscow a shadow of its former self. Anyone watching the regiments depart would have noticed two things: The men were often in terrible physical shape, "crawling rather than marching." And they had grabbed an enormous pile of loot, which they had loaded onto every available cart, droshky, chaise, and carriage: trophies such as flags captured from the Turks and the cross of Ivan the Great from the Kremlin, Oriental rugs, entire wardrobes, ornate furniture, even ornaments used in the coronation of the tsars and a gem-encrusted Madonna. Most officers commanded a single cart, while generals had six or more to haul their swag. Common soldiers had packed their knapsacks with anything jeweled or golden (though many mistook gold leaf for solid gold artifacts) for resale back home or exotic dresses and capes for their wives or girlfriends. Some of the hams, mutton, shoe leather, and fur caps necessary for a march of 2,000 miles through hostile and often barren country were also loaded on carts, but far less than was needed. The more enterprising of the soldiers had bullied Russian peasants into carrying their take; these long-bearded men were the final pieces of booty the army was carrying back to Paris. The carriages jostled for room, five across on the road.

The army was depleted physically, but the soldiers still carried themselves as conquerors, "one of those armies of antiquity laden with spoils and slaves, returning from some horrible destruction," as Ségur wrote. Behind the caravans came an assortment of refugees: French actresses, Russian whores, servants, sutlers, and criminals fleeing the prisons. As many as 50,000 stragglers accompanied the Grande Armée on its way out of the blackened city.

The enormous cavalcade inevitably led to delays. One officer estimated that the army took six hours to travel a distance that a single carriage would have covered in one. But there was an air of carnival to the day. "It was afterwards justly said," Eugène Labaume wrote, "that our retreat commenced with a masquerade and ended with a funeral."

With Moscow being abandoned for a second time, 1,850 of the sick awaited their fate in the Foundling Hospital. Captain Thomas-Joseph Aubry of the 12th Regiment of Chasseurs, who had been wounded at Borodino and caught typhus while recovering in Moscow, described how the past few weeks had gone:

> The typhus made appalling inroads in our ranks. We were forty-three officers in our ward. All of them died, one after the other, and delirious from this dreadful disease, most of them singing, some in Latin, others in German, others again in Italian—and singing psalms, canticles, or the mass. When this happened they were nearly always in their death agony . . .

As soon as the Young Guard, forming the rear of the retreating army, had cleared the Moscow gates, the patients looking out the hospital windows saw vigilantes combing through the abandoned buildings looking for stragglers. Frenchmen were run through with bayonets and their bodies dumped in the Moskva. When the Cossacks reached the hospital entrances, the sick troops fired down on them with the muskets left by their beds.

According to Aubry, 1,800 of the 1,850 French soldiers in the hospital died from typhus—a nearly 100 percent mortality rate. Aubry himself escaped the epidemic and recovered fully in Siberia. But almost all of the sick patients who were surrendered to the Russians perished.

The evacuated men typically fared little better. The winnowing of baggage began almost immediately on the army's escaping the suburbs of Moscow. Men opened their knapsacks and dumped out whatever they thought expendable: often the ammunition and cleaning equipment or spare uniforms went first and the baubles survived. But the sick, too, were excess weight, and drivers frequently sped over bumps in the road in order to knock them off their carts. They would lie by the side of the rode, delirious, stretching their hands out to the passing troops. The Russian captives who had been used to haul the loot and who strayed back to the rear guard because they were too weak or hungry met a more merciful fate. They were shot in the back of the head, smoke wafting out of the fresh bullet holes as the French soldiers glanced quickly down and then marched on.

And the army was barely out of Moscow.

The Emperor's forces left by two routes: the main body went southward down the old Kaluga road, while IV Corps marched in a parallel line down the new Kaluga road to the west. Napoleon had prepared assiduously for the march to Moscow, collecting books, topographical surveys, and atlases on everything Russian, but his research on the current route was incomplete. The generals found their maps were often inaccurate and they had to blunder their way through towns and hamlets with unpronounceable names. One unit actually kidnapped a peasant and forced him to act as their guide, "but he was so stupid that he only knew the name of his own village." Once reached, the thoroughfare presented its own problems. The mud surface quickly became deeply rutted, and the narrow bridges resulted in bottlenecks when they held up or in long delays when the timbers snapped under the loads. A few days into the retreat, a torrential rain turned the road into a swamp, and travel times decreased again.

Three retreat routes would eventually be considered by Napoleon: the southern route that would bring them through virgin territory toward the city of Kaluga; the due-west Moscow-Smolensk road that the Grande Armée had used to reach the capital; and a third way, southwest to the town of Medyn, with a dogleg that would eventually lead the army back to Smolensk. Each had its advantages and risks: The untouched Kaluga route would provide fresh supplies of rye and livestock, but the Russian army blocked the way. The Smolensk route would allow Napoleon to avoid a confrontation with Kutuzov, but it had been stripped bare of all supplies on the approach. And the Medyn route promised sustenance to the remaining men, but it was unfamiliar terrain, risking unpleasant surprises and a possible encounter with the enemy.

Now it was Napoleon who avoided battle. Two days into the march, he suddenly swerved from the old Kaluga road and marched westward to join up with Prince Eugène and IV Corps, which was headed toward the key junction town of Malo-yaroslavets. He had intended to freeze Kutuzov into position and then skirt along his left flank and secure the resources-rich depots of Kaluga before the Russians could catch him. He even sent a colonel to Kutuzov to follow up on Lauriston's request for a meeting with Alexander, as if his armies were still waiting patiently in Moscow instead of hurrying south. But Kutuzov had Cossacks, peasants, and French informers to keep him abreast of the emperor's movements. Definitive evidence that Napoleon was in retreat came on October 23, when a messenger reported to Kutuzov that information from captured officers indicated that the French had abandoned Moscow and that the emperor and his staff were camped at Fominskoye, forty miles from the capital. The Russian commander knew instantly that the campaign had turned in his favor. He wept and, turning to face an icon of Jesus mounted in the corner of the room, cried a few words of thanks: "Oh Lord, my creator! At last you harkened to our prayer, and from this minute Russia is saved!"

However damaged, Moscow was returned to its inhabitants and Napoleon was on the run. But before the last soldiers of the

Imperial Guard quit the capital, they received final orders instructing them to destroy the Kremlin with explosives. They began rig-
ging the ancient buildings, hurrying to escape the vigilantes and
Cossacks now slipping back into the city. On the road, a French
captain near the town of Charopovo heard a "tremendous report"
from the north; had many of the explosives not failed to ignite, the
sound would have carried miles farther. It was an act of rage and
spite on Napoleon's part, revenge for the inhuman war he felt the
Russians had pursued. Eugène Labaume regretted the action and
pitied Moscow. "She experienced from the native of an obscure
and remote island the most lamentable of human vicissitudes," he
wrote. To him, it was a signal that Napoleon's claim to be fighting a
civilizing war—bringing French culture and ideals to the savages—
was finally acknowledged to be a fiction.

AT MALOYAROSLAVETS, THE LEAD elements of both armies
clashed, turning the town into a blood-spattered hellhole. The
French won the encounter, but Kutuzov retreated only two miles
away to the city of Kaluga. Now Napoleon had to choose which
route to take.

The emperor quickly called a conference with his marshals.
After a heated, almost violent discussion, Napoleon dismissed his
marshals with a dejected air and sat alone to make the decision. As
at Borodino, the key issue became manpower: Napoleon no longer
had the troops to sacrifice in a bruising push through Kutuzov's
lines on the way to Kaluga. The Grande Armée was like a sick man
whose every ounce of fat had been burned away by fever: there
was little or nothing to spare. And about a third of his forces were
now spread out on missions: 10,000 of the Young Guard and
other troops were still guarding the evacuation of the last units
from Moscow; 8,000 members of VIII Corps were trudging the
route along the Smolensk road; and the valiant Poles under Poniatowski were on their way to secure Vereya and Medyn. He was

down to 72,000 effectives and the number decreased daily due to disease. "The time has come now for us to turn all our thoughts to saving the remains of the army," Napoleon told Davout. He had sworn that he would never return to Germany by the "desert we ourselves created." Finally, he decided on the Smolensk road.

Rickettsia had again deprived him of live options. Had the Grande Armée finished off the Russians at Borodino, they could have retreated at their leisure down the Kaluga road and eaten their fill. Or, had Napoleon not lost thousands more since Borodino, he might have considered his army strong enough to break through the Russian lines. But those possibilities had vanished. Now his men would have to traverse a moonscape.

The French turned their heel on the Russian army and headed directly north, toward Borowsk and then Mozhaisk, where they would swerve west and head toward Smolensk (two hundred miles away) and finally Vilna, both of which cities were supposed to hold enormous depots of food and ammunition, as well as structures that could shelter the army from the winter, which wouldn't stay over the horizon forever. After that, there was the Niemen River, the fateful border, and then Germany and France. It was an incredibly conservative decision for the emperor, one that showed how dispirited the offensive genius had become. Both commanders flinched from another engagement, but it was Napoleon who would pay dearly for his decision to preserve the remaining troops. The Grande Armée was the emperor's personal guaranty of power, and he wanted to save as many men as possible. He ordered Poniatowski to abandon the Medyn route and head for Smolensk by the burned-over road, and Ney and Prince Eugène followed suit.

The imperial party made it to the outskirts of Mozhaisk on October 28, and here Napoleon was confronted with the sight of the wounded left after Borodino and fresh numbers of sick arriving from Moscow. He refused to leave them behind and ordered they be placed "wherever they could hang on": on top of wagons, inside the carts sent out on foraging missions, on commandeered droshkies. But the sick men weighed down already overburdened vehicles and slowed their journeys over the rutted roads. "We were going back to the deserted and devastated road by which we had come full of illusion of enthusiasm," wrote one Frenchman. Drivers were pushing their horses fifteen hours a day and to lighten the load did everything to knock the patients off their wagons. Caulaincourt estimated that of the hundreds loaded onto vehicles, only 20 made it to Vilna in Lithuania. No one wanted to be left behind; for many of the sick, it wasn't if they were going to die, but how. And being taken by Cossacks or peasants was the worst imaginable fate.

Captured soldiers were now being routinely executed by the Russians, with General Aleksey Yermolov enforcing a particular personal hatred against the Polish troops. At Viazma, 50 French troops were burned alive "by a savage order." The choice of the Smolensk road also meant that the army was retracing its steps through hamlets and villages that it had raped, pillaged, and terrorized its way through on the way forward. Any trace of sympathy for Napoleon as a potential liberator was gone. Many areas now boasted peasant militias. If the battles between Kutuzov and Napoleon still retained shreds of the knightly code in treatment of the wounded and respect for bravery, the mini–guerrilla war that the Grande Armée now experienced was without rules, red in tooth and claw.

The Russian peasants actually paid the Cossacks to get their hands on French soldiers (2 francs a head was considered a fair price) and made the prisoners the center of a grotesque revenge. There were several popular methods for brutalizing the prisoners. Men were hoisted on pulleys with their hands and feet tied together. After the soldier was suspended high in the air, the rope was let go and the prisoner smashed to the ground, snapping bones and causing grave injuries to the internal organs. The soldier would be hoisted and dropped repeatedly until he became a jellied bag of bone and viscera.

Other captives were marched naked through nights of −4 degree weather. They were burned alive and their skulls caved in with rifle butts. They were thrown into mass graves while still alive and then buried by peasants. (Sir Robert Wilson saw a drummer boy exempted from such a fate jump into the pit to die with his comrades.) The sack method was also popular: Prisoners were wrapped in sacks dipped in water, with a pillow underneath to partially shield the man's organs, prolonging his agony. The townspeople would be handed hammers and rocks and invited to bash at the man's midsection, until he died of internal bleeding. But perhaps the most bestial "game" had naked French soldiers spread-eagled and tied across huge logs, their heads extended over the edge. The serfs would dance and sing, and when they passed the captive they would smash his bowed head with cudgels until the skull broke open. Denis Davidov, the legendary partisan fighter, recalled what happened when he captured some elite French troops. Another leader named Figner arrived on the scene and begged Davidov to allow some new Cossack recruits to kill the prisoners, so that they would be "blooded." An appalled Davidov refused.

One of the few instances of mercy came when the Cossacks captured an officer of the Imperial Guard. They immediately stripped him of his fur coat and were about to take his uniform as well when, "to his boundless astonishment," they stopped, staring at one of the medals pinned to his jacket. Others were summoned, and seeing his awards nodded in confirmation. The Cossacks satisfied themselves with a little money and a few pages from his diary and then let him go. They had mistaken the Hessian Order of Merit for the Tsar's Order of Vladimir, a highly prized award created by Catherine II in 1782, which featured identically colored ribbons. A bit of silk had saved the man's life. Even Napoleon feared capture by the peasants.

After a close encounter with Cossacks near Maloyaroslavets, he carried a small bag of poison around his neck.

The nights were growing frigid, and men slept around roaring campfires, those farthest from the flames waking with hoarfrost coating their capes and mustaches. Mozhaisk is generally regarded as the turning point, where suffering overwhelmed all human and regimental bonds. The soldiers now barely resembled human beings. Captain Charles François painted a portrait of his mates: "Our heads were hideous, our faces yellow and smoke-begrimed, filthy with the soil of our bivouacs, blackened by the greasy smoke from conifers; eyes hollow, our beards covered with snot and ice." The sound of corpses being "ground to pieces under the horses' feet" became the routine music of the retreat, as did the voices of

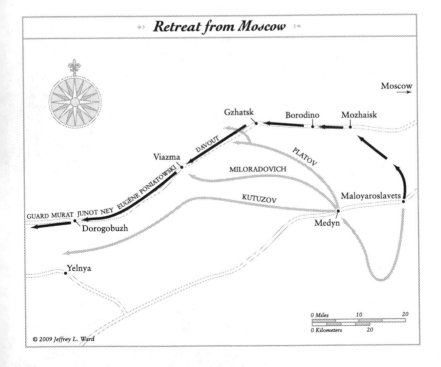

Retreat from Moscow

© 2009 Jeffrey L. Ward

the unfortunate. "On all sides we heard the cries and groans of those who'd fallen and were struggling in the most terrifying death-throes," wrote one soldier, "dying a thousand times while waiting to die."

The Imperial Guard's Sergeant Bourgogne came across a family led by a grizzled soldier and his wife who had lost everything, including two of their children. The wife was sitting in the snow with her dying husband's head resting in her lap. "She didn't cry, her grief was beyond that," he recorded and then passed on. As the mercury plunged even further, to 30 below, in addition to the almost benign sight of typhus victims lying by the road were added more hideous ones: Naked men gathered around a burning hut, the flesh on their backs roasted when they attempted to warm them; men feasted on strips of meat cut from the body of a dead comrade they had cooked over a fire. A newborn child was ripped from her mother's hands and thrown into the snow. Men staggered into campfires, thinking they would get warm, and were immolated.

On October 29, Napoleon arrived in the town of Gzhatsk, the roads leading to it littered with dead Russian prisoners. These men had been taken by the Grande Armée at Borodino and Moscow and either used to pull wagons or carry enormous packs, or simply treated as traditional POWs. The alternative was letting the captives starve to death. If they had been set free, they would have become spies reporting how desperate, ill-nourished, and ripe for attack the French forces were.

The Grande Armée was strung out along the Smolensk road, with Napoleon traveling quickly at the head of the retreat, followed by the Imperial Guard, Junot's VIII Corps, III Corps, and Prince Eugène and his IV Corps, with Davout and I Corps bringing up the rear. The route was icy and filled with hollows that the horses slid down and then were unable to climb out of, finally sinking dejectedly into the cold mud at the bottom. This was the signal for the soldiers following the convoy to fall on the animals and slash them with their knives and bayonets, tearing off chunks of flesh to be roasted over open fires. Napoleon, who had begun his career as an artillery officer, insisted that the remaining guns not be abandoned, even though dragging them through pits of mud and up and down icy hills slowed the retreat. He maintained the illusion that he was leading a conquering army instead of a desperate rabble, and so the gunners would find other horses, sometimes unhitched from the officers' own wagons, and fasten them to the heavy guns. Troops harnessed themselves to the iron pieces and pulled alongside the horses, even as the Cossacks— their cannon loaded onto sleds—lobbed shot onto the roadway.

On October 28, elements from the vanguard had marched past Borodino, where thousands of rotting bodies were still strewn across the field of battle. The Polish officer Heinrich von Brandt noted not only "this cursed place, still covered in corpses" but the mass graves that looked like "an immense flock of giant sheep." Lieutenant Mailly-Nesle of the 2nd Carabiniers, who was traveling with the imperial staff, passed close enough to see the faces of the cadavers, remarkably preserved. "Almost all had their eyes fixedly open," he remembered. "Their beards had grown out of all measure for this epoch. And a bricklike and Prussian-blue color, marbling their cheeks, gave them an abominably filthy and messy aspect." The wounded from the Battle of Borodino who had been installed at the abbey of Kolotskoe "let out lugubrious and heartbreaking screams" or threw themselves at the wheels of the caravans as their comrades passed them by.

There was a spectrum of illnesses and chronic maladies now competing on the return march: acute rheumatism, "lung catarrh" and tuberculosis, enteritis, pneumonia, and even scurvy. Snow blindness caused the men's eyes to bleed and often led to their wandering off the road. But typhus remained the dominant killer.

The diary of the Belgian surgeon de Kerckhove reads like a report from a plague year. "Typhus strongly advancing. We left behind a huge crowd of sick and dying men. . . . Typhus and dysentery making the most murderous ravages. . . . Ney had with him . . . seventeen thousand sick, wounded, and lonely men." In the frigid weather, he noticed a new development. Typhus victims who were exposed to very cold temperatures looked fully recovered. All the symptoms seemed to retreat except for dryness of tongue and the zombie-like stupor that marked so many cases. It was only when the sufferer found shelter and a warm fire that "fever appeared violently, along with all the symptoms of the disease." The men would topple over and die.

Intriguingly, there is strong evidence that the common soldiers suffered a worse fate than officers: many of Napoleon's top generals and majors escaped the epidemic, and there are anecdotal accounts of officers surviving while their men perished from disease. There are several reasons why this might have been true: The officers had better access to food, lodging, and medical services, which helped them remain healthy. And officers often traveled and slept separately from their men: they had their own carriages and their own tents during bivouacs, meaning that infected lice had far fewer opportunities to find their way into their clothing.

ON OCTOBER 31, AS HE reached Viazma, Napoleon was greeted with more bad news. To the north, battles had been ongoing between his Bavarian VI Corps and Russian forces under General Wittgenstein. The duel had spun off into a small, almost separate war. Now the Bavarians had been whittled down by hunger and disease to just 5,000 soldiers and along with II Corps had been pushed out of the city by Wittgenstein in a ferocious battle. The Russians had paid dearly for the victory—12,000 of their soldiers had been killed—while the French had lost only 6,000. But now Wittgenstein was free to descend from the north and cut off the retreat at any number of choke points.

Napoleon was quite literally losing the army itself. Headcounts were disastrously low. "You want to fight," Marshal Ney told him in exasperation, "yet you have no army!" Napoleon had 40,000 men left. He would pick up more from garrisons and detached forces as he headed west, but they couldn't come near to replacing the lost soldiers.

Smolensk, as Moscow had before it, now took on an oversize importance in the mind of Napoleon and his men. It was to be their salvation, and the sick and wounded, especially, made "superhuman efforts" to reach it. Napoleon abandoned the idea of a confrontation with Kutuzov and raced toward the city that would harbor the survivors of a rapidly unfolding debacle.

CHAPTER 15

Graveyard Trees

ON JULY 8, 1941, THE FOURTH PANZER ARMY OF THE THIRD Reich rolled into the town of Borisov, in what was then the Soviet Union. One of its commanders, General Gunther Blumentritt, found himself on the road to Moscow, without a Soviet soldier in sight to oppose his tanks. With some other staff officers, the general strolled down to the banks of the Berezina River and stared meditatively at the surging waters, remembering their history and what had happened here. One of his underlings pointed out something in the clear water, what appeared to be wooden struts sunk below the surface. They puzzled over what the structure could be, until it came to them that these were the remnants of bridges built by Napoleon's engineers a hundred and thirty years earlier.

A chill must have run down Blumentritt's back; he knew the story of Napoleon's campaign. He had been opposed to the invasion of the Soviet Union from the beginning and here was a reminder of a leader far more brilliant than Hitler who had poured out the lifeblood of his army on a nearly identical campaign. Armies had been marching back and forth across these lands for hundreds of years, leaving their detritus—bones, medals, buttons—in layers of soil beneath Blumentritt's feet.

The path seemed almost fated to destroy armies. One reason was *Rickettsia*. The other was winter.

THE BUGBEAR OF the campaign's critics, the Russian winter, arrived in force on November 6. Soldiers noticing a change in the quality of light tilted their faces to the sky and found it changing from cerulean blue to menacing gray-black as a cold mist swept in from the marshes. The mist grew thicker and suddenly snowflakes were falling, at first lightly and then in driving sheets. The carts bogged down in the wet snow and the landscape changed, the hollows soon covered by deep drifts. Men wandered off the road and fell through the crisp white surface and were lost. The icy wind picked up and drove the snow horizontally, until the men had to turn and march backward, their thin uniforms freezing on their bodies from sweat and melted snow. Many of the soldiers were still dressed in light summer trousers, with no gloves to protect their hands and shoes that were falling apart.

Landscape became destiny. Writer after writer in their memoirs recalled the bleak, elemental scenery against which the disaster unfolded, as if designed for the purpose. The historian Ségur saw the snow as "an immense winding sheet" slowly enveloping the army, while Captain Eugène Labaume of IV Corps wrote that "the farther we advanced the more the earth seemed to be in mourning." Other soldiers used to the well-cultivated French countryside, where one always seemed to find evidence of humankind's hand or a tolerant nature, remarked on how the world itself seemed drained of color and life, a bled-out corpse. Snow covered the ground in drifts whose distance it was impossible to gauge, the line between earth and sky disappeared, the line of sight pierced only by black-trunked firs, which the men called "graveyard trees." The last touch was the swarms of crows circling overhead, swooping down to feast on fallen men, staining the snow with blood flecked from their beaks.

With the snows came the end of command structure for many of the men on the Smolensk road. Many never received an order after November 6; for all intents and purposes, they were no longer members of an army but individuals trying to return home on their own. Carbines lined the route, tossed away by soldiers who couldn't bother to carry them anymore. "A great number of sick or wounded or men too feeble to keep up with their units are just throwing away first their packs, then their muskets," reported Césare de Laugier, an adjutant major with IV Corps. Doctors were rarely sighted and food wagons and depots were raided by the troops in the advance guard, leaving nothing for the rest. Men shot and smothered each other for food, stole at will, and even impersonated Russians, calling out the Cossack war cry of "Hurrah!" to scare competitors away from homes that might contain a bit of grain or the promise of shelter for a night.

This became the iconic image of the 1812 campaign: ragged soldiers wandering through the snowy wastes of the Russian hinterland. But by the time winter arrived, Napoleon had lost 85 percent of his frontline soldiers. The snow would cover a multitude of sins and mistakes; it was a white mantle drawn over the final act of a tragedy. The retreat now had as much in common with disastrous expeditions such as Ernest Shackleton's Antarctic adventure as it did a military exploit. Ice, hypothermia, starvation, and disease stalked the men; at times, the enemy was an afterthought.

The other piece of bad news that arrived with the blast of arctic air was a bulletin from Paris. There had been a coup attempt led by a half-mad general and ex-governor of Rome named Claude de Malet. He and a coterie of republicans had attempted to seize control of the government in a coup that often resembled opéra bouffe. He had managed only to arrest two of Napoleon's ministers and the prefect of police before being himself clapped in chains, but the rumors of the emperor's death that were regularly sweeping through Paris and letters home from soldiers detailing the unfolding disaster had given the conspirators enough momentum to challenge Napoleon's rule.

The ditches beside the Smolensk road began to fill with the booty of Moscow. Men desperate to reduce the amount of calories they were burning tossed away the things that once were going to ensure a comfortable retirement. Along the road one saw silver candelabra, gold crucifixes, the *Complete Works of Voltaire* bound in Moroccan leather, wall hangings laced with silver thread, "cases filled with diamonds or rolls of ducats." Carts and droshkies stuffed to the roof with swag were abandoned or pushed off the road by military police to speed up the march. Lieutenant Nicolas-Louis Planat de la Faye recalled one sutler's wagon being overturned, out of which a beautiful set of books and a magnificent harp spilled out, "to a great burst of laughter from all present." The enormous harp had represented the lifestyle the men had expected to sink into once they reached home; now, tumbling into a snowbank, it was a token of present realities. An even more outrageous artifact was lost by Davout when his wagon was commandeered by a band of Cossacks. Tucked inside was a map of India, which had been a possible next stop after the conquest of Moscow.

The men were thin from hunger. They slept rough in the open air or built flimsy huts made of sticks and tree branches. They marched like automatons, the tips of their noses growing marble white with frostbite. "We resemble our lackeys," wrote the novelist Stendhal, an officer in the commissariat, who was still among the luckiest men on the retreat, having preserved his carriage. "We are far removed from Parisian elegance." And they had donned whatever relic of the Moscow bazaar they had left. Gaunt soldiers wore silk dresses over their uniforms; fur capes and throws; chartreuse, lilac, or white satin capes. "If the circumstances hadn't been so sad," wrote Louise Fusil, a famous French actress who had fled her

Moscow theater, laughter would have greeted the sight of an "old grenadier, with his mustache and bearskin, covered in a pink satin fur." Some wore remnants of carpets stolen from glossy Muscovite floors. Many of the greatcoats were singed by the campfires or sported black-edged holes where embers had fallen on sleeping soldiers and burned through.

Soldiers who had only weeks before been eating caviar and reclining on fur cloaks in Moscow were now turned into omnivores, "starving lunatics." Everything went into the cooking pot. One colonel had managed to corral eighty head of cattle and his regiment marched with them and butchered them as needed, but the vast majority of the troops were reduced to a meager diet consisting of anything that fell into their path: Russian dogs, the native white bears, cats, rock-hard cabbages and roots, leather dipped in water to soften it, even human flesh. The men ate their own fingers that had been amputated because of frostbite, and drank their own blood. Horse meat was the staple, and sometimes men who had no knives and whose hands had become frozen solid would kneel at the side of a fallen steed and tear at the flesh with their teeth "like famished wolves."

"I have never suffered so much," Dr. Larrey wrote his wife. "The campaigns in Egypt and Spain were nothing when compared to this one; and we are by no means at the end of our troubles." As he approached a small town late in November, the Russian partisan leader Denis Davidov saw "mountains of dead men and horses . . . piles of enemy soldiers, barely alive, lay in the snow or sought shelter in the carts." One could hear the impact as the runners of his sleigh snapped arm bones and crushed the skulls of the French lying in the road. Later, wagoners would stuff corpses into ruts and potholes in the road, paving the road with carcasses. The dead were used as tables, chairs, road-building material, and insulation. Doctors stuffed cadavers into cracks in hospital walls and across windows whose panes were broken, to keep out the wind.

The only things that seemed to thrive in the subfreezing temperatures were lice. As the temperatures plunged, the parasites burrowed closer to the skin, invading the armpits and the groin, and then emerging at night by the thousands. "As long as we were out in the cold and walking, nothing stirred," wrote one lieutenant, Karl von Suckow, "but in the evening, when we huddled round the campfires life would return to these insects which would then inflict intolerable tortures on us." The body louse was demonstrating what a brilliant choice *Rickettsia* had made in selecting it as a vector. It was able to thrive when even the famously hardy black rat would have perished.

After a soldier died, the parasite had three and a half days (the longest a louse can survive without feeding) to find another host. The fact that fellow soldiers and Cossacks stripped dead men for their clothes, providing a fresh meal for the louse, meant that it was one of the creatures on the retreat best equipped to survive the intense cold.

REMARKABLY, FEW OF THE soldiers cursed Napoleon for the situation they now found themselves in. Cries of "Vive l'Empereur!" were now rarely heard, but the luster earned at Austerlitz still held. "No one among us dreamed of reproaching him for our setbacks," wrote Captain François Dumonceau of the 2nd Guard Lancers, "and in our eyes he still retained the prestige of a supreme arbiter."

One can only marvel at the generosity of the soldiers. It wasn't so much the hazy political motives behind the Russian invasion or the dead left scattered all over the line of march that gives rise to a suspicion that Napoleon had broken faith with his troops. Members of the Grande Armée weren't primarily concerned with whether wars were just or unjust, whether the empire was truly threatened by Alexander or not. They didn't evaluate the worth of their sacrifice by the political goals of the campaign. It was in the fighting itself, in the personal camaraderie and the opportunity to perform heroically that they sought meaning and even joy, and in this arena Napoleon had always been exemplary: He maneuvered his soldiers brilliantly for victory, rewarded valor with immediate promotions, and fought close to his men, consumed by the intricacies of the battle, his body and spirit given over to the engagement. His men were content, even proud, to starve and suffer and march hundreds of miles over impossible terrain to die in legendary battles for a man like that. But in Russia, he had been intellectually lazy, negligent in the basic things that allowed the men to get to the battlefield for their chance at honor, and instead had allowed them to die ingloriously of cold, want, and *Rickettsia,* the afflictions of criminals. And yet most of the men never abandoned their idea of him as a great commander.

On November 9, Napoleon entered Smolensk, now covered in layers of snow. He had expected his commissariat to have assembled enough supplies here to last for months, giving him the option of wintering in the city while receiving reinforcements from Paris and his allies. But he found that the enormous stores that had been stockpiled in the city had been eaten away by the stragglers left behind on the advance, by the 15,000 sick and wounded who had been installed in the city's bursting hospitals, and by reinforcements on their way to Moscow. Cattle had died on the way, caravans had been intercepted, and the surrounding countryside hadn't yielded nearly as much wheat and beef as Napoleon had estimated it would. In short, there were enough supplies at Smolensk for a brief break in the march, but nowhere near enough to sustain an army for an entire season.

More bad news arrived at a dizzying pace: An infantry brigade filled with new reinforcements from France had been intercepted on the Medyn road and forced to surrender. Vitebsk, where another massive supply of food had been directed, had fallen to the

Russians. When Berthier, Napoleon's chief of staff, heard the news, he muttered over and over again, "Not possible, not possible."

The emperor's reaction was considerably more pointed. He burst out in a tirade against his commanders, especially Davout and Marshal Claude Victor, who had been stationed with his IX Corps in Smolensk as an emergency reserve force: "See how they sacrifice the safety of my armies to themselves! All of them, do you see? Davout's half-mad and of no further use. Victor comes to Smolensk to destroy to no purpose the stores prepared here. . . . No, no, there isn't one of them one can entrust with anything. . . . If I dared to, I'd have them all shot."

The soldiers' hopes of an end to their suffering had been dashed and disappointment quickly turned to rage. Troops turned bandit and forced commissary officials to hand over food at gunpoint. Units squabbled over sides of beef and bags of flour and stragglers banded together to rob fellow soldiers of supplies. General Rossetti noted in his diary: "This city where we thought to find the end of our sorrows cruelly deceived our most dear expectations, and became, on the contrary, the witness to all our disgrace and despondency."

Typhus and dysentery victims had willed themselves to the city, freezing on top of open wagons or hobbling through miles of mud for a chance at a bed and a doctor. But they were turned away. "The hospitals, the churches, and other buildings couldn't hold the sick who showed up in the thousands," wrote Rossetti. "These unfortunate ones, exposed to the rigor of a freezing night, remained on carts, in caissons, or died looking in vain for refuge." Corpses piled up in the streets. Disease was spreading even more quickly now that troops were pouring into the city. Lamurzier reported that patients suffering from exhaustion were "stuck together with contagious patients," and some were even lying among the dead bodies. Infected lice would have been pouring off those bodies in the thousands, looking for new homes. "A horrible, death-dealing stench . . . was poisoning the air," wrote a French commissary. "The dead were killing the living."

If Mozhaisk was the generally acknowledged beginning of the intense suffering experienced on the march, Smolensk was the gateway to disorder and a rising panic. The Imperial Guard grabbed much of the remaining supplies for themselves, increasing the bitterness of the regular troops. As more and more regiments poured into the outskirts of Smolensk and set up camp around the burned-over city, temperatures plunged to −10 and lower. Men sold their last remaining pieces of loot from Moscow in a thronging bazaar that sprang up, bartering necklaces and bracelets studded with gems for bread or a small cut of meat. Those without anything to trade broke into food depots, which had to be guarded around the clock.

Napoleon spent five days in Smolensk, a delay that was more a function of his continuing indecision than an effort to allow his men to find what sustenance and rest they could. He was still thinking of finding a secure place to winter and assemble his forces for a spring campaign. On November 14, the vanguard marched out toward Borisov. Marshal Ney had now taken up the rearguard position, just behind Davout and Prince Eugène. But the road was clogged with the flotsam of Napoleon's mammoth army: he had brought so many troops to Russia that he now had to drive through the sickened remainder. The bedraggled mix of unit-assigned soldiers, stragglers, troops-turned-bandits, riffraff from Moscow, hangers-on, wives, girlfriends, streetwalkers, French refugees, and servants began the next leg of their journey without a beacon like the promise of Smolensk.

One well-born French soldier from Breton dying of "fever," most likely typhus, begged his mate to carry a note back to his family in France. It was an elegy reduced to the barest details.

Farewell, good mother,
My friend;
Farewell, my dear,
My good Sophie!
Farewell Nantes, where I was born;
Farewell, beautiful France, my fatherland;
Farewell, dear mother:
I am going to die—
Farewell!

The ranks grew thinner every morning. On November 12, the Hessian memoirist Captain Roeder took a count of his company (which had marched into Russia with 442 men and 26 officers) and recorded the results: "Missing: 1 drummer, 2 schutzen [infantrymen], 43 guardsmen. Absent sick: 31 guardsmen, 1 sergeant, 2 bandsmen. Present sick: 10 guardsmen, 2 sergeants. To march out: 8 sergeants, 1 drummer, 7 schutzen, 42 guardsmen." The final numbers included men who had fallen in with his company from other units; of his original contingent of 468 men, only 34 troops were left.

On November 15, as he led the vanguard to the next major town on the Smolensk road, Krasny, Napoleon and the Guard had to batter their way through Russian forces, who had cut the route ahead of him. The Guard were now like a bullet shot into water: the Russians would give way to the irresistible momentum of a superior fighting force, but once the corps was through, the surrounding forces would immediately close up behind them as if nothing had happened.

Prince Eugène was caught in one such attack: the Russians cut off his units from the main line of troops. Facing certain extermination, he followed the advice of a Polish colonel and, starting at ten o'clock at night, led his men off the road and through the nearby woods to circle around the enemy. Marching through deep snow in silence interrupted by the muffled exclamations of men tumbling into hidden ravines and the metallic *snick* of gunmetal scraping across belt buckles, the survivors expected at any moment to be ambushed. When a Russian scout challenged the half-visible unit that loomed toward him in the blackness, the Polish colonel barked, "Shut up, you fool. Can't you see we're Ouvarov's corps and that we're off on a secret expedition?" Miraculously, the ruse worked and the men made it to safety.

Only Ney, who had taken on the suicidal mission of guarding the extreme French rear, remained separated from the rest of the army. Eager to reach the supplies and protection of Orsha, seventy-five miles away, Napoleon marched on, leaving Ney and the rear guard to fend for themselves. Ney was apoplectic when he realized that he had been abandoned, left with 6,000 men and six cannon to face 80,000 Russian infantry and a robust artillery. Ordered to surrender, Ney drove his men at the center of the Russian formation, with artillery shells tearing through the ranks. "At each step, death was becoming more inevitable," wrote Colonel Fezensac, who was leading the 4th Line into battle. "Yet our march wasn't slowed down for a single instant." Entire divisions such as the 2nd disappeared as the Russians raked the charging men with canister and grapeshot.

As night fell, Ney was in danger of being wiped out the following day. The road to France was blocked by a force he couldn't hope to outfight. Napoleon, days ahead in Orsha on the Dnieper River, waited for news of his rear guard, sending messenger after messenger inquiring about the marshal and telling his advisers that he would give the 300 million francs in his treasury to have Ney with him again. For four days there was no word. The men of the Grande Armée, which had found enough food and shelter in the river town to stave off hunger, now brooded on the fate of III Corps. "The wreck of the army . . . ," Ségur wrote, "shared Napoleon's grief."

Like Prince Eugène, Ney had decided to use the darkness in a last-gasp effort to escape almost certain annihilation. The marshal aimed for the Dnieper River, taking a substantial risk that his men would be able to find the right road in the darkness and that, once arrived at the riverbank, they'd find the water frozen and fordable. Marching out as dusk was falling and temperatures plunged, Ney luckily happened on a lame peasant who directed the French to a riverside town. Camped out in the frigid cold, they could hear the river ice creak and snap. In the morning, there was a rush for the other bank. Scrambling down the icy incline, the men searched in the diffuse morning light for routes where the ice seemed thick enough to support them. Horses and their riders plunged into the icy water and were never seen again. Others who had broken through the ice cried out to their comrades. "Their complaints tore at our hearts, already overwhelmed by our own perils," remembered General Jean-David Freytag. Water splashed on the men immediately began to freeze, and when they reached the opposite bank, the soldiers found it was twelve feet high and coated with ice. Many tried to make the climb but, exhausted, slipped down to the foot of the slope and waited for death.

The next day and night the French troops who survived the crossing picked their way across the Russian countryside and endured terrifying raids by Cossacks and barrages of grapeshot from pursuing Russian units. The ranks were winnowed down and the Russians who swept past their flanks called out for them to surrender. The column was twice surrounded by Russians, but Ney marched them out through gaps in the line before the enemy had a chance to fall on them. Trapped at one point with their backs to a thickly wooded forest, low on cartridges, the French saw a messenger advancing under a white flag. The envoy brought a message, saying the French were surrounded by 100,000 men and faced only death. To the request to lay down their arms, Ney replied, "Go and tell your general a Marshal of France never surrenders." The men had not eaten for days, their boots were waterlogged, and they were racked by illness, but Ney got them through the Russian lines by sheer force of will.

Finally, on November 20, they reached Orsha, completing one of the most intrepid marches in military history, a feat achievable only through Ney's indefatigable leadership. Prince Eugène rushed to Ney and threw his arms around the marshal, while his soldiers broke ranks and rushed to embrace the spectral men. "In this moment we forgot past ills, men's egoism, the cruelty of fate and future perils," wrote Césare de Laugier, the adjutant major in IV Corps. Napoleon's regiments were thrilled with the news, "drunk with delight," as the diplomat Caulaincourt wrote, and the emperor himself was visibly moved by Ney's feat.

But the relief was only momentary. Even Napoleon now saw clearly the suffering of his men. "The misery of my poor soldiers breaks my heart!" he said at Orsha. "But where can we rest, without ammunition, food, or artillery? I am not strong enough to stay here."

SERGEANT BOURGOGNE OF Napoleon's elite Guards was one of those poor soldiers who had fallen ill. On arriving at the Berezina, approximately sixty miles west of Orsha, he collapsed on the riverbank and found that he was feverish. His body shook and his mind began to travel far from the grim scene around him. "I was delirious for a long time," he remembered. "I fancied I was at my father's house, eating potatoes, bread and *butter à la flamande,* and drinking beer." Near to the campfire was another soldier who had put on his full dress uniform as if he were going on parade. Bourgogne asked him what he was doing, but the man laughed and said nothing. "That laugh was the laugh of death, as he succumbed during the night."

Bourgogne was now traveling with two regiments, down from a force fifteen times that size only two weeks before. To their ailments was now added snow blindness and eye problems caused by men sitting too close to smoky fires for hours on end. The sightless men had companions guiding them along the road, or if they had no friends to be their eyes, they were left to blunder off into the drifts.

Dr. Larrey, now stumbling along on foot with the rest of the troops, still had no real idea of what was killing them. His latest theory was ice water: "The snow and icy water that the soldiers swallowed, hoping thereby to allay their hunger, or to quench their thirst," he wrote, "produced by irritation of the mucous membrane of the stomach, largely contributed to the death of these individuals, since the little heat left in the viscera was absorbed." It was certainly possible to lower one's core temperature by gulping large amounts of frigid water, but that can hardly account for the mass dying-off that had occurred in the ranks. The doctor did offer up some contrarian sociophysiological thoughts on who lived and who died: "I noticed that people with dark hair and an emotional, labile temperament, mostly from the countries of southern Europe, stood up better to the severe cold than did fair-haired men of phlegmatic temperament and coming for the most part from northern countries," he wrote. "The circulation of the first group is no doubt more active; their vital forces have more energy; it is likely, too, that, even in conditions of extreme cold, their blood retains much better the principles of animal warmth identified with their pigmentation." The Mediterranean temperament also allowed the men to remain more cheerful than their dark-browed brothers from the north, according to the doctor's observations. But if there were significant differences between the survival rates of different racial groups, it's more likely it had to do with the preparation and resourcefulness of their officers, the thickness of their coats, and the fitness of the soldiers.

Heinrich von Brandt and his Polish regiment, which would be reduced from 2,000 to just 60 after the retreat, reached the city of

Borisov on the banks of the Berezina River on November 15, ahead of Napoleon and the Imperial Guard. They were marooned there for five days as they waited for the word to advance. Rumors flew that the Russians controlled the other bank of the river. The town was filled with refugees, terrified civilians, troops that had become separated from their units or whose units had ceased to exist, and "a clutter of scoundrels who filled the cafés and bars and did nothing but drink and play at cards." There was no rule of law, no command structure, and the town had degenerated into the kind of frontier anarchy in which von Brandt and his companions occasionally had to draw their weapons in order to survive. Von Brandt and his troops fled the town before the French expatriate general Count Charles de Lambert and the Russians took it on November 20, and they found themselves in Bobr, which was filled with deserters and stragglers, "marauders of the most dangerous kind." The Grande Armée, he concluded, "to all intents and purposes, no longer existed."

As he approached Borisov, unaware that it had been taken by the Russians, Napoleon turned his thoughts toward the Berezina. It was the last river to ford, and one of the last choke points, before reaching Vilna and then, seventy-five miles on, the Niemen, where all his troubles had begun. When he studied the maps, a familiar name jarred his memory: Poltava, where the Swedish army had been massacred in 1709. "Ah yes!" he cried. "Poltava! . . . Like Charles XII!" It was black humor, but he had read Voltaire's account of the Swede's disaster intently and knew how close he was to sharing that fate.

The various Russian armies—the headstrong Admiral Pavel Chichagov in the southwest, Wittgenstein in the north, and remains of the First and Second armies along with the Cossacks tailing Napoleon—were all poised to converge at Borisov. The depots at Minsk had already fallen to Chichagov's 60,000 men. All signs

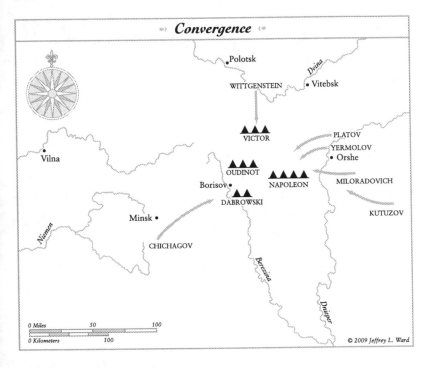

Convergence

Polotsk

Dvina

WITTGENSTEIN   • Vitebsk

Vilna

VICTOR

PLATOV
YERMOLOV
• Orshe

OUDINOT   NAPOLEON   MILORADOVICH

Borisov •

DABROWSKI   KUTUZOV

Minsk •

Niemen

CHICHAGOV

Berezina

Dnieper

0 Miles   50   100
0 Kilometers   100

© 2009 Jeffrey L. Ward

pointed toward a Russian pincer movement at the river, where Kutuzov would spring his long-delayed trap and annihilate the French army before it could escape to Lithuania and the Niemen.

"Kutuzov is leaving me alone now in order to head me off and attack me," Napoleon said. "We must hurry." He knew there was only a single bridge at Borisov, guarded by a single Polish division. If the Grande Armée didn't reach it in time, they could find their way blocked and their escape thwarted. In one of the statements that give the measure of Napoleon's sangfroid, he remarked, "This is beginning to be very serious." It had, of course, been serious for many weeks, but Kutuzov's incompetence as a strategist and as a fighter gave the emperor some hope of outmaneuvering the Russians. Still, the numbers and the terrain were wholly in favor of the enemy.

Napoleon didn't realize he'd been beaten to the choke point by Lambert's men. The Russians, believing their lines secure, then found shelter and relaxed their guard. Unknown to them, French troops were streaming toward the city, and when they arrived they found the Russians unprepared for an attack. The fighting was savage but one-sided: the Russians lost 9,000 men and in their negligence would have handed Napoleon a golden opportunity to slip over the Berezina unmolested had they not torched the single bridge as they fled to the western bank. The river, packed with mushy, unstable ice, was effectively unfordable. New bridges would have to be built under the guns of the Russians and the old one quickly repaired.

On November 23, the French command received the news while they were just under forty miles from the Berezina. Napoleon briefly considered a thrust northward to surprise Wittgenstein's army and then a turn west. But the roads were unfamiliar, the terrain was marshy and rough, and his troops were in no condition for the maneuver. Instead he decided to race to Borisov and attempt to rebuild the destroyed span, throw some pontoon bridges across the river, and get away before Kutuzov could smash his forces against the icy water. "The names 'Chichagov' and 'Berezina' passed from mouth to mouth," remembered Captain Johann von Borcke. The lead elements of the French forces arrived in Borisov on November 23, with Napoleon a day behind. The engineers tasked with building pontoons for the thousands of troops rushing up behind them gaped at the currents sweeping great tumbling chunks of ice downstream.

But French cavalry units had stumbled on a point in the river seven miles upstream that the army might be able to ford en masse. Their general lobbied Napoleon to change course and head for the crossing point. If the army could ford the Berezina there, Napoleon might be able to squeeze his armies between Chichagov in the south and Wittgenstein in the north instead of fighting his way through.

Bad information and the lack of coordination among the Russian commanders allowed the French this small window of opportunity. As Napoleon made his move northward, Chichagov was receiving contrary reports about the French intentions. His scouts reported sighting enemy units below Borisov, and bulletins from both Kutuzov and Wittgenstein warning him of a possible attack on his southern flank, combined with eyewitness reports from villagers of Frenchmen gathering logs and other bridge-building materials in the area, confirmed the impression that Napoleon intended to ford the river *below* the town. He stationed 1,500 of his men in Borisov, then led the rest of his troops out of the town and turned due south. The log gatherers were actually cuirassiers sent on a jaunt to trick Chichagov. The ruse worked.

What should have been a classic pincer movement became a trap clattering open, at least momentarily. But it would still be a perilous escape. Knowing this, Napoleon burned the reports from Paris that had reached him on the retreat and created a new personal security detail, the "sacred squadron," made up of 500 commissioned soldiers, to protect him from the very real possibility of becoming a prisoner of state.

The French troops hurried north and managed to get 750 sappers to the crossing point on November 24 to begin the construction of two bridges, one for the cavalry, wagons, and artillery and the other for the infantry. With them they had six wagons packed with essential materials that were almost abandoned earlier in the retreat: hammers, crowbars, and iron sheets, along with four wagons packed with coal and portable forges to make the nails and cross braces. Wood came from the huts and stables in the village, which were torn apart to provide planks; steel rims from the abandoned wagons were turned into clamps and spikes. Carrying them over their heads, the pontoneers walked out into the dangerously cold river, about a hundred feet wide and six feet deep at this point, their boots slipping over the smooth rocks on the river bottom. Fifteen minutes was all that any soldier could stand in the currents, and many succumbed to hypothermia or stumbled and were carried away by the river. The Dutch soldiers worked knowing that on the elevations across the river, Cossack pickets were patrolling the far banks, and their bobbing heads were easily within Russian cannon range.

The Cossacks spotted the pontoneers at their work, setting trestles in water up to their chins, and sent riders to Chichagov with reports of the suspicious activity. If the messengers returned with Chichagov's main force, using the heights of the opposite bank to sweep the river with canister and musket fire, the Grande Armée would have been lost. But Chichagov, notorious for refusing to admit his mistakes, took the activity for a feint and stayed where he was, prowling the banks south of Borisov for a sign of Napoleon.

The emperor remained calm as the work progressed. Marshal Ney remarked that if Napoleon got the army out of this fix, he would never doubt the emperor's luck again. But Murat, more high-strung than his colleague, bent under the strain, bursting in on Napoleon as he worked in a house on the riverbank. "I consider it impossible to cross here," he burst out. "You must save yourself while there is still time!" The emperor brushed the suggestion aside as beneath him. He was eager to reach Paris, but abandoning the army at a choke point while the enemy lurked all around would have been a black mark on his name.

At dawn on November 26, the French watched the opposite bank, half expecting to see Chichagov's ranks serried back from the water's edge. Surely the incessant pounding of the sappers' hammers and the shouts of the engineers had brought the main body of the general's forces to the crossing point. But the light revealed only abandoned campfires and a black line of troops curling into the tree line on the road south to Borisov. "It isn't possible!" Napoleon cried in astonishment. But it was. Chichagov had abandoned the position. The emperor sent 100 chasseurs and Polish lancers to drive off

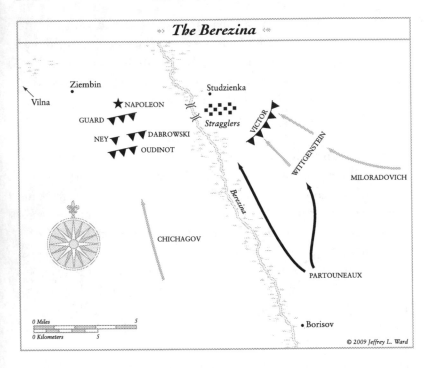

the handful of Cossacks left behind and later secured the bank with 400 troops ferried over on rafts.

By noon, the first bridge was finished. The second, intended for the cavalry and wagons, would take four more hours. Napoleon sent cavalry and infantry units across to cover the retreat's southern flank, in case Chichagov changed his mind and moved northward. The Guard followed soon after, followed by the "sacred squadron" with Napoleon in its midst, then Davout, Ney, Murat, and Eugène. The men hurried across the rickety bridge, whose planks rested just inches above the water, with the trestles that anchored the bridge sometimes sinking under the weight of the troops, dipping the planks into the frigid water. Horses had to cross at intervals, for fear that their cumulative weight would collapse the "matchbox" structure. From the woods, the thousands of stragglers watched for their chance to make it across, their numbers growing as the hours passed. The wheels of the carriages, artillery pieces, and officers' wagons rattled along the uneven roadway of the second bridge, scraping off the pine branches and horse dung that had been used as a surfacing material.

Trestles sank or tumbled over on both bridges, planks cracked, and sappers rushed back into the water to improvise a fix and keep the soldiers moving, bashing the ice floes away with their axes. The anxious men fought over their place in line, shoving each other back from the first planks. As the day progressed, a north wind picked up and snow began to fall, at first gently, then in sheets. Napoleon, dressed in his campaign uniform with white breeches and a gray overcoat, his boots freshly shined, watched from the shore.

The bulk of the army had made it to the western bank by evening on November 27. Only a few units and Marshal Victor's brigades, who were arriving at the Berezina after battling Wittgenstein, remained. The military police who had guarded the entrance to the bridge and controlled the flow over it began letting the stragglers onto the structure, but they weren't rushing to cross, not yet. There was no sign of a Russian attack and it was safer to cross the bridges, which increasingly sagged and buckled as the crossing went on, during daylight.

On the morning of November 28, the window began to close. A contingent of 30,000 Russian soldiers, sent north by Chichagov, encountered French forces on the western bank of the Berezina. Shells splintered trees and musket fire clipped off pine branches as the Russians pressed to close off the escape route toward Vilna. Ney rushed some of his 13,000 men as reinforcements, but Chichagov, now fully convinced that Napoleon had duped him, was sending his entire army north and the volume of enemy fire directed toward the French seemed to increase by the half hour.

The Grande Armée, bone-thin and riddled with disease, turned to stop the attack. Cries of "Vive l'Empereur!" echoed through the forest as Polish, Swiss, Croat, Portuguese, and Dutch troops held off the numerically superior Russians. When the Swiss regiments ran out of ammunition, they leveled their bayonets and plunged through the knee-deep snow, scattering the Russian infantry as they went. One Swiss soldier, Louis de Bourmann, was advancing with his 2nd Regiment when an officer dismounted ahead of him to lead his men on foot. "A Russian musket ball went through his throat," recalled one of his men. "He gave a cry, stifled by blood, and fell backwards into my arms. . . . Without losing consciousness, he said these simple words to his fellow-citizen: 'Bourmann, I've died here as a Christian.' " The soldiers' efforts stood out on one of the Grande Armée's finest days. The Swiss charged the Russians seven times with only bayonets to defend themselves. The mysterious bond that held Napoleon's army together despite every incentive to disintegrate held fast.

At the same time, Wittgenstein was descending on Victor's men on the eastern bank, the long-awaited pincer finally closing on the French. Wittgenstein had already rolled up one of the brigades that had held Borisov until November 27, then blundered north into the Russian lines. Now he concentrated an artillery barrage against the 8,000 remaining troops and the mini-city of stragglers and human flotsam that huddled amidst the gray smoke of the campfires. Rumors had been circulating since three in the morning that an attack on the rear guard was imminent, and the entrance to the first bridge had become jammed with thousands of men, women, and children desperate to avoid being captured and being sent to camps in the frozen North.

The bombardment only increased the frenzy. The mass of people rippled and surged, throwing men into the icy river and packing the crowd so tightly that no one could move forward or back. One was simply carried along, feet never touching the bridge. Karl von Suckow of the Württemburg III Corps found himself "surrounded on all sides, caught in a veritable human vise. . . . Everyone was shouting, swearing, weeping, and trying to hit out at his neighbors." The road leading to the bridge became littered with corpses of men and horses, their flesh pulverized under the hordes pressing toward the river. All the while Russian round shot struck the crowd, leaving craters of mud and severed limbs. The stragglers rushed from one bridge to the other, battling crowds headed in the other direction.

Observers on the western bank could hear a constant bellowing, "like the distant roarings of a tempest at sea, cries, yells, wagons exploding, an undefinable uproar which filled us with terror." The Imperial Guard began directing cannonades at the Russian batteries, and finally Marshal Victor and his IX Corps mounted an attack that pushed the guns out of range. They managed to hold their ground as night fell and the Russian fire lessened. The lanes leading to the bridge were cluttered with piles of cadavers and dead horses; Victor and his men had to cut a route through them with their sabers while military police pushed back the despairing mobs of stragglers who had failed to cross during the day. By six o'clock that night all of his troops were across except for some mounted troops and 200 soldiers bringing up the rear.

Astonishingly, although the bridges were now open, some of the hangers-on elected to spend another night on the eastern bank, despite the entreaties of IX Corps' Marshal Victor and General Jean-Baptiste Eblé, who even went around the campfires warning the people that the bridge was about to be blown up to slow the Russian pursuit. The hopeless men and women simply looked at Eblé, past comprehension or caring. The general tramped back across the bridge and made ready the cache of combustibles that would destroy the crossing at seven a.m.

The next morning, Eblé waited on the western bank, watching the scene unfold across the river. After sleeping under the falling snow, the remaining soldiers had again rushed to the bridges' entrances and clogged them as the Russians closed in. Men slashed their way through the mob with bayonets, and the roar resumed. Finally, as the Russian gunners began to find the range of the rear guard waiting to blow the bridge, Eblé ordered the fuses lit, and planks shot into the air as the western reaches of the bridges exploded. One soldier, miles away from the Berezina, remembered hearing a collective scream from the doomed multitudes when they saw the explosives ignite.

The last of the stragglers were tipped into the water and froze to death or were killed by the Russian grapeshot that kicked up sprays of water. The blue-lipped bodies of women and children, some of them newborns, floated downstream, a sight remembered by many of the retreating soldiers, and clotted masses of bodies were grouped along each shore. The Cossacks arrived on the riverbank and began stripping the bodies of the dead and the living. Many of the sick and wounded who had somehow managed to survive the ghastly trip from Borodino or Moscow never made it over the bridge.

Crossing the Berezina cost the Grande Armée and its followers about 25,000 dead, while the Russians lost some 15,000. The Russians took entire regiments prisoner, with Wittgenstein's units capturing 13,000 men, leaving Napoleon with only about 40,000 men (his ranks having been swelled by garrisons, stragglers who had rejoined the march, and Victor's and Marshal Gouvion Saint-Cyr's men). Even with the scenes on the bridge that haunted many survivors' memories more than any other aspect of the retreat, it's still remembered as something of a miracle, a late, brilliant flashing-out of Napoleon's genius. His maneuvering was clever, but it was now his men that were the vessels of his reputation. Without being whipped to it, his soldiers fought for him with something more than the robotic stupor of half-dead men guarding the only route to survival; they performed with an esprit de corps that transcended nationality and the ridiculous piling-on of misfortune. But the fact that such a nightmare is counted as a victory of the campaign shows the perilous state that the Napoleonic enterprise had reached by November 29.

"THE ARMY IS LARGE, but in a state of terrible dissolution," the emperor wrote on November 29, emphasizing that the troops needed to find plentiful supplies in Vilna in order to have a chance. "Food, food, food! Without that there is no atrocity that this undisciplined mob will not visit upon the city." Napoleon was still considering some kind of garrison within Russian territory—Vilna was the last possibility—to be reinforced for a spring offensive. He was also beginning to think strategically about how to best present the disaster that had overcome his army to his allies and enemies in western Europe. He ordered all foreign diplomats out of Vilna, so they couldn't report on the state of his troops, and instructed his commander there to proceed as if the retreat was orderly and the Grande Armée in robust health. But the emperor knew that word of his defeat must be spreading through the capitals of Europe.

On December 3, he issued the 29th Bulletin, the first in almost three weeks. For the first time, he revealed the "frightful calamity" that had occurred, and blamed it mostly on weather and the lack of food. There were hints that the dead had been at fault for dying so easily. "Those men, whom nature had not sufficiently steeled to be above all the chances of fate and fortune, appeared shook, lost their gaiety—their good humor, and dreamed but of misfortunes and catastrophes; those whom she has created superior to everything, preserved their gaiety, and their ordinary manners, and saw fresh glory in the different difficulties to be surmounted." Napoleon famously ended the dispatch with the assurance that "His Majesty's health has never been better."

By December 5, Napoleon had decided to return to Paris. There he would raise a new army of 300,000 men and return to Russia to finish the war. The hardened survivors of 1812 would become the core of the offensive of 1813. He brought his marshals together and gave his final speech of the campaign, for the first time admitting his own culpability to his generals in apologizing (according to some present) for leaving Moscow too late. But he was still breathing the last fumes of his Russian dream, believing that the Polish population would rise up and attack the Cossacks besieging the garrison at Vilna, that the French army would triple in size once food and clothing was supplied to the survivors and reinforcements arrived, and that the Russians would find it hard to supply the forces around the city. He told the marshals that he felt he had stayed away from Paris as long as possible; if things turned for the worse, there could be another coup attempt or his fragile alliances with Austria and Prussia could collapse. Then as now, defeat in the military sphere meant a realignment of power elsewhere, especially in political relations with allies whose interests and ambitions ran counter to France's. Disguised to avoid capture, the emperor departed at ten that night, with his former Russian ambassador, Caulaincourt, in a carriage guarded by mounted Neapolitan and Polish soldiers.

THE ARMY FAILED to realize Napoleon's vision of a miraculously revived force. Some 20,000 more men died on the road to Vilna, and troops began burning entire houses on the route to stave off the cold, which reached its nadir at −36 degrees. The remainder of the troops, looking like survivors of some medieval famine, surged into the sophisticated city of shops and stylishly dressed merchants, which was quickly looted and trashed by the half-crazed throngs. The thirteen-year-old son of a French surgeon described it as "nothing but a vast hospital, with men arriving sick with typhus and dysentery." The floors of one hospital were covered with the feces of the soldiers, "dying there in great numbers."

Some 20,000 troops entered Vilna; only 10,000 marched out. One parish reportedly had 8,000 dead dumped in its churchyard, the vast mound hurriedly disguised with snow.

By the time they reached Kovno in central Lithuania, the disappearing army was down to 7,000. And when they crossed the Niemen back into Germany, with the indestructible Ney the last man over the bridge before it was burned, there were only a few thousand left of Napoleon's frontline troops (other reserve forces had crossed earlier), many of them infected with *Rickettsia*, journeying home as fatal messengers, only to infect the loved ones who had waited for them for so long.

Rendezvous in Germany

WORD OF THE FRENCH DEFEAT ELECTRIFIED EUROPE. When the diplomats and Polish officials and aristocrats who had been herded into Vilna saw the emperor's forces in person, the news could be held in no longer: Napoleon's army had mostly vanished. In Germany, students and ragamuffins paraded through the town streets chanting a ditty that mocked the once-fearsome Grande Armée:

> *Drummers without drumsticks*
> *Cuirassiers in female garb,*
> *Knights without a sword,*
> *Riders without a horse!*
> *Man, nag and wagon*
> *Thus has God struck them down!*

"It seems to me that the spell has been broken as far as Napoleon is concerned," wrote the Dowager Empress Maria Fyodorovna. "He is no longer an idol, but has descended to the rank of men, and as such he can be fought by men." The glamorous balls and state receptions that Napoleon initiated on his return to Paris couldn't muffle the rumblings of disaster that emanated even from within his own ministries.

The emperor tried to sweep the details under the rug, claiming that only 400,000 of his troops had crossed the Niemen and that only half of those were French, which allowed him to peg his own casualties at an absurdly low 50,000. It was a fantasy, and few believed it.

As the survivors marched west and south, they were "shunned like lepers," as word of the epidemic in their midst spread before them. Many of the troops were quarantined in the various towns they traveled through, and the locals often locked them in for the night so they couldn't spread the contagion. When the German infantryman and diarist Jakob Walter caught typhus along with his brothers-in-arms, the good people of a small settlement near Stuttgart, Germany, escorted them to the town hall, then bolted the door. When the lads escaped and made their way to a local inn, alarm bells rang and the citizens threatened to call the local militia to bring them back to their quarters at gunpoint.

The men, no matter their nationality, were called "Russians" and "Moscow bums." The diarist and Württemberg lieutenant H. A. Vossler remembered:

> Wherever we went we were gaped at like freaks, for we were among the few who had escaped the universal disaster. Everywhere we were made to give, over and over again, an account of our own adventures, of the plight of the army, and of the appalling hardships we had suffered. Yet such is human nature that there were always some who felt our tale was not harrowing enough and argued that we could not therefore have experienced the campaign and the retreat in its entirety.

Dr. Larrey, who had, in one of the heartening scenes at the Berezina, been passed by hand over the heads of his cheering troops to the western bank, finally noted in his memoirs that contagious disease had impacted the Grande Armée. "Epidemic maladies successively attacked a great part of those who had escaped the foregoing catastrophe," he wrote. Days later, he succumbed on the way back to Paris. "I had scarcely concluded my arrangements, when I was suddenly seized with symptoms of the catarrhal fever attendant on congelation, a species of typhus having the greatest analogy to hospital fevers. . . . This malady made rapid progress, and rendered in a very few days my situation extremely dangerous." He barely survived. For other soldiers who came down with the disease, he prescribed leeches, cupping, bleeding from the jugular vein, and "application of the skin of an animal flayed alive."

When he reached Leipzig, Larrey received a panicked letter from a commander from the Russian invasion who was alarmed at the rapid spread of typhus. His suggestions to combat the outbreak were rather shocking, as they came so late in the game. "My report . . . pointed out the hygienic measures to be adopted for impeding the development of this fever," he wrote, "for arresting its progress, and preventing its contagious influence."

Captain Roeder, the passionate widower whose diary mirrored the experience of so many men on the march, somehow survived the campaign. When he reached Vilna, he was astonished to still be alive. "It is morning and I have slept in a bed, completely undressed!" he wrote in his diary. "Great God! Is it possible I have survived all these hardships! . . . Father in Heaven, how I thank thee! Look, oh look in mercy on thy grateful son! Help me to reach the frontier. Let me see my own again!"

But typhus caught up with him and by February 6 he was writing his beloved Sophie a farewell note.

> I feel that I shall not be able to recover from this sickness and that I cannot live another week unless my feeble constitution can perform another miracle, and how can one

reckon upon that in a town where death is everywhere? So I must take leave of you, beloved Sophie; once I dreamed that I might have lived a few sweet years with you. But it is not God's will. My life is reaching the last link of a terrible chain of misery, and indeed I am infinitely weary of it.

He survived, somehow, but to reach Sophie he had to run a gauntlet of spies, corrupt officials, smugglers, and murderous criminals. A Jewish innkeeper smuggled him across the Russian border into Poland, and he found himself packed into a doss-house full of peasants, one of whom repeatedly pointed a loaded gun at him for amusement. Escaping to Prussia (now under the control of Sweden after Napoleon's defeat), he was thrown into prison as a spy and held for months.

Finally, in June, the captain was released and made his way back through a seething northern Germany that was now free of Napoleon's control and on the verge of an uprising. "Matters have almost reached the point where they were in France at the outbreak of the rebellion," he wrote nervously in the city of Bergen. On June 25, Roeder reached his home in Göttingen, one of a tiny number of survivors of what he now called "that accursed Russia." He gave his overjoyed children all that was left of the immense bounty taken from Moscow: a silver ruble and a single Swedish krona. To his wife, Sophie, he records at the end of the diary that "to her all I had to give was myself." He was an incomparably lucky man.

As Napoleon hurried back to Paris, one of the last enigmas of the 1812 campaign unfolded. Riding in sleighs and carriages with Caulaincourt, the emperor had fluctuated in mood from pensive to jovial throughout the journey, but the closer he got to Paris the more buoyant he became. As he left the town of Glogau in a freezing sleigh and traveled across northern Germany on the night of December 13, Napoleon began wondering what would happen if they were captured, and he remembered the fate of a predecessor whose dreams were canceled by typhus. "If we are stopped," he told Caulaincourt, "we shall be made prisoners of war, like Francis I." He and Caulaincourt checked their pistols and kept them close by. Despite the danger, Napoleon's mood soared: at times the walls of the sleigh echoed with the pair's uncontrollable laughter.

The episode of the sleigh ride is justifiably famous, used by many camps in the field of Napoleonic studies, either as a testament to the emperor's heartlessness or his mental instability, or as a leading example of Bonaparte as existentialist. Caulaincourt thought he was fully delusional at times. How could he be so giddy when his army lay shattered back in Vilna and his empire hung by a thread? But it's impossible to reduce those hours to a single set of causes; they display the astonishing range of Napoleon's character, his unparalleled response to life. One moment he was expressing deep bitterness at his betrayal by friends and allies, the next he was breathless with laughter at the thought of being displayed in a Prussian cage like a captured macaque. After months of being trapped in a traveling mausoleum, the emperor could feel life—a new army, fresh enemies, sex, Paris, challenges, and appetites— approaching with each freezing mile. Perhaps he was even thrilled at the thought that he was again the underdog, and would have to strain every fiber of his being to produce miracles with which to astonish the world. It's hard to escape the conclusion that he had been bored on the Russian campaign. What was said of Junot— that his eye "no longer lit up at the sight of a battlefield"—was also true for the emperor. But now, he had to remake his legend over again. To the forty-three-year-old Napoleon, it must have tasted something like youth.

· · ·

THE FINAL NUMBERS of the campaign of 1812: Between 550,000 and 600,000 members of the Grande Armée (including reinforcements) crossed the Niemen. About 100,000 were captured by the Russians, of whom only 20,000 eventually were repatriated to their home countries. The total number of dead among the Grande Armée can be conservatively put at 400,000 (although other estimates range as high as 540,000). Less than a quarter of them died as the result of enemy action. The rest of this magnificent force, the majority of Napoleon's effectives, died of disease, cold, hunger, and thirst. Individual regiments and corps saw the majority of their members dead or missing. Incredibly, the cosseted Imperial Guard emerged from Poland with only 1,500 of its original 47,000 members.

As author Adam Zamoyski has pointed out, the losses were made more painful by the small populations of European countries at the time. A figure of 300,000 French casualties would be the equivalent of 700,000 today. The Polish losses of 75,000 would translate to 750,000 in modern terms, and one can extrapolate such terrible numbers for most of the nations that took part. The Russians lost an equivalent number of soldiers, slightly more of them in battle, and the death of civilians by disease, famine, and violence easily lifts the number of dead for the 1812 campaign well over the 1 million mark.

The Grande Armée didn't keep precise statistics of the manners of death of its soldiers. It is impossible to pin down the number of typhus victims, but it's clear that disease was the lead killer on the campaign, and typhus the most lethal disease present. And typhus had not only killed men outright. By encouraging Alexander to avoid a treaty (as he felt the French army was dying on the march), by hamstringing Napoleon at Borodino and Maloyaroslavets, and by greatly weakening the survivors, it had initiated a series of calamities that killed more men on the retreat. *Rickettsia*, not Kutuzov and not "General Winter," had tripped the emperor's army into its Russian grave.

Napoleon still had resources and talents to draw on for the battle for his empire he now knew was coming. But the invasion of Russia had given *Rickettsia* its greatest spurt of life in a thousand years, a dark flower of death spread across Europe. It wouldn't release its hold on the continent, or the emperor, so easily.

THE DEBACLE IN RUSSIA acted as fresh oxygen on buried embers, especially in Germany, where militias sprang up and young Germans vowed to overthrow the French usurper. On March 13, 1813, the new alliance of Russia and Prussia declared war, and the losses in Russia echoed in France: many of Napoleon's best officers and veteran soldiers were dead, and their green replacements couldn't match their experience or hardiness. And to get those new recruits, Napoleon was forced to new extremes, including an April 3, 1813, edict that required each son of a noble family to recruit and equip his own unit of soldiers, which cost him crucial support among the richest families. Younger and younger boys were drafted, but *Rickettsia* and the Russian army had simply decreased the pool of eligible and willing troops. The emperor's 1813 recruitment target was 650,000 men. He got 137,000. France's appetite for war was sated.

Napoleon eventually cobbled together an invasion force of 200,000 and marched in April 1813. He managed two quick victories, a brilliant tour de force at Lützen and a difficult one at Bautzen in May. But typhus reappeared in the ranks almost immediately and carried away tens of thousands of men, again hobbling his forces.

His enemies united in the Sixth Coalition ultimately assembled 800,000 men to Napoleon's eventual total forces of 650,000. An armistice was signed on June 4, and Napoleon was presented with terms that would have been unthinkable before Russia. The French Empire would be dissolved, and Napoleon would retreat to the nation's pre-1792 borders, threatened on all sides by enemies. With 90,000 men on the sick list, Napoleon signed.

The downfall was swift. Sweden broke its alliance with France and then, on August 12, Napoleon's most important ally, Austria, switched sides. Napoleon attacked the Russians and Austrians on August 26 and won a brilliant victory at Dresden. But two quick defeats followed, leading to the crucial Battle of Leipzig on October 16, where 500,000 troops fought outside the historic city, the largest single battle until the beginning of World War I. According to the military surgeon and scholar Von Linstow, by the time of the engagement Napoleon had lost 105,000 men on the campaign by forces of arms, but 219,000 to disease, chiefly typhus. Now he had to face an allied force of 320,000 men with half that number in his own ranks. On the 1813 campaign, Napoleon had occasionally equaled the verve and brilliance of his greatest battles, but *Rickettsia* again sapped him of vital strength.

Napoleon lost 46,000 men at Leipzig in a horrendous defeat and retreated across the Rhine with only a rump force of 40,000. Paris fell on March 31, 1814, and six days later Napoleon abdicated the throne, which was returned to the Bourbons in the form of the gout-afflicted, thoroughly unimpressive Louis XVIII. The disgraced Corsican was sent into exile on Elba. His 1815 return to power ended on June 18 at Waterloo, where he was defeated by the Duke of Wellington in his long-sought confrontation with the British, and he was again exiled, this time to St. Helena.

His last days were spent in sickness. His aide recalled the former emperor, weak and feverish, days before his death:

> Tears came into my eyes when I saw this man—who had been so feared, who had so proudly commanded, so absolutely—beg for a spoonful of coffee, ask for permission to have it. . . . At present, he was as docile as a little child.

Despite several rescue efforts, including one launched from Texas, Napoleon died on May 5, 1821, most likely from stomach cancer.

On St. Helena, the emperor had been working on his memoirs, but he hadn't yet reached the year 1812.

WHAT IF THE CAMPAIGN of 1812 had been typhus-free? If Napoleon had utterly destroyed the Russians at Borodino and Alexander had capitulated?

The consequences would have radiated out through time and territory. Napoleon would have marched back to Paris at the head of a triumphant army of several hundred thousand men. Russia would have been neutralized as a threat for a number of years and his Continental enemies—Prussia, Portugal, Spain—would have been cowed into submission. There would have been no Sixth Coalition to face him in 1813 and Napoleon's grip over Europe would have been firm.

On his return to Paris, Napoleon's attention would have turned to the rebellion in Spain and to his ultimate nemesis: England. Certainly his ego would have expanded to gargantuan dimensions and ambitious plans would have consumed him. Eventually, a showdown with England was inevitable, but Napoleon would have been in far better shape than he was at Waterloo, a battle he should have won. He could conceivably have finally defeated his nemesis and marched into London, utterly changing the face of nineteenth-century world affairs.

No doubt, he wouldn't have stopped there. In 1813, Napoleon had eight more years to live and with England and Russia in his grasp—two nettlesome captives, to be sure—he would have looked west and east for new conquests. An expedition to India would not have been out of the question, nor would an invasion of South America. Napoleon's claim that he wanted nothing more than to sit peacefully at Versailles and administer his existing empire peacefully should not be taken seriously.

Hubris and self-willed blindness played a huge part in Napoleon's debacle in Russia, and it's possible that they could have led him into fresh disasters. The English occupation would have made the Spanish one seem tame. German nationalism would have bubbled to the surface, and Prussia would not have stayed quiet forever. The emperor would have had a contentious eight years, but there's little doubt that, with his major enemies vanquished, Napoleon would have reshaped European history in his remaining time.

As for Russia, a defeat would have spooled out a rich carpet of new patterns and shapes. If Alexander had signed a treaty with Napoleon, he could very well have been overthrown, either in a coup led by members of the aristocracy and military elite, or—the cataclysmic option—in a true peasant uprising. With his military in disarray, the tsar would have been powerless to prevent it and he would most likely have suffered the same fate as his hated father. The freeing of the serfs and the toppling of the imperial system could have arrived a hundred years before they finally did, and Lenin and Stalin could have been born into a nation already transformed by revolution from below.

This is pure speculation, a few possible outcomes among hundreds that could have proceeded from a typhus-free invasion of Russia. Napoleon's all-in approach to the campaign made it a high-stakes historical moment, and guaranteed that the results of the war would unroll for decades. But there is no question that the emperor's defeat altered history in a thousand ways. And so there can be no doubt that *Rickettsia,* in helping to achieve it, shaped our modern world.

THE EPIDEMIOLOGICAL LEGACY of the Russian campaign resonated for years. As the army had swept through Lithuania and Russia, it had acted both as fresh material for the spread of typhus and as a conduit, a multiplier, spreading the disease to previously uninfected hamlets and cities along the way. The civilian epidemic began in the summer of 1812, and by the time Napoleon turned and began his retreat, it was advancing through populations near the French route. Russians would bury or incinerate 243,612 corpses during the early part of 1813.

"We found whole families stricken down with typhus," wrote the Prussian army doctor Krantz, "in whose dwelling soldiers, showing no signs of disease, had stayed overnight." In Berlin, there was an almost poignant reminder of what could have been had Larrey and his fellow doctors instituted at least some hygienic practices. As the typhus brought into Germany by the returning soldiers took hold and began to rage through the city, the Charité Hospital instituted a rigorous program to stop the disease within its own corridors. Typhus patients were given their own ward on the second floor, and special grating was installed to bar uninfected patients from entering while still allowing fresh air to enter. The clothes of the sick brought to the hospital were removed and soaked in hydrochloric acid for days, before being tossed into vats filled with boiling water and lye. The patients were dressed in fresh linen and placed in the typhus ward, which was thoroughly cleaned and disinfected daily. The doctors and nurses, before entering the ward, donned special black capes made of glazed linen (which, in theory, any infected material would have trouble sticking to), and as they exited, they doused their faces and hands in cold water and also gargled. As a result, *Rickettsia* was confined to the typhus ward and the rest of the hospital and its staff remained free from infection.

The Belgian doctor de Kerckhove, as acerbic as ever, contemplated the spread of *Rickettsia*. "It was a fatal present which we gave them," he wrote, "and which caused such a high mortality among the inhabitants of the country through which we passed. Wherever we went, the inhabitants were filled with terror and refused to quarter the soldiers." *Rickettsia* visited a new level of suffering on civilians during wartime, which had in the past largely escaped the military carnage if they weren't in the direct route of the armies or weren't trapped with defenders in besieged cities. Distance from the line of march had brought relative safety. In terms of civilian impact, the available armaments had not yet caught up with the creation of mega-armies, but the very size of these new forces extended both their geographic reach and the lethality of the pathogens they carried. Epidemics did the work that would be later taken over by the V-2 rocket and the night raids of B-52s.

The northeast of France, near the border with Germany, was particularly hard hit by the epidemiological aftermath of the Russian campaign. One town named Mors was almost depopulated by the epidemic. In December 1813, the microbe reached the town of Pont-à-Mousson, a city of abbeys that would be ravaged by Luftwaffe bombing raids in 1945. But now it was the pathogen that struck with the arrival of the sick and wounded from Napoleon's latest campaign. A Frenchman remembered:

> Who of us will not remember as long as he lives those harrowing scenes, which one cannot describe without shuddering? Who will ever forget those hundreds of wagons filled with unhappy wounded men who had no medical care since Leipzig; and packed in with them were sick men suffering from dysentery, typhus fever, etc., almost all of them succumbing to inanition, weakness, and filth, as well as disease. Those unfortunate men begged only for a place in a hospital already filled with dying men, only to receive in reply a forced refusal. And so they were under the cruel necessity of going further to pass away, with the result that they infected all the towns and villages along their route, wherever they were granted a gracious hospitality.

Typhus brought the war home to thousands of villages and towns throughout Europe and traveled thousands of miles. It was, for the microbe, its greatest triumph in five centuries of conquest.

Then, inexplicably, it disappeared.

After 1814, the disease ceased to be a major epidemic killer in Europe, outside of Ireland and the eastern border countries. The contagion moved to the more vulnerable populations of the planet in Africa and the Middle East, especially. It was as if, having spurred the downfall of the greatest conqueror it ever faced, it now retired from the field.

And its pursuers followed it. The search for the killer's nature would be picked up again far from the nations it had tormented for so long.

Author's Note:

The Doorway of the Hospital at Tunis

IN JANUARY OF 1909, IN THE SMALL VILLAGES MILES FROM THE capital of Tunisia, men began to fall sick. The symptoms were fever, headache, lethargy, and spots on the trunk, legs, and arms. The relatives of the stricken men knew from experience that there was little to do but wait the disease out. Death would take those it wanted.

In the spring, the disease started to appear in the city itself. Men—it seemed mostly to be men, and young men especially—began turning up at local hospitals or were found prostrate in the "Moorish" cafés frequented by locals, as well as in the *zaouias,* the Sufi spiritual schools where people from the countryside traveled for instruction in mystic Islam. Men would wander into the local hospitals and collapse, their faces puffy and darkened, their eyes staring or manic, days from death. In April, the numbers rose steadily; in May, there was a sudden spike in cases. Doctors sent the overflow patients to a lazaret outside of the city, as their wards were overwhelmed. Some 4,000 Tunisians caught the disease, 836 in the capital. And 32.6 percent of them died.

Typhus was endemic in Tunisia. It had become a part of the natural cycle, as expected a part of the seasons as rain or the raising of crops. But 1909 was different for two reasons: Typhus had bloomed into a serious epidemic. And Charles Nicolle was waiting for it.

Nicolle was a French doctor who had come to Tunisia to head up the Pasteur Institute and make his name. He was a scientist to the marrow, a believer in the precise inductive reasoning that had led the master to his great contributions to germ theory that finally banished miasmism as a medical philosophy. Nicolle even admitted he wished to become the "next Pasteur."

Sailing for the North African colony, Nicolle was in one way following in the footsteps of Napoleon; the Pasteurians saw themselves as benign imperialists, venturing to the corners of the earth to spread rational French science and culture by persuasion and not war. The "civilizing mission" that Napoleon had marched under, promising progress and liberty when in fact he most often brought tyranny, was the same banner that brought Nicolle to this outpost of the French Empire.

Nicolle began his pursuit of the disease's cause only a year after arriving in Tunisia, when he and two colleagues planned a research trip to one of the small villages, Djouggar, about fifty miles outside the capital, that acted as incubators for the disease. But days before their departure, Nicolle began spitting up blood and was unable to make the journey (the illness, a lung ailment, turned out not to be serious). His collaborators, the doctor in charge of the village and his servant, set out for the outlying town. While there, both caught typhus, and when they returned, after days of agony, both died of the disease. *Rickettsia* had claimed two more of the countless pursuers it had killed without granting them a basic insight into its secrets. "Without this incident," Nicolle later wrote, "my first contact with typhus would doubtlessly have been my last."

Nicolle soon learned that most of the doctors in Tunisia eventually caught the disease, and one-third of them died of it. This was made even more disturbing by the fact that animals never seemed to succumb, so that one couldn't study typhus safely in lab specimens or keep the pathogen alive between epidemics. Humans alone seemed to carry the pathogen and die from it, and to get close to it one had to take the chance of catching it. Nicolle needed to figure out typhus's modus operandi not only to make his name but also to have a fair chance of staying alive. And despite hundreds of years of study and millions of victims, the accumulated scientific knowledge of the disease's cause was near zero. Humankind essentially knew nothing definitive about what caused the disease, how it spread, or how to stop it.

For three years, the expatriate doctor had been following the clues that typhus left in its annual cycle. It arrived in the rural districts outside Tunis in winter, then spread to the "doss-houses and the prisons" of the small villages and towns by early spring. From there it would reach into Tunis itself through the jails and the tightly packed neighborhoods populated by natives. By June or July it was gone. It favored a particular type of person: Many of the victims belonged to the underclass of the French colony— single men who worked as day laborers or farmhands, or begged in the streets for alms, barely able to live on the small coins dropped in their hands. Women and children were far less likely to come down with the disease. And curiously, one of the established facts about typhus's spread, that it flourished in confined spaces, seemed exactly the opposite of what was happening in Tunisia. The disease spread across the country not in winter, when families stayed in their closely packed homes and villages, but in the spring, when people began to move and travel. Why?

And, if the pattern of infection was so consistent and followed a perennial route, why did the disease reach epidemic proportions in some years (such as 1906 and 1909) but not in others (1907 and 1908)? After looking at other factors that affected the poor— especially food supplies and weather—Nicolle and his collaborator, Ernest Conseil, realized that the most severe typhus years coincided with famines that sent unemployed single men flocking to the cities.

The local hospitals were known to be flash points, as so many of the doctors and staff who came in contact with typhus victims eventually died from the disease. That argued for person-to-person infection. But when Nicolle and Conseil looked more closely at the data, they realized that not everyone in the hospitals was catching the disease; even though typhus victims were mixed in with other patients, the other patients failed to fall ill with the fever. There was clearly a dividing line over which the pathogen didn't cross. It was killing people in the receiving wards, but somehow it was stopped before reaching the upper floors.

Clearly, the microbe wasn't spread by simple human-to-human contact. Nicolle began to suspect that the vector was an insect. Following the postulates developed by the pioneering researcher Robert Koch, he began injecting monkeys with blood from infected patients in 1906. The first trials failed, and Nicolle theorized that it was the fault of the test subjects: monkeys were too distant from their human cousins to have the same susceptibilities to disease. He sent for a chimpanzee, physiologically the creature closest to man. The chimp had to be imported from Marseille at the exorbitant cost of 550 francs. As Nicolle waited for the *Pan troglodytes* to reach Tunis, June arrived and the number of typhus cases began to fall off. The epidemic, as it did every summer, was fading; if the chimp didn't arrive soon, Nicolle would have no infected blood with which to inoculate it, and he would have to wait until the next plague swept Tunisia.

Finally, the chimp arrived in its crate and Nicolle quickly injected it with blood from an infected thirty-five-year-old Tunisian man. Now he watched and waited. At first, nothing happened. The chimpanzee stared back at the French scientist with its warm, placid brown eyes, revealing no signs of sickness. Nicolle went home and dropped off to sleep. When he returned in the morning, the chimp still regarded him with the same bored and perfectly healthy gaze. But twenty-four days after receiving the infected blood, his test subject began to display unmistakable signs of fever. The chimp was the first nonhuman vertebrate victim of *Rickettsia* ever observed.

Nicolle worked quickly. He took blood from the chimp and

infected a macaque, a Chinese monkey. Nothing happened. For twelve days, Nicolle watched the macaque closely. On the thirteenth day, the monkey's eyes began drooping and a thermometer revealed that he was running a high fever. Nicolle had isolated the microbe. Now he had to locate the vector.

The doctor had narrowed his search for the typhus carrier to one insect: the common body louse. In Tunisia, especially in the rural districts, lice were the only parasites universally found on the body and clothing of "the wretches" who spread the disease. Nicolle placed a number of healthy lice on the fur of the sick Chinese monkey. After giving them time to feed on their host, he transferred the lice to a healthy monkey. Within days, it had fallen ill with typhus. Nicolle had proved that the body louse had been from time immemorial the carrier of the fatal disease.

IN HIS SPEECH accepting the Nobel Prize for Medicine in 1928, Nicolle compressed years of medical detective work into a flash of understanding. "Often, when going to the hospital, I had to step over the bodies of typhus patients who were awaiting admission to the hospital and had fallen exhausted at the door," he wrote. But once upstairs these febrile men infected no one. "The contagious agent was therefore something attached to his skin and clothing, something which soap and water could remove. It could only be the louse. It was the louse." Perhaps this image—the scientist suddenly struck by a world-changing idea while stepping over the bodies of the poor and desperately ill—made for a more thrilling story. Perhaps Nicolle felt the pressure to give the solving of the riddle a classic "eureka" moment in line with public expectations of how medical breakthroughs were made. But the process had been far more involved and much more a classical inductive pursuit than the story expressed.

Nor did Nicolle mention his most controversial step. Attempting to create a simple vaccine, he ground up the bodies of infected lice and mixed them with the blood serum of men who had survived typhus. He injected the vaccine into his arm, but didn't develop any symptoms. Driven to complete the holy grail of typhus research, he then walked up to the children's ward of the hospital and injected the mixture into two Arab boys, without advising them or their parents of what was happening. The two fell sick but luckily survived.

The protocol was complete. After five hundred years, *Rickettsia*'s secret was out.

Had it not been for Nicolle's discovery, the pathogen would have soon had one more chance at a battlefield coup: World War I. As the doctor wrote in his Nobel speech:

> If in 1914 we had been unaware of the mode of transmission of typhus, and if infected lice had been imported into Europe, the war would not have ended by a bloody victory. It would have ended in an unparalleled catastrophe, the most terrible in human history. Soldiers at the front, reserves, prisoners, civilians, neutrals even, the whole of humanity would have collapsed.

The last phrase is speculative, of course, but Nicolle had solid evidence of a possible conflagration should typhus have run unchecked during the war. Unable to delouse their army with the same proficiency as the Allied forces, the Russians saw the scourge revisit the towns and cities of Russia in the first great epidemic since the Crimean War, when 900,000 had died from *Rickettsia*. During 1914–18, it hit the armies of the Balkans and Russia itself and as many as 3 million troops and civilians died. If typhus had burned through western Europe as well, with the size of the armies roaming the Continent, that number could have risen to 10 million or more. (As it turned out, the Allies were spectacularly successful at combating the pathogen: only 104 cases of typhus were reported among Allied troops during the entire conflict.) After the war, Lenin declared, "Either socialism will defeat the louse, or the louse will defeat socialism." In fact, the contest was a draw. Stalin and his minions couldn't control the disease, and it went on killing.

The Red Army had been shocked at the ferocity of the epidemic and decided to try to harness the power of the tiny microbe that had nearly collapsed their eastern front. In 1928, a secret program was initiated to weaponize *Rickettsia* under the auspices of the GPU, which later became the KGB. They decided that the best way to spread typhus in enemy armies would be to spray them with an aerosolized version of *Rickettsia* dropped from airplanes.

The Red Army's scientists first inoculated chicken eggs at the Leningrad Military Academy. According to the epidemiologist Ken Alibek, who defected from the former Soviet Union in 1992, thousands of chicken eggs arrived at the institute every week during a time of widespread hunger in the country. The researchers also injected rats and other test animals in their labs, let the *Rickettsia* multiply in their bodies, then extracted the pathogen and mixed it with liquids in huge blenders. The concoction was turned into a powder and a liquid, ready to be inserted into bombs that could be dropped over the enemy.

In 1938, the USSR's defense commissar warned that the Red Army stood ready to use typhus "against an aggressor on his own soil." What nature had achieved spontaneously against Napoleon the Soviets were now ready to deploy as a man-made weapon. The United States responded by beginning its own biological weapons research at Fort Detrick in Maryland, under the leadership of George Merck of the famous pharmaceutical company.

We have no reliable evidence that the Russians ever used typhus on the Germans. But one group of Polish resistance guerrillas apparently did utilize the pathogen against the Nazis: in a report from the Polish Secret Army to the Combined Chiefs of Staff of the Allied Forces dated September 7, 1943, the liaison officer (using the wrong name for the pathogen) detailed under "Activities of retaliation" the use of "typhoid fever microbes and typhoid fever lice" in a "few hundred cases." If true, the rickettsial weapon most likely came from Russian stockpiles.

For the Germans, typhus became a tool. The disease ran rampant in the concentration camps, where the Nazis deliberately used it as an instrument of genocidal germ warfare. Scholar Naomi Baumslag estimates that 1.5 million prisoners of the camps died of the disease, and it was at Bergen-Belsen that typhus would claim its most famous victim in five hundred years.

Anne Frank arrived at the concentration camp on October 28, 1944. She had barely escaped death at Auschwitz earlier in the fall, where, having just turned fifteen (the cutoff for immediate death), she was spared a trip to the gas chambers and was separated from her father. Her head was shaved, and she was stripped naked, disinfected, and tattooed with her camp number. When she was later transported to Bergen-Belsen, she arrived already ill and malnourished along with her sister Margot. Anne survived, working in the bullet factory and sleeping in the unheated, desperately crowded barracks, until March 1945, when just weeks before the Allied liberation of the camp, a typhus epidemic raged through the camp. About 1 in 5 of the 500 prisoners in her barracks caught the disease. Near the end, Anne told the barracks leader, Irma Sonnenberg Menkel, "I am very sick" and soon was unable to make the roll call. "She didn't know that she was dying," Menkel remembered. Anne soon fell into the coma-like stupor that marks the final stage of the disease. Along with Margot, she was among the approximately 17,000 men and women who perished in the epidemic.

TODAY, *RICKETTSIA* STILL ROAMS the poorest sectors of the Third World, claiming victims especially in the cold mountainous regions of South America and Africa, where infected lice burrow into the clothing of villagers too poor to afford decent medical care. It is now rare in the industrialized world, but in a startling development a new vector has been discovered for the pathogen: *Glaucomys volans,* the flying squirrel, common in the continental United States. Nesting in attics, these rodents are the only known vertebrate reservoir for *Rickettsia* other than humans, and they have caused small outbreaks of epidemic typhus across the country. The furry, nocturnal animal that can be seen gliding from tree to tree, especially in gloaming of Southern moonlight, has been for thousands of years humankind's brother under the skin.

Typhus will never roam the planet as it once did. A plague of flying squirrels might be the plot of a B horror flick, but rickettsial hordes of them are unlikely to invade the real world. The only threat that typhus realistically still poses is as a weaponized biological agent. Defectors have reported that North Korean leader Kim Jong Il has experimented with *Rickettsia,* along with anthrax, cholera, and the bubonic plague, research conducted at the appropriately sinister-sounding Germ Research Institute of the General Logistics Bureau of the Armed Forces Ministry. Various intelligence services report that the North Koreans have even conducted live experiments with biological agents on islands off the country's coast. One defector claimed that she was present at an experiment in which 50 inmates of the regime's concentration camps were exposed to biological agents and died horrifying deaths.

If the stories of North Korean stockpiles are true, it's a fitting end for *Rickettsia,* stored in the vaults of a tiny, grotesque dictator, a cut-rate Napoleon. The microbe has always encountered men with lurid ambitions. Emperors, kings, and generals found that their armies could conquer everything except this one last natural barrier to the thing they wanted most.

But things have reversed themselves. *Rickettsia*'s nemesis, science, which conquered the microbe after five hundred years of pursuit, has now saved it. The pathogen has been processed into powders and aerosols, uniting the ancient and the new, and giving

Rickettsia its only hope for a return to the wider world. It waits for what it has always waited for. War. Disaster.

The organism that helped stop Napoleon on the road to the fabled capital of Russia now exists in the most neglected areas of the world, places so poor as to be hardly worth conquering. But it also sits, close to extinction, locked in dark, infrequently visited rooms, filling at the end of its life the opposite role that it played in 1812: not as a barrier to power but as a dazzling weapon, one dark day, to seize it. Its wager on the incurably violent human race hasn't quite played out.

Glossary

boyar: A member of the Russian nobility.
carabinier: A cavalryman.
chasseur: A rapid-reaction infantryman.
cuirassier: A cavalry soldier wearing a cuirass, or breastplate armor.
droshky: An open, four-wheeled carriage.
flèche: An earthwork with angled walls in the front and an open back where troops could assemble.
flying ambulance: A small, enclosed ambulance pulled by horses and designed to advance onto the battlefield for evacuating the wounded.
jaeger: A sharpshooter or skirmisher often deployed in front of the main line of troops.
lazaret: A hospital, especially one specializing in infectious cases.
pontoneer: A member of the bridge-building corps of troops.
redan: A V-shaped defensive earthwork.
sapper: An explosives expert.

MAJOR PLACE-NAMES

Berezina: A western tributary of the Dnieper River, now part of modern-day Belarus.
Dnieper: A major Russian river that flows from a point 160 miles west of Moscow south to Odessa on the Black Sea.
Niemen: A river that previously formed the border between Poland and Russian Lithuania and now bisects the southwestern corner of Lithuania.

Saxony: A duchy and kingdom in the southeast region of modern-day Germany.

Smolensk: A major city in western Russia, located on the Dnieper River.

Vilia: An east-west tributary of the Niemen.

Vilna: Modern-day Vilnius, the capital of Lithuania.

Vitebsk: A city now located in Belarus, near the northeastern border with Russia.

Westphalia: An early-nineteenth-century kingdom located between the Rhine and the Weser rivers in the north-central part of modern-day Germany.

Württemberg: An early-nineteenth-century kingdom located in the southwestern part of modern-day Germany whose traditional capital was Stuttgart.

Notes

Introduction: Old Bones

3 " 'wouldn't stop coming out of the ground' ": "Reading the Bones" by Eve Conant, *Newsweek*, September 9, 2002, p. 1.

3 "There had been whispers": Ibid., p. 1.

3 "a grave filled": Ibid., p. 2.

4 "Or perhaps these were the corpses": Ibid.

4 "When archaeologists": Ibid., p. 2.

4 "As they excavated": "Napoleon's Lost Army: The Soldiers Who Fell," by Paul Britten-Austin, www.bbc.co.uk/history.

5 "None of the remains": "Reading the Bones," p. 2.

5 "Napoleon's troops breaking into": "Digging Napoleon's Dead," by Jarret A. Lobell, *Archaeology*, Sept/Oct. 2002.

Chapter One: Incarnate

8 "when men ran through": Herold, *Age of Napoleon*, p. 37.

9 " 'He wanted to put' ": Quoted in Herold, *Mistress to an Age*, p. 214.

10 " 'From that moment' ": Quoted in Duggan, p. 11.

12 " 'The belief that they were invincible' ": Quoted in Zamoyski, p. 84.

13 " 'The genie of liberty' ": Quoted in Conklin, p. 11.

15 "Napoleon would say later": Napoleon to Metternich, quoted in Troyat, p. 94.

16 " 'He is a truly handsome,' ": Quoted in Horne, p. 2.

16 " 'Love for the Tsar,' ": Quoted in Cronin, p. 305.

17 "French manufacturers": McLynn, p. 495.

17 "even aristocratic families": Horne, p. 233.

17 " 'In Hamburg' ": Ibid., p. 296.

18 " 'Sooner or later' ": Schom, p. 436.

18 " 'The world is clearly' ": Ibid., p. 475.

19 " 'I care nothing,' ": Quoted in McLynn, p. 499.

19 " 'torrents of blood' ": Quoted in Troyat, p. 139.

Chapter Two: A Portable Metropolis

21 "The army that the emperor": The number of men encompassed in the invasion of Russia is the subject of perennial disputes. I have depended most heavily on the work of Adam Zamoyski in *Moscow 1812* for estimates of troops.

21 "semaphore signals": McLynn, 344.

21 "It formed": The number of Napoleon's troops and hangers-on who crossed the Niemen is estimated at 600,000. The figures for Tokyo and Istanbul are circa 1800; Tokyo's population was 685,000 and Constantinople's total was 570,000. Chandler, Tertius. *Four Thousand Years of Urban Growth: An Historical Census*. New York: Edwin Mellen Press, Ceredigion, 1987.

22 "Each had to be able": Horne, p. 98.

22 For an extended discussion of Napoleon's marshals, see Chandler, David A., *Napoleon's Marshals*.

25 For a discussion of unit sizes in Napoleon's armies, see Muir.

26 " 'which permitted the speed' ": McLynn, p. 505.

27 " 'It was an impossible dream' ": Ibid., p. 506.

27 For a discussion of the Russian officer class, see Cate, p. 115.

27 " 'The headquarters of the Emperor' ": Clausewitz, p. 3.

30 " 'malignant spotted fever' ": Villalba, quoted in Zinsser, p. 243.

30 "Only 3,000": Ibid.

31 "The conflict drew together": This account draws mainly from Arfaioli's *The Black Bands of Giovanni*.

31 " 'Therefore I cannot but see' ": Quoted in Brandi, p. 220.

33 "Nearly three hundred years": Seward, p. 136.

33 "The historian David Bell": See Bell's *The First Total War* for an explication of his ideas about the evolution in the culture of war.

34 " 'a war to the death' ": Ibid., p. 3.

Chapter Three: Drumbeat

35 "His statistical expert": McLynn, p. 496.

35 "By the first months": Ibid.

35 " 'It would be a crime' ": Quoted in Zamoyski, p. 72.

36 " 'I have come,' ": Caulaincourt, *Memoirs*, p. 129.

36 " 'Whether he triumphs' ": Quoted in Zamoyski, p. 79.

37 " 'We will die or conquer' ": Troyat, p. 46.

38 "The army itself was a pageant": For a discussion of uniforms, see Haythornwaite, Philip and Chappell, Mike, *Uniforms of Napoleon's Russian Campaign*, London: Arms & Armour Press, 1996 and Haythornwaite and Fosten, Bryan, *Napoleon's Line Infantry*, London: Osprey, 1983.

39 "and the grenadiers": Quoted in Nicolson, p. 24.

39 "Franz Roeder was a captain": For an account of Roeder's service, see *The Ordeal of Captain Roeder*.

40 " 'which may be partly caused' ": Roeder, p. 50.

40 " 'creeping nervous fever' ": Ibid., p. 51.

40 " 'I share the thoughts' ": Brett-James, p. 11.

40 "10,000 wills": Ibid., p. 13.

41 "But the forty-six-year-old": For the inexperience of the novice doctors, see Larrey's letter of January 1812, quoted in Howard, p. 69.

41 " 'Medicine is the science' ": Quoted in Fournier, p. 163.

41 " 'I dress' ": Quoted in McLynn, p. 37.

42 " 'I'm trying to rise' ": Quoted in Cronin, p. 314.

42 " 'Walcheren has for its defense' ": Quoted in Howard, p. 64.

43 " 'hunchbacks and cripples' ": Howard, p. 24.

43 "The pathogen had aided": Prinzing, p. 101.

43 " 'a malignant, nervous and putrid' ": Howard, p. 201

43 " '[The dead] were thrown' ": Ibid., p. 164.

44 " 'Like an enormous fire' ": For a description of typhus at Mantua, see the testimony of Napoleon's surgeon J. Baptiste-Turiot, quoted in Schom, p. 62.

44 "Spanish prisoners": Prinzing, p. 103.

44 "During the Wars": Ibid., p. 96.

Chapter Four: Crossing

46 "In his diary": Roeder, p. 62.

47 "In the noise": Accounts of soldiers falling out of the ranks and dying are found in Larrey's memoirs and Kerckhove's account, among others.

47 "Some victims": The description of the symptoms are collected from first-hand accounts of typhus victims in the medical literature. The description of "a very uncommon feeling" is from Dr. Smyth's own experience of the disease in *The Description of the Jail Distemper.* Other symptoms come from Johnson's description of his own illness in *Practical Illustrations of Typhus and Other Fevers,* as well as Bartlett, Smith, et al. All of the accounts are listed in the bibliography under Primary Sources.

49 " 'Of the illness' ": The patient is John Reed, the journalist and Bolshevik activist. The writer is his wife, Louise Bryant, in a letter dated November 14, 1920, published in *The Liberator,* February 1921. Reed died of typhus on October 19, 1920, with Bryant by his side. He was buried in the Kremlin Wall Necropolis.

49 "The mistake was compounded": Prinzing, p. 102.

50 "To understand what": This brief overview of nineteenth-century attitudes toward disease is informed by several sources, including Roy Porter's *The Greatest Benefit to Mankind,* J. Rosser Matthews's *Quantification and the Quest for Medical Certainty,* McNeill's *Plagues and Peoples,* and several essays, including "Fevers and Science in Early Nineteenth Century Medicine," by Leonard Wilson.

52 " 'loaded with' ": Quoted in Howard, p. 201.

53 "In 1811": See North's *A Treatise on a Malignant Epidemic.*

53 "The doctor's name": For an account of Lind's experiments, see Winslow, p. 295 and Roddis, pp. 57–64.

55 "One of Lind's": Roddis, p. 64.

55 " 'enjoy a better' ": Quoted in the article "Thumpers!" by Henrik Bering, *Policy Review,* June–July 2005.

Chapter Five: Pursuit

60 " 'He has come' ": Ségur, p. 27.

60 " 'I have never' ": Larrey, p. 12.

62 "The Belgian doctor": All quotes from de Kerckhove are from his *Histoire des maladies observées à la Grand Armée française, pendant les campagnes de Russe en 1812 et d'Allemagne en 1813,* Janssens, 1836. Translated for the author by Rose-Marie Coulombel.

62 " 'Nothing announced' ": de Kerckhove, p. 8.

62 " '60,000 [troops]' ": Larrey, *Surgical Memoirs.*

62 " 'in the first weeks,' ": Clausewitz, p. 110.

62 " 'was already stricken' ": Wilson, p. 29.

63 " 'dragged themselves behind' ": de Kerckhove, p. 30.

63 "Napoleon was losing 4,000 to 6,000 soldiers": McLynn, p. 511.

63 "Another 30,000": Zamoyski, p. 163.

63 "Pleurisy, jaundice": de Kerckhove lists these and a few other diseases as being present on p. 20.

63 " 'Under these circumstances' ": Vossler, p. 51.

63 "Dysentery ruled": The timing of the dominance of each disease is impossible to chart with absolute precision, but both de Kerckhove and Ebstein (pp. 42–4), quoting the doctor Lamazurier, support the late summer as the time when typhus became strongest. "In the second half of August," Ebstein writes, "typhus became the dominant disease, but it didn't yet reveal its terrible contagiousness."

63 "with 80,000 sick": Zinsser, p. 162.

63 "although recent outbreaks": Jane Perlez, "A Stubborn Killer of Refugees: Dysentery," *New York Times*, August 5, 1994.

64 "At one hospital": von Scherer's findings are summarized in Rose, p. 15.

64 " 'Typhus was present' ": de Kerckhove, p. 48.

65 "One major": This letter is contained in Paul Britten Austin's monumental collection of eyewitness accounts of the invasion, which will be referenced throughout. P. 238.

65 " 'Napoleon doesn't give a damn' ": Austin, *The March on Moscow*, p. 238.

66 " 'What misery' ": Roeder, p. 94.

67 " 'This did not remain' ": Clausewitz, p. 110.

Chapter Six: Smolensk

70 " 'It was truly heartbreaking' ": Caulaincourt, p. 50.

73 " 'Each night' ": Quoted in Dodge, p. 501.

73 "3,400 men": Riehn, p. 192.

75 " 'terrifying' increase": de Kerckhove, p. 65.

75 "between 200 and 500 rubles": Parkinson, p. 3.

76 "One Bavarian officer": Labaume, p. 69.

76 "50,000 men": Cate, p. 205.

76 "800,000 silver rubles": Ibid.

77 " 'War's a game' ": Austin, *The March on Moscow*, p. 159.

77 " 'The campaign of 1812' ": Ségur, p. 19.

78 " 'I shall send you' ": Cate, p. 170.

78 " 'Well, what are we' ": Ségur, p. 22.

Chapter Seven: The Sound of Flames

80 " 'The number of sick' ": de Kerckhove, p. 41.

80 " 'Never was there' ": Caulaincourt, p. 66.

81 " 'This news filled' ": Quoted in Zamoyski, p. 207.

84 "He was down to": McLynn, p. 511.

84 " 'One man after another' ": Walter, p. 44.

85 " 'The thought of the coming day' ": Walter, p. 49.

86 " 'shattered great heaps' ": Brett-James, p. 86.

87 "triple-vented shell": Austin, p. 194.

87 " 'A second earlier' ": Brett-James, p. 86.

87 "The regimental bands": The lineup is for a line infantry band of 1802, which would have been largely unchanged for 1812. See *Grove's Dictionary of Music and Musicians,* by Eric Blom, George Grove, and Denis Stevens, 1955, p. 770.

88 "One cannonball": Ségur, p. 32.

88 " 'Everything which doesn't make haste' ": Austin, p. 196.

89 " 'An eruption' ": Caulaincourt, p. 77.

89 " 'You German' ": Quoted in Zamoyski, p. 219.

89 " 'It is painful' ": Quoted in Cooper, p. 95.

90 " 'The flames became' ": du Faur, p. 54.

90 " 'The mirage of victory' ": Ségur, p. 33.

90 " 'Never can you' ": Labaume, p. 54.

90 "The fire had carbonized": Nicolson, p. 56.

91 " 'And yet' ": Roeder, p. 145.

91 "Pisani approached the body": See Pisani's account of Smolensk in *Con Napoleone nella Campagna di Russia,* beginning on p. 124.

91 " 'Here the wounded' ": Ebstein, p. 20.

93 " 'You are unworthy' ": Brett-James, p. 83.

93 " 'Amidst the stumps' ": Ségur, p. 35.

94 " 'Even if' ": Quoted in Horne, p. 145.

94 " 'imperative need' ": Brett-James, p. 98.

95 " 'The terrible deprivations' ": Ebstein, p. 62.

95 " 'Write to the generals' ": Cooper, p. 89.

98 " 'Once more' ": Caulaincourt, p. 82.

99 " 'Once again' ": Ibid., p. 83.

99 " 'The two armies' ": Clausewitz, p. 131.

Chapter Eight: Smoke

100 "An autopsy": The dissection was carried out by Dr. Robert Jackson and the description is included in his wonderfully detailed *An Outline of the History and Cure of Fever*, 1798.

101 "Among them": For a detailed discussion of the origins of *Rickettsia*, see Gray, Michael W., "Rickettsia, Typhus and the Mitochondrial Connection," *Nature*, November 12, 1998, p. 109–10.

102 " 'a molecular theater' ": For a discussion of the *Rickettsia* genome, see Friedman, Roberta, "Bacterial Revelations," *Natural History*, June 2001.

104 "The body louse in Africa": Ibid., p. 177.

105 " 'These thunders' ": Donne, *Devotions*.

106 "more Irish would die": Porter, p. 29.

106 "But the discovery": See Wilford, John Noble, "Lice from Mummies Provide Clues to Ancient Migrations," *International Herald Tribune*, February 6, 2008.

106 "a mysterious illness in 1083": Zinsser, p. 242.

106 "During the Middle Ages": The discussion of typhus's early history is informed, among other sources, by Zinsser, pp. 242–81.

108 " 'Throughout all the people' ": Translated from the original Latin for the author by Luco Grillo.

Chapter Nine: At Borodino

110 " 'Beloved, is it that' ": Roeder, p. 125.

111 "now down to 1,500": Roeder, p. 138.

111 "eating less than he should have": Riehn sees a drastic change in available supplies once the army crossed from Poland into old Russia: "The march now led through fertile regions, where the rye stood tall in the fields. . . . food was not a problem." pp. 232–3.

111 " 'This poor army' ": Quoted in Parkinson, p. 137.

113 " 'I was young' ": Ibid., p. 91.

113 " 'one stupidity' ": Brett-James, p. 110.

113 " 'I had no other course' ": Ibid., p. 110.

114 " 'The nobility' ": Quoted in Parkinson, p. 47.

114 " 'But I hope' ": Ibid., p. 1.

115 " 'The day was cloudy' ": Quoted in Zamoyski, p. 249.

115 " 'a hatcher of intrigues' ": Quoted in Parkinson, p. 118.

116 " 'plunged in grief' ": Brett-James, p. 148.

117 "Men escaping": Cate, p. 261.

118 " 'The objective' ": Parkinson, p. 14.

121 "The Russian commander": Cate, p. 284.

121 " 'This invention' ": Rose, p. 45.

121 "The device": Ségur, p. 91.

121 " 'In a fortnight' ": Caulaincourt, p. 90.

121 "The emperor even": Napoleon touched on this idea in an interview with the Russian emissary Count Orlin. Cooper, p. 90.

122 " 'It will lose me' ": Caulaincourt, p. 92.

124 " 'Our outposts were' ": Brett-James, p. 121.

125 " 'Fortune is a shameless courtesan' ": Ibid., p. 120.

125 " 'There were many' ": Labaume, p. 70.

126 "Ognik ('Fire')": Parkinson, p. 137.

129 " 'Weak and starved' ": Ségur, p. 62.

129 " 'The voice of the court' ": Clausewitz, p. 142.

Chapter Ten: Clash

130 " 'Soldiers! Here is the battle' ": Quoted in Zamoyski, p. 265.

131 " 'Trusting in God' ": Quoted in Nicolson, p. 74.

131 "when Soviet generals": Ibid., preface.

134 " 'When she caught sight' ": Austin, p. 279.

134 "Lieutenant Roth von Schreckenstein": Brett-James, p. 124.

137 " 'sluggish, apathetic' ": Ségur, p. 69.

137 " 'What's the Emperor' ": Ibid., p. 71.

138 " 'ceased to exist' ": Parkinson, p. 142.

138 " 'No!' he told' ": Ségur, p. 65.

139 "When one of his officers": Ségur, p. 68.

140 "The most conservative": The figures are from Zamoyski, p. 287.

141 " 'And if there is' ": Quoted in Ségur, p. 72.

142 "Franz Ludwig August von Meerheimb": Brett-James, p. 135.

143 " 'Whole files,' ": Ibid., p. 127.

144 " 'I had been through' ": Ibid., p. 128.

144 "The Russian general later remarked": Zamoyski, p. 273.

144 " 'He appeared destitute' ": Clausewitz, p. 141.

145 " 'the bad condition' ": Ibid., p. 142.

147 " 'My battle' ": Ségur, p. 68.

147 " 'For strong, healthy' ": Austin, p. 296.

148 "the captain": Brett-James, p. 129.

149 " 'Do what you' ": Austin, p. 300.

151 " 'It would be difficult' ": Quoted in Zamoyski, p. 278.

151 " 'In one hand' ": Austin, p. 306.

153 " 'gashed' ": Vossler, p. 67.

153 " 'It was horrible' ": Quoted in Dyer, p. 234.

155 " 'It is another question' ": Clausewitz, p. 168.

155 " 'People will be' ": Brett-James, p. 130.

Chapter Eleven: The Hospital

157 " 'All the villages and houses' ": Quoted in Howard, p. 133.

159 "Imagine the journey": This account of a typical hospital is drawn
     largely from the memoirs of Larrey, de Kerckhove, and common soldiers,
     as well as the eyewitness accounts collected in Brett-James and Austin
     and Howard's study of the Grande Armée medical service.

163 " 'horribly disemboweled' ": Austin, p. 311.

163 "As the night progressed": The description of typhus patients is drawn
     from the same primary sources listed in the second note for page 49.

164 "The men often gave off": The odors are mentioned specifically in
     Bartlett, p. 189, where the author writes of "pungent, ammoniacal and
     offensive [smells] especially in severe cases, and in fat, plethoric indi-

viduals; sometimes, for a few days before death, the smell resembled that of putrid animal matter." Similar descriptions are given in other firsthand accounts.

164 " 'The face was sometimes' ": For de Kerckhove's description of typhus symptoms, see his memoir, pp. 406–9.

165 "opium or Hoffman's drops": Austin, *The March on Moscow*, p. 176.

165 "*chirurgiens de pacotille*": Howard, p. 2.

166 "As he tended": de Kerckhove's description of his treatment regimen starts at page 406 of his memoir.

Chapter Twelve: The Last City

172 " 'We had never suffered' ": Brett-James, p. 109.

173 " 'With which low bitch' ": Ibid., p. 133.

173 " 'used a dead horse' ": Parkinson, p. 159.

174 " 'Everyone was still' ": Quoted in Zamoyski, p. 284.

175 " 'Six hundred wounded Russians' ": Brett-James, p. 142.

176 " 'You see what they want' ": Ibid., p. 155.

179 " 'We kept on' ": Ibid., p. 150.

180 " 'What blackguard' ": Ibid., p. 160.

181 "140,000 from France": Zamoyski, p. 311.

181 " 'Not only' ": Ibid., p. 312.

183 " 'Farewell, delightful haunts' ": Troyat, p. 153.

183 " 'They will wait' ": Brett-James, p. 172.

184 " 'It would be difficult' ": Caulaincourt, p. 113.

185 " 'a small machine' ": Bourgnone, p. 23.

185 " 'Even the gallery slaves' ": Labaume, p. 91.

185 "There was, at last": Memoirists from de Kerckhove to Ségur to Jakob Walter recount the abundance of food in Moscow.

185 " 'as round and large' ": Walter, p. 57.

186 " 'It [would be] difficult' ": Larrey, p. 44.

188 "The fire was now so close": For an account of Napoleon's escape from the Moscow fire, see Ségur, pp. 109–11.

189 "a contingent of 10,000": Ebstein, p. 40.

189 " 'Want, sickness' ": Wilson, p. 57.

190 "They received a contingent": Howard, p. 219.

190 "The troops who had been on the campaign": Rose, quoting the Prussian doctor-memoirist Krantz, attests that reinforcements or rear units who came in contact with the main body of the Grande Armée often fell ill almost immediately. "The Prussian soldiers of York's corps had not been with the Grand Armée in Moscow, and there was no typhus among them until they followed the French on their road of retreat from Russia. [Krantz:] 'From this moment on, however, the disease spread with the greatest rapidity in the whole Prussian army corps,' and this spreading took place with a certain uniformity among the different divisions . . . In the first East Prussian regiment of infantry, when it came to the Vistula, there was not a single case of typhus, 'while after a march of 14 miles on the highway which the French had passed before them there were 15 to 20 men sick in every company, every tenth or even every seventh man. In those divisions which had been exposed to infection while in former cantonments, the cases were much more numerous, 20 to 30 in every company.' "

190 " 'During our first days' ": de Kerckhove, p. 88.

190 "typhus 'ripped' ": Ebstein, p. 48.

190 " 'Thousands of sick soldiers' ": de Kerckhove, p. 88.

190 "The diseases awakened by the war": For estimates of Russian casualties from disease, especially typhus, see Bernhardy's report, quoted in Ebstein, p. 66. For Davidov's account, see *In the Service of the Tsar Against Napoleon*.

Chapter Thirteen: Decision

193 "General de Marbot acknowledged": See *The Memoirs of General the Baron de Marbot*. Published online at http://www.fullbooks.com/ The-Memoirs-of-General-the-Baron-de-Marbot8.html, section 8.

195 " 'One could have heard' ": Quoted in Troyat, p. 155.

196 " 'At every step' ": Brett-James, p. 187.

197 " 'if we met with the slightest' ": Caulaincourt, p. 145.

198 " 'What?!' he cried": Ségur, p. 120.

199 " 'I want peace' ": Ibid., p. 122.

200 " 'What a frightful' ": Ségur, p. 126.

200 " 'A thick fog descended' ": from *Hilaire Belloc: An Anthology of His Prose and Verse*, London: R. Hart Davis, 1951, p. 233.

202 " 'oriental despotism' ": Schom, p. 180.

203 " 'The mortality continues' ": Parkinson, Wenda, p. 190.

Chapter Fourteen: Two Roads

205 "By the beginning of November": Zamoyski estimates Napoleon's forces as he departed Moscow at "no more than 95,000 and probably less." Riehn's estimate is rather higher, at 109,000. Clausewitz recorded 90,000.

205 " 'had scarcely' ": Howard, p. 214.

205 " 'These unfavorable circumstances' ": Larrey, p. 6.

206 "There is no question": Ségur.

207 "The historian Jean Morvan": Howard, p. 36.

210 "In the famous": These facts are drawn from *The Great Starvation Experiment: Ancel Keys and the Men Who Starved for Science*, by Todd Tucker, Minneapolis, Minn.: University of Minnesota Press, 2008.

211 " 'chronic disorders' ": See, for example, Smyth's *Description of a Jail Distemper*, p. 14, where the doctor writes: "Even those who escaped from the more immediate danger of the disease recovered in general very slowly, were a long time weak and subject to returns of fever, or they fell into chronic disorders which in the end proved no less fatal."

211 "they could quite easily drop back": There are numerous accounts of this mini-army of stragglers trailing the main body of troops, among them Ségur, who wrote, on p. 21, at Vitebsk, "The interminable lines of sick and stragglers must be given time to rejoin their regiments or get into hospitals."

213 " 'The typhus made' ": Brett-James, p. 210.

214 "The generals found": Labaume, p. 120.

216 " 'She experienced' ": Ibid., p. 121.

217 " 'The time has come' ": Ségur, p. 145.

218 " 'We were going' ": de Kerckhove, p. 100.

219 " 'to his boundless' ": Roeder, p. 188.

220 " 'Our heads were hideous' ": Austin, p. 213.

221 " 'On all sides' ": Ibid.

221 " 'She didn't cry' ": Bourgogne, p. 147.

222 " 'let out' ": de Kerckhove, p. 100.

222 " 'Typhus strongly advancing' ": Ibid., pp. 142, 155.

224 " 'You want to fight' ": Quoted in Zamoyski, p. 407.

Chapter Fifteen: Graveyard Trees

225 "On July 8": Cooper, p. 1.

228 " 'We resemble our lackeys' ": Brett-James, p. 230–1.

228 " 'If the circumstances' ": Austin, p. 98.

229 " 'old grenadier' ": Austin, p. 98.

230 " 'As long' ": Quoted in Zamoyski, p. 451.

230 " 'No one among us' ": Austin, p. 101.

232 " 'See how they' ": Austin, p. 123.

233 " 'A horrible, death-dealing stench' ": Quoted in Ségur, p. 185.

234 " 'Farewell, good mother' ": Bourgogne, p. 199.

234 "On November 12": Roeder, p. 168.

236 " 'Their complaints tore at our hearts' ": Austin, p. 197.

237 " 'The misery of my poor soldiers' ": Ségur, p. 206.

237 " 'I was delirious' ": Bourgogne, p. 196.

238 " 'I noticed,' ": Larrey, p. 68.

239 " 'Ah yes!' ": Ségur, p. 231.

240 " 'This is beginning' ": Caulaincourt, p. 235.

246 " 'A Russian musket ball' ": Austin, p. 290.

246 " 'surrounded on all sides' ": Ibid., p. 300.

250 " 'nothing but a vast' ": Austin, p. 366.

Epilogue: Rendezvous in Germany

253 " 'Drummers without drumsticks' ": Quoted in Cate, p. 392.

254 "As the survivors marched": For an account of the attitudes of townspeople toward the infected soldiers, see Walter, p. 108.

254 " 'Wherever we went' ": Vossler, p. 99.

255 " 'Epidemic maladies' ": Larrey, p. 67.

255 " 'application of the skin' ": Ibid., p. 88.

255 " 'It is morning' ": Roeder, p. 191.

255 " 'I feel that I' ": Ibid., p. 207.

256 "As Napoleon hurried": For Caulaincourt's account of the sleigh ride, see his memoirs, pp. 271–323.

258 "It is impossible": That disease was the lead killer in the Russian campaign is supported not only by the accounts of doctors and common soldiers on the campaign, but by a second wave of medical historians. In *Napoleon's Doctors*, Martin writes, "In Russia, typhus can be easily identified in the eyewitness accounts of an army which lost perhaps over 200,000 soldiers solely from disease." And that typhus was dominant among a host of contagious illnesses is confirmed by specialist secondary authors such as Prinzing, in his excellent *Epidemics Resulting from Wars*, who writes that "the most common disease even in Moscow was typhus fever" (p. 116). The analysis is seconded by Zinsser, who writes that "typhus remained the dominant disease" during the invasion (p. 163). Zinsser does perhaps overemphasize the rate of infection at the end of the campaign when he asserts, "The vestiges of the army which escaped from Russia were almost without exception infected with typhus." There are accounts of units that were free from the disease on the march home, and the DNA evidence from the skeletons at Vilnius don't support an infection rate that high.

260 "According to the military surgeon": For an extended discussion of typhus's effects on the armies of 1813–14, see Prinzing, pp. 127–34. He
writes: "After the battle of Dresden (August 26–27) from which Napoleon again emerged victorious, but especially during the short siege of
Dresden (from the middle of October to November 11), the epidemic
increased in both extent and fury. The increased mortality went from
184 in January to 960 by November. In the course of the year 1813, no
less than 21,090 soldiers died in Dresden, while in the same year 5,194
residents died."

260 " 'Tears came' ": Quoted in McLynn, p. 654.

263 " 'We found' ": This quote is from *Bemerkungen ueber den Gang der
Krankheiten welche in der königlich preussischen Armee vom Aus-
bruch des Krieges im Jahre 1812 bis zu Ende des Waffenstillstandes (im
Aug.) 1813 geherrscht haben. (Remarks on the Course of the Diseases
Which Have Reigned in the Royal Prussian Army from the Beginning
of the War in the Year 1812 until the End of the Armistice [in August]
1813)*. The text is included in Rose (unpaginated).

263 "In Berlin": Prinzing, p. 125.

264 " 'Who of us' ": Ibid., p. 153.

Author's Note: The Doorway of the Hospital at Tunis

267 This account draws mainly from Kim Pelis's biography of Nicolle.

271 "In his speech": The text can be read in full at http://nobelprize.org/
nobel_prizes/medicine/laureates/1928/nicolle-lecture.html

272 "During 1914–18": The "3 million" total is not uncontested, and some
analysts believe it is overstated. But the Statistical Bulletin of the
Metropolitan Life Insurance Company, quoting a Russian physician and
epidemiologist, estimated that there were 25 million cases of typhus in
Russia, with more than 3 million deaths, in the years 1918–1922 alone.

273 " 'Either socialism' ": Quoted in *The Western Medical Tradition: 800
BC–1800 AD*, by Lawrence Conrad, Cambridge, Mass.: Cambridge
University Press, 1995.

273 "The Red Army's scientists": For a full account of the Russian biological weapons program, including the typhus experiments, see Ken Alibek and Stephen Handelman's *Biohazard: The Chilling True Story of the Largest Covert Biological Weapons Program in the World—Told from the Inside by the Man Who Ran It*, New York: Dell, 2000.

274 For Irma Sonnenberg Menkel's account, see "I Saw Anne Frank Die," *Newsweek*, July 21, 1997.

Sources

Primary Sources

Armstrong, John. *Practical Illustrations of Typhus and Other Fevers.* Bedlington, Boston, 1829. Physician to the Fever Institution of London.

Bartlett, Dr. Elisha. *The History, Diagnosis and Treatment of Typhoid and of Typhus Fever.* Lea and Blanchard, Philadelphia, 1842.

Brett-James, Antony. *1812: Eyewitness Accounts of Napoleon's Defeat in Russia.* MacMillan, London, 1966.

Caulaincourt, Armand de. *Memoirs of General de Caulaincourt, Duke of Vicenza.* Cassell and Co., London, 1935.

———. *With Napoleon in Russia.* William Morrow, New York, 1935.

Clausewitz, Carl von. *The Campaign of 1812 in Russia.* Da Capo, New York, 1995.

Davidov, Denis. *In the Service of the Tsar Against Napoleon: The Memoirs of Denis Davidov, 1806–14.* Greenhill Books, London, 1999.

Dimsdale, W. P. *Extract from an account of cases of typhus fever, in which the affusion of cold water has been applied in the London House of Recovery.* London, Printed for the Society for Bettering of the Condition of the Poor, W. Bulmer & Co., London, 1803.

Donne, John. *Devotions Upon Emergent Occassions*, originally published 1624, Cosimo Classics, 2007.

Ebstein, Wilhelm. *Krankheiten im Feldzuge gegen Russland (1812).* F. Enke, Stuttgart, 1902.

Faur, Faber du. *With Napoleon in Russia.* Greenhill Books, Newbury, 2006.

Hunter, William. *The Serbian Epidemics of Typhus and Relapsing Fever in 1915.* Reprinted from the *Proceedings of the Royal Society of Medicine, 1919*, vol. XIII, John Bale, London, 1920, pp. 29–158.

Jackson, Dr. Robert. *An Outline of the History and Cure of Fever, Endemic and Contagious, More Expressly the Contagious Fever of Jails, Ships and Hospitals.* Mundell & Son, Edinburgh, 1798.

Kerckhove, J.L.R. *Histoire des maladies observées à la Grand Armée française, pendant les campagnes de Russe en 1812 et d'Allemagne en 1813.* Janssens, 1836.

Labaume, Eugène. *A History of the Invasion of Russia by Napoleon Bonaparte.* Adamant, Chestnut Hill, 2008.

Larrey, Baron DJ. *Surgical Memoirs of the Campaigns of Russia, Germany and France.* Translated by John Mercer. Casey & Lea, Philadelphia, 1832.

North, Elisha. *A treatise on a malignant epidemic, called spotted fever; with remarks on the nature of fever in general.* T&J Swords, New York, 1811.

Pisani, Filippo. *Con Napoleone nella campagna di Russia; memorie inedite di un ufficiale della grande armata, pubblicate, con introduzione e note, a cura di Carlo Zaghi.* Istituto per gli studi di politica internazionale, Milan, 1945.

Robertson, Dr. Robert. *Observations on Jail, Hospital, or Ship Fever. From the 4th April, 1776 until the 30th April, 1789. Made in various parts of Europe and America and on the Indeterminate Seas.* Self-published. Greenwich, MDCCLXXXIX.

Roeder, Franz. *The Ordeal of Captain Roeder.* St. Martin's, New York, 1961.

Ségur, Count Phillippe-Paul de. *Napoleon's Russian Campaign.* Time Inc., New York, 1965.

Smith, Dr. Nathan. *Practical Essay on Typhous Fever.* E. Bliss and E. White, New York, 1824.

Smyth, James Carmichael, M.D., FRS, Fellow of the Royal College of Physicians and Physician Extraordinary to his Majesty. *The Description of the Jail Distemper, as it appeared amongst the Spanish prisoners at Winchester, in the year 1780.* J. Johnson, London, 1803.

Villalba, Joaquin. *Epedimiologia española o historia cronologica de las pestes, contagios, epidemias y epizootias que han acaecido en españa desde la venida de los cartagineses, hasta el ano 1801.* Don Mateo Repulles, Madrid, 1802.

Vossler, H.A. *With Napoleon in Russia 1812.* Translated by Walter Wallich. Constable, London, 1998.

Walter, Jakob. *The Diary of a Napoleonic Foot Soldier.* Introduced by Marc Raeff. Doubleday, Garden City, 1991.

Wilson, Leonard. "Fevers and Science in Early Nineteenth Century Medicine." *Journal of the History of Medicine and Allied Sciences 1978* XXXIII(3): 386–407.

Wilson, Sir Robert. *Narrative of events during the Invasion of Russia by Napoleon Bonaparte.* Murray, London, 1860.

Secondary Sources

Arfaioli, Maurizio. *The Black Bands of Giovanni: Infantry and Diplomacy during the Italian Wars, 1526–28.* Pisa University Press, Pisa, 2005.

Austin, Paul Britten. *1812: Napoleon's Invasion of Russia.* Stackpole, Pennsylvania, 2000.

Baumslag, Naomi. *Murderous Medicine: Nazi Doctors, Human Experimentation and Typhus.* Praegar, Westport, 2005.

Bell, David. *The First Total War.* Houghton Mifflin, New York, 2007.

Bell, Madison Smartt. *Toussaint Louverture.* Pantheon, New York, 2007.

Bourgogne, Adrien. *Memoirs of Sergeant Bourgogne.* 1812–13. William Heinemann, London, 1859.

Brandi, Karl. *The Emperor Charles V.* Jonathan Cape, London, 1939.

Cartwright, Frederick. *Disease and History.* Thomas Y. Crowell, New York, 1972.

Cate, Curtis. *The War of the Two Emperors: The Duel Between Napoleon and Alexander, Russia 1812.* Random House, New York, 1985.

Chandler, David A. *The Campaigns of Napoleon.* Macmillan, New York, 1966.

———. *Napoleon's Marshals.* Weidenfeld Military, London, 2000.

Conklin, Alice L. *A Mission to Civilize: The Republican Idea of Empire in France and West Africa, 1895–1930.* Stanford University Press, Stanford, CA, 2000.

Cooper, Leonard. *Many Roads to Moscow: Three Historic Invasions.* Coward-McCann, New York, 1968.

Cronin, Vincent. *Napoleon.* HarperCollins, New York, 1994.

Diamond, Jared. *Guns, Germs and Steel.* W.W. Norton, New York, 1999.

Dodge, Theodore Ayrault. *Napoleon: A History of the Art of War.* Houghton, Mifflin, New York, 1907.

Duggan, William R. *Napoleon's Glance: The Secret of Strategy.* Nation Books, New York, 2003.

Dunn-Pattison, R.P. *Napoleon's Marshals.* Empiricus Books, London, 2001.

Dyer, Gwynne. *War: The Lethal Custom.* Carroll & Graf, New York, 2005.

Elting, John. *Swords Around a Throne.* Free Press, New York, 1988.

Fournier, August. *Napoleon I: A Biography.* Henry Holt, New York, 1911.

Gordon, Benjamin Lee. *Medieval and Renaissance Medicine*. Philosophical Library, New York, 1959.

Herold, J. Christopher. *The Age of Napoleon*. American Heritage, New York, 1963.

———. *Mistress to an Age: The Life of Madame de Staël*. Grove Press, New York, 2002.

Horne, Alistair. *How Far from Austerlitz? Napoleon 1805–1815*. St. Martin's Press, New York, 1997.

Howard, Dr. Martin R. *Napoleon's Doctors: The Medical Services of the Grande Armée*. Spellmount, Stroud, 2006.

Johnson, Steven. *Ghost Map: The Story of London's Most Terrifying Epidemic—and How It Changed Science, Cities and the Modern World*. Riverhead, New York, 2006.

Karlen, Arno. *Man and Microbes: Disease and Plagues in History and Modern Times*. Tarcher/Putnam, New York, 1995.

MacDougall, J.D. *A Short History of Planet Earth*. Wiley, New York, 1996.

Major, Ralph. *Fatal Partners: War and Disease*. Doubleday, Doran and Co., Garden City, 1941.

Matthews, J. Rosser. *Quantification and the Quest for Medical Certainty*. Princeton University Press, Princeton, 1995.

McLynn, Frank. *Napoleon: A Biography*. Arcade, New York, 2002.

McNeill, William H. *Plagues and Peoples*. Anchor Books, New York, 1989.

Muir, Rory. *Tactics and the Experience of Battle in the Age of Napoleon*. Yale University Press, New Haven, 2000.

Murchison, Charles. *A Treatise on the Continued Fevers of Great Britain*, third ed. Longmans, Green, London, 1884.

Nicolson, Nigel. *Napoleon 1812*. Harper & Row, New York, 1985.

Parkinson, Roger. *The Fox of the North*. David McKay, New York, 1972.

Parkinson, Wenda. *This Guilded African: Toussaint L'Ouverture*. Salem House, London, 1982.

Pelis, Kim. *Charles Nicolle, Pasteur's Imperial Missionary: Typhus and Tunisia*. University of Rochester Press, Rochester, N.Y., 2006.

Porter, Roy. *The Greatest Benefit to Mankind*. Norton, New York, 1999.

Prinzing, Dr. Friedrich. *Epidemics Resulting from Wars*. Oxford: At the Clarendon Press, London, 1916.

Raoult D., Dutour O., Houhamdi L., Jankauskas R., Fournier P.E., Ardagna Y., Drancourt M., Signoli M., La V.D., Macia Y., Aboudharam G. "Evidence for louse-transmitted diseases in soldiers of Napoleon's Grand Army in Vilnius." *Journal of Infectious Diseases.* January 2006. 1; 193(1): 112–20.

Raoult D., Woodward T., Dumler J.S. "The history of epidemic typhus." *Infectious Disease Clinics of North America.* 2004 Mar;18(1): 127–40.

Richardson, Glenn. *Renaissance Monarchy: The Reigns of Henry VIII, Francis I and Charles V.* Oxford University Press, New York, 1992.

Riehn, Richard. *1812: Napoleon's Russian Campaign.* Wiley, New York, 1991.

Roberts, A. "The Fifth Little Horseman." *Nursing Times.* Nov 2–8, 1983; 79(44): 49–53.

Roddis, Louis H. *James Lind, Founder of Nautical Medicine.* Henry Schumann, New York, 1950.

Rose, Dr. Achilles. *Napoleon's Campaign in Russia Anno 1812, Medico-Historical.* Self-published. New York, 1913.

Schom, Alan. *Napoleon Bonaparte.* HarperCollins, New York, 1997.

Seward, Desmond. *Prince of the Renaissance. The Golden Life of Francois I.* Macmillan, New York, 1973.

Siraisi, Nancy G. *The Clock and the Mirror: Girolamo Cardano and Renaissance Medicine.* Princeton University Press, Princeton, N.J., 1997.

Troyat, Henri. *Alexander of Russia: Napoleon's Conqueror.* Dutton, New York, 1982.

Weir, Alison. *Henry VIII: The King and His Court.* Ballantine, New York, 2001.

Winslow, Charles-Edward Amory. *The Conquest of Epidemic Disease: A Chapter in the History of Ideas.* University of Wisconsin Press, Madison, 1980.

———. *Man and Epidemics.* Princeton University Press, Princeton, N.J., 1952.

Yeomans, A. *Typhus Fever.* Oxford University Press, New York, 1947.

Zamoyski, Adam. *Moscow 1812.* HarperCollins, New York, 2004.

Zinsser, Hans. *Rats, Lice and History: The Biography of a Bacillus.* Little Brown, Boston, 1984.

Acknowledgments

My first pilgrimage in researching this book was to the Countway Library of Medicine at Harvard University, whose staff proved immensely helpful. Jack Eckert, in particular, was patient and knowledgeable on a wide variety of arcane subjects. I'd also like to acknowledge the New York Academy of Medicine and its fabulously deep archives. And Keith Oliver, research officer at the Napoleonic Association, was a close and insightful reader of the manuscript.

Thanks to my agent, Scott Waxman, for his typically ardent efforts on behalf of my work. And to Rick Horgan and Julian Pavia at Crown, who sharpened the story's focus and made it cleaner and tighter.

Love and thanks, as always, to my wife, Mariekarl, and my children, Asher and Delphine. Finally, I'd like to acknowledge the encouragement of Jerry Hodson, the brother-in-law every writer dreams of having.

Index

About the Author

STEPHAN TALTY is the author of the critically acclaimed *Mulatto America* and the bestselling *Empire of Blue Water*. A widely published journalist, he has contributed to *The New York Times Magazine*, *GQ*, *Men's Journal*, and *Details*, among others.

Also by
Stephan Talty

"Talty's vigorous history of seventeenth-century pirates of the Caribbean will sate even fickle Jack Sparrow fans. . . . A pleasure to read from bow to stern."
—*Entertainment Weekly*

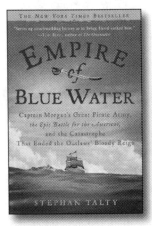

The passion and violence of the age of exploration and empire come to vivid life in this story of the legendary pirate who took on the greatest military power on earth with a ragtag bunch of renegades. Awash with bloody battles, political intrigues, natural disaster, and a cast of characters more compelling, bizarre, and memorable than any found in a Hollywood swashbuckler, *Empire of Blue Water* brilliantly re-creates the life and times of Henry Morgan and the real pirates of the Caribbean.

Empire of Blue Water
Captain Morgan's Great Pirate Army, the Epic Battle for the Americas, and the Catastrophe That Ended the Outlaws' Bloody Reign
$14.95 paper (Canada: $16.95)
978-0-307-23661-6

Available from Three Rivers Press wherever books are sold

Printed in the United States
by Baker & Taylor Publisher Services